Brought to You By

Lawrence R. Samuel

Brought to You By

Postwar Television Advertising

and the American Dream

UNIVERSITY OF TEXAS PRESS

Austin

Requests for permission to reproduce material from this work should be sent to
Permissions, University of Texas Press, P.O. Box 7819, Austin, TX 78713-7819.

∞ The paper used in this book meets the minimum requirements of
ANSI/NISO Z39.48-1992 (R1997) (Permanence of Paper).

Library of Congress Cataloging-in-Publication Data

Samuel, Lawrence R.
Brought to you by : postwar television advertising and the
American dream / Lawrence R. Samuel.
p.   cm.
Includes bibliographical references and index.
ISBN 0-292-77762-0 (alk. paper) — ISBN 0-292-77763-9 (alk. paper)
1. Television advertising—United States—History.   I. Title.
HF6146.T42 S25   2001
659.14'3'0973—dc21   2001018114

Contents

Acknowledgments

Many thanks to Jim Burr, Allison Faust, Nancy Bryan, and the other fine folks at the University of Texas Press as well as copy editor deluxe Sue Carter for bringing *Brought to You By* to fruition. Thanks also to Mark Hirsch, Ann Miller, Richard Wentworth, Douglas Armato, Susan Ferber, and the anonymous readers, all of whom contributed valuable ideas along the way. I greatly appreciate the efforts of the staffs at the Museum of Television and Radio, University of Southern California Cinema-Television Library, UCLA Film and Television Archive, Library of Congress Print and Photographs Division, the National Museum of American History Archives Center, the John W. Hartman Center for Sales, Advertising, and Marketing History at Duke University, and Campbell-Ewald, who helped lead me to important materials. I still owe a debt of gratitude to Lary May and John Fiske, both of whom were instrumental in helping me forge my own views of social history and cultural theory. Kudos to Sheree Bykofsky and Janet Rosen for being the first ones to recognize this was a story worth telling. Extra special hugs to Mary Ellen Muckerman and to my mom for their support and love.

Introduction

Brought to you by . . .

Beginning of *The Jack Benny Program, Playhouse 90,* and many other television shows

Between the years 1946 and 1964, American television—and much of American culture—was brought to you by television advertising. The aim of this book is to show how television advertising was ground central for the postwar American Dream, both shaping and reflecting our national ethos of consumption. *Brought to You By: Postwar Television Advertising and the American Dream* is designed to fill a gaping hole in the history of advertising and complete a missing chapter of twentieth-century American social history. The postwar years were what I believe to be the most exciting and dynamic period of advertising in America, as the development of the most powerful medium in history dovetailed with a patriotic celebration of consumerism and, of course, with the baby boom. Although television advertising of this era is a fascinating and important cultural site, the subject is conspicuously absent from both popular and scholarly literature. There are many good books on postwar television, but precious few resources dedicated to television advertising. This is unfortunate because it was television advertising that brought television to us and, in the process, assumed a central role in postwar culture. One cannot truly understand postwar America, I believe, without understanding the cultural history of one of its loudest voices.

Television advertising is especially fertile ground to study the social and cultural dynamics of postwar America because it was the perfect medium for and a perfect metaphor of the times, steeped in the values of consensus, conformity, and, of course, consumption. Television advertising quickly emerged as a new vocabulary all Americans could share, a common language that often crossed the social divisions of gender, race, class, and geography. By the early sixties, both doctors and construction workers could tell you that Ajax was stronger than dirt and that every litter bit hurts, and people in

Casper, Wyoming knew just as well as New Yorkers that Timex watches could take a licking but still keep ticking. Television advertising was thus part of the larger standardization of American consumer culture in the postwar era, when national brands, retailers, franchises, and chains flattened out regional differences and bridged demographic diversity. Adding to this homogenizing effect, Michael Kammen has noted, was the fact that viewers in any given market received only a handful of television stations (at most three or four networks and two or three locals), far fewer than the dozen or more radio stations any urbanite could pick up. In addition to its creation of a "universal" base of knowledge was the proven ability for television advertising to make people take action. As one of the most influential forms of propaganda in history, television commercials were seemingly capable of motivating people to do things they otherwise would not consider. Why else gulp down Geritol if one didn't truly believe that it woke up "tired blood"?[1]

Most important, however, was commercial television's role in reviving the national mythology of the American Dream, that is, every citizen's birthright to achieve success, realize prosperity, and enjoy the fruits of consumer culture. A revival of the American Dream in the postwar era was vital because of the cultural roller coaster of the previous quarter century, when business and its economic foundation of consumer capitalism were first celebrated and then seriously challenged. In his book *The Good Life and Its Discontents,* Robert J. Samuelson observed the dramatic change in the public's view of business that occurred between the wars. "In the 1920s," he writes, "the country had gotten visibly richer, and the effect was to fortify the power and prestige of business, which was credited for the American boom." However, Samuelson continues, the Depression "discredited private business and the faith that the normal workings of capitalism—what we now customarily call 'the market'—would automatically improve Americans' well-being." As the public image of business became restored during the war, a function of capital's alignment with the government, it was time for an equivalent recovery of the "the market." It was time for Americans to, in Samuelson's words, "yearn for private pleasures [versus] public agendas."[2]

A full revival of market-driven capitalism, however, demanded that Americans be retaught to not want to save money, to replace things that still worked. After all, Americans had just spent the last four years scrounging for scrap metal, planting victory gardens, and putting their savings into war bonds. War bond propaganda had, of course, been a ubiquitous presence on the home front, appearing on everything from milk cartons to menus, urging Americans to invest their savings in the nation. Posters carrying headlines such as "Do Your Part to Win the War" (1942) and "Doing All You Can Brother?" (1943) had trained Americans to think of consumerism as selfish and decadent, antithetical to wartime sacrifice. The specter of Depression-era bank foreclosures and pervasive unemployment also lingered, scenarios that reinforced a consumption ethic focused on essentials only. Put most simply, most Americans just did not know how to be very good consumers in 1945. As David Halberstam pointed out in his book *The Fifties,* "For most Americans, the idea of buying luxury items was a relatively new concept, as was the idea of buying on time" immediately after the war. If the country was to make a full recovery and realize its destiny as "the city on a hill," then thrift—a patriotic value during both the Depression and war—would have to be recast as unpatriotic, a violation of the national commitment to keep the economy moving. Instead of scarcity, restraint, and delayed gratification, the nation's best interests now resided in the values of abundance, pleasure, and immediate gratification. "After the privations of the Depression, after the hardships and shortages of a war," Karal Ann Marling writes in *As Seen on TV,* "... victorious Americans deserved nothing but the best."[3]

Importantly, the new American Dream had to be articulated and perceived as a less elitist and divisive form of consumer capitalism than that of the unbridled, unchecked economy of the 1920s, which had let the nation down. Business, however, had learned a valuable lesson over the last decade and a half, integrating the democratic, populist spirit of both the New Deal and wartime experience into its own self-image and into its communications with consumers. Now indelibly linked to the middle class, the American Dream promised that every citizen—at least every white citizen—was entitled to his or her share of what Marling called "the standard consumer package"—a family, car, and suburban home full of modern appliances. Amazingly enough, much of this mythology would be realized during the postwar years, as market capitalism flourished and became integral to the American experience as never before. The 1950s, Kammen has posited, "marked the true beginning of mass consumption as we know it," as "mass markets swiftly became a 'real fixture' in national life." With Americans' self-confidence and exceptionalism renewed, the "old puritanism was drastically weakened," as Halberstam put it, ultimately creating "an astonishing age of abundance." The American Dream, seeded in the 1920s, pruned in the 1930s and early 1940s, blossomed from the late 1940s through the early 1960s.[4]

This major transformation of American identity occurred, not coincidentally, with the debut of commercial television. Commercial television, we all know, dovetailed perfectly with the domestic, family-oriented, consumption-based lifestyle that characterized American culture during the baby boom. In his book *Time Passages,* George Lipsitz has described the unique role that television assumed as a voice of consumerism during the postwar years. "In the midst of extraordinary social change," he writes, "television emerged as the most important discursive medium in American culture . . . charged with special responsibilities for making new economic and social relations credible and legitimate." These "special responsibilities" involved nothing less than the restoration of the American Dream, which had emerged in the prosperous 1920s, when a new broad middle class was offered and eagerly embraced the pleasures to be found in consumption and leisure. With the ideology of consumer capitalism damaged by the scarcities of the Depression and the rationing of the war, however, it was in both Corporate America's and the federal government's interest to revive Americans' faith and belief in an acquisition-based lifestyle. From an economic standpoint, the revival of the American Dream would result in greater corporate profits and a larger tax base. From a social standpoint, major national concerns—fears of another depression, militant labor, and ethnic, class, and racial divisions—could all be eased by a populist belief in "abundance and prosperity for all." From a political standpoint, a thriving, bountiful marketplace too was America's best strategy to combat threatening ideologies of socialism or communism.[5]

Again, however, the impetus to embrace consumerism without restraint after the war's end ran counter to many Americans' experience over the previous decade and a half, when the values of indulgence, hedonism, and debt fell out of moral favor. The war might have got us out of the Depression from an economic standpoint, but it did a poor job in training Americans to part with their money on unnecessary things or go into debt, the keys to a thriving marketplace. With high-paying factory jobs, many homefronters were indeed flush with cash, but outside of basic needs and entertainment, there were few opportunities to spend this money. Going to the movies or to a nightclub with cash in one's pockets was one thing; buying a new house, a new car, and a set of new major appliances—all on time—was quite another. Intent on achieving this latter, more complex version of American-style capitalism, the federal government and business put a number of policies into place after the war to encourage consumerism and, as a by-product, long-term debt. Easier credit for consumers to purchase homes, autos, and appliances was made possible, a strong incentive for Americans to once again take on significant debt. Allowing low down payments on new homes via federal loans, combined with the income tax deduction for mortgage interest, essentially ensured that the millions of newly marrieds (already eager to move out of crowded apartments) would gobble up the ticky-tacky houses being built in the nation's suburbs soon after the war. The single-family house was, of course, the key to unlocking unchecked consumerism, a generic box requiring dedicated time, effort, and money to make it home sweet home. Connecting suburban developments to the jobs (and grandma) within their respective core city (and to each other) via new roads further encouraged young families to begin life on the new American frontier.[6]

The realization of the new, improved American Dream, however, would not be possible without the presence of a clear, consistent, powerful voice encouraging citizens to occasionally leave their consumer paradises to actually buy things. Television, a broadcasting medium whose technology existed well before the war but would have to wait for a market to develop, was now in the right place at the right time. Recognizing its potential as the ideal advertising medium to spark a retooled American Dream by persuading citizens to abandon their frugality, the federal government and Corporate America each supported research and development of commercial television. "Conscious policy decisions by officials from both private and public sectors shaped the contours of the consumer economy and television's role within it," Lipsitz states. Antagonistic during the New Deal years, capital and the government had forged a happy alliance during the war in order to win the military war overseas and the economic war on the home front. This alliance would carry over into the postwar era, directly impacting the formation and flourishing of commercial television.[7]

Rather than act as bystander and allow business alone to lead the televisual charge, the government thus actively took a number of steps to make the medium happen in order to serve national economic, social, and political interests. First, government scientists shared technological advances made in the medium for military purposes with their counterparts in the private sector. Second, the Internal Revenue Service extended its wartime policy of allowing corporations to write off media costs from their taxable income, a major incentive to take a chance with the new medium. This less-than-glamorous tax loophole proved to be instrumental in allowing the sponsor system to transfer from radio to television, as corporations were able to build up their cash reserves and concentrate their institutional power to ensure they—versus radio networks—would hold most of the programming cards. Third, the government's prosecution arm brought anti-trust charges against the major movie studios, breaking up the studio system and forever ending their leading role, so to speak, in American popular culture. Fourth, and perhaps most important, were a series of actions taken by the government's communication arm, the Federal Communications Commission (FCC). The FCC was awarded the power to oversee the network system in television, as it had with radio. The agency was also given the responsibility to license local television stations, a huge determinant in who would retain control of and profit from the new medium. The FCC's decision to suspend the issuing of new station licenses during the seminal years of 1948 to 1952 guaranteed that the radio-television networks would control broadcasting rights at a local level as well. The radio model, in which advertisers created and owned the programs, thus transferred neatly over to television, assuring that the medium would be, first and foremost, a commercial one. "Government decisions, not market forces, established the dominance of commercial television," Lipsitz concludes — so much so that it was "virtually the official state economic policy."[8]

The ability of television advertising to spread the ideology of the American Dream resided in its roots as the first exclusively commercial medium in history. Print media — newspapers and magazines — grew out of a tradition of journalism and initially earned their sole revenues from direct sale to the reader. Radio too was in its early days advertising-free, its sole mission to serve the public's interest. Although television also had a legal mission to serve the public's interest, it was clearly and always intended to be a commercial medium, at least after World War II. This unique, innate, and unapologetic characteristic of television differentiated it from all other media, and quickly established it as the best marketing tool Corporate America ever had (and has, for now at least). Also unlike radio, of course, television delivered the then incredible dimension of sight, offering marketers the stuff of their wildest dreams — the chance to demonstrate their products in consumers' homes. The television quickly became a central appliance in the American living room or den (90 percent of households had at least one in 1960 — a penetration rate it took radio thirty years to achieve), with the latter typically relegated to basements, attics, and garages. "Because of the incredibly swift ascent of television, radio became a supplementary source of entertainment by the late 1950s," Kammen observed. In less than a decade after its debut, in fact, commercial television would overtake radio, magazines, and newspapers as an advertising medium, and, in the process, it would play a vital role in extending the arc of consumer capitalism.[9]

The sheer reach of television was enough to convince advertisers that God must also be a capitalist. With the co-axial cable linking coast to coast in 1951, advertisers could now show their products to 15 to 25 million Americans at once. Television was viewed as a surrogate salesman invited into the viewer's living rooms, an electronic display room filled with the cornucopia of the good life. "Never before had so many people heard so often that happiness and security rested in ceaseless acquisition," observed Douglas T. Miller and Marion Nowak in their book *The Fifties: The Way We Really Were.* The populist, egalitarian nature of television was in part due to its being "free," unlike other forms of entertainment such as the movies or theater. More than that, however, commercial television was, like many postwar institutions, designed entirely around middle class (or perhaps "classless") values. Also like other postwar institutions grounded in consensual values, television was authoritarian, monolithic, and paternalistic, interested only in a body of individuals versus individuals themselves. "The American people, indeed, were no longer regarded exactly as people," Miller and Nowak concluded, as "in the eyes of advertisers and network executives, they became . . . the audience." From a televisual perspective, at least, Americans were less citizens, more consumers, a huge transformation in the idea of national identity. Despite this "top-down" orientation of commercial television, it is important to keep in mind that each consumer, then and now, views any and all texts individually, and holds ultimate power in his or her acceptance or rejection. "It is precisely this relative freedom of television audiences," Ien Ang has written, "to use television in ways they choose to which has been conveniently repressed in the industry's imaginings of its consumers." Television advertising of the postwar era was thus a clear example of the paradoxical, often misunderstood nature of consumerism, that even the most "top-down" messages are instantly converted into "bottom-up" terms.[10]

In addition to its unsurpassed role in consumer culture, television advertising intersected with many other dimensions of postwar life, helping to redefine everything from how politicians got elected to the way we traveled. Even the civil rights movement intersected with the path of television advertising, as blacks fought for their share of the American Dream by demanding they see people who looked like themselves in commercials. Until 1963, in fact, sponsors, networks, and ad agencies essentially denied the existence of African Americans, as classic an example of institutional racism as one can imagine. The most enduring legacy of this era of television advertising, however, was its intimate relationship with children, which picked up where radio left off. The first era of American television advertising coincided precisely with the presence of more children in any one time or place in history. "I want my Maypo!" was just one of many demands echoing in kitchens across the country in the fifties and sixties, shouted out by millions of children who would one day be known as baby boomers. Research showed that kids as young as three were as drawn to television advertising as Tony the Tiger was to Sugar Frosted Flakes. Television advertising would ultimately teach the baby boom generation to be professional consumers, and bestow upon many of the Me Generation their shop-till-you-drop, I-go-go-go-because-I-owe-owe-owe philosophy of life. From 1946 to 1964, advertisers pounced on these 76 million mini-consumers, realizing they controlled much of the spending power of American households. And unlike radio advertising, television advertising to kids was often the driving force of huge national marketing campaigns aimed to sell licensed merchandise or cross-promote other media products.[11] Lone Ranger, Howdy Doody, Davy Crockett, and Daniel Boone tchotchkes flew off warehouse shelves faster than you could say "Heigh-ho Silver," incentives for kids to persuade their moms to buy a certain brand of breakfast cereal or snack. Until boomers go off to the big Peanut Gallery in the sky, they will continue to trace their consumption roots to their weaning on television commercials.

Post-boomers—Generations X and Y—may be surprised to learn that through the first decade or so of the postwar era, many television commercials, like the shows themselves, were presented live as part of the programs. Trained in the conventions of radio, show hosts such as Jack Benny, Arthur Godfrey, and Jack Paar delivered the sponsor's commercials from the stage, effortlessly weaving between showmanship and salesmanship. Guest stars ranging from Frank Sinatra to Jerry Lewis also integrated product plugs into their performances, sewing a seamless quilt of artistic creativity and advertising. Even respected journalists like John Cameron Swayze and Walter Cronkite personally endorsed products on their newscasts, blurring the lines of "truth" and opinion. This mixing and matching of entertainment and advertisement brought together the realms of popular culture (the cultural dynamics of leisure) and consumer culture (the cultural dynamics of consumption) in new and more powerful ways. Unlike radio, whose popularity peaked in an economic downturn, television flourished during an economic boom, multiplying its impact as an agent of consumerism. The sponsorship system of early commercial television, in which corporations and their advertising agencies dictated programming decisions, created a cultural soup of leisure and consumption during a pivotal point in the twentieth century. "Sponsors of television programs during the fifties swiftly began to exercise an increasing amount of control over not merely the kind of program they made possible, but its content as well as its manner of presentation," Kammen has noted.[12] This concentration of power and synergy also served the principles of the American Dream, casting materialism with a heavy dose of entertainment and entertainment with an equivalent dose of materialism.

Although it was articulated most clearly in television, the sponsor system was, of course, not indigenous to the medium. Having thirty years of experience in broadcasting, the power triumvirate of media networks, advertisers, and ad agencies traded heavily upon the organizational structure and selling techniques already established in radio. Despite networks' attempts to the contrary, this structure—in which the networks sold fifteen-minute or more blocks of time to sponsors—was transferred from radio to television. Historians such as William Boddy and Michele Hilmes have documented the ways in which agencies quickly seized the reins of television programming as the medium became commercialized after World War II. "In network television," Hilmes notes, "economic stability rested on the carryover of the relationship among sponsor, agency, and network so successful during the previous three decades of radio." Agencies like Young & Rubicam and J. Walter Thompson wisely invested in program content for their clients, betting that television would someday be a viable advertising vehicle. Over the next decade, advertising agencies (on behalf of their client sponsors) would hold tight control over programming, a legacy of the power they had assumed during radio's heyday. Sponsors and agencies determined what shows would reach the air and wielded creative control over program content. Everyone involved in a show, from star to gaffer, worked for the sponsor, whom Erik Barnouw anointed a "modern potentate."[13]

By the latter half of the fifties, however, the networks had taken much of this power away from agencies and sponsors, as a host of economic and legal factors redefined the nature of the industry. The trends toward multiple sponsorships, Hollywood production of filmed (versus live) shows, and sponsor "rating-itis" all chipped away at advertisers' virtual omnipotence during the first decade of commercial television. These forces, compounded by the quiz show scandals of 1959, spelled doom for sponsors' retaining the crown jewel of the industry, the "time franchise," in which a single advertiser commanded creative control over a particular scheduling slot. The sponsorship system would eventually give way to the "magazine format," in which advertisers purchased time from networks based on audience demographics (as for magazines and newspapers). As editorial authority shifted from sponsors to networks, television shows were no longer created by advertisers, but rather, were carefully packaged media vehicles designed to reach a specific target market. Each network's broadcast schedule became, in Christopher Anderson's words, a "coherent, integrated text in which each component was designed to hold a viewer's attention." Ironically, however, advertisers' exit from the entertainment side of the business only served to strengthen their position in the marketplace by allowing them to focus on what they did best—selling products and services to consumers. With the networks now custom tailored for marketing efficiencies, television of the early sixties became what Michael Curtin has called "a display window for a national consumer culture." The rules of the game may have changed, but consumerism remained the heart of the American Dream, at least until many of the children weaned on it began to question its ethical and moral value.[14]

In addition to documenting the cultural sweep of commercial television, revisiting the world of advertising of the postwar years is a prime opportunity to validate or debunk many of its mythologies. Our collective memory and our perception of this world have been heavily influenced by popular culture, with its images of three-martini or Gibson lunches and a less-than-completely full set of industry ethics. The figure of the Madison Avenue account executive, canonized in fiction (e.g., Sloan Wilson's 1955 *The Man in the Gray Flannel Suit*), nonfiction (e.g., Vance Packard's 1957 *The Hidden Persuaders*), film (e.g., *The Hucksters,* starring Clark Gable in 1947; *Will Success Spoil Rock Hunter?* starring Jayne Mansfield and Tony Randall in 1957; *Lover Come Back,* starring Doris Day and Rock Hudson in 1961; and *Good Neighbor Sam,* starring Jack Lemmon in 1964), and television itself (e.g., *Bewitched*), is part truth, part fiction. The Madison Avenue account executive really was the man in the gray flannel suit, albeit a much less cartoonish figure than either of *Bewitched*'s two Darren Stevenses. The client or sponsor of the postwar era also lingers as a cultural icon, as does the sponsor's wife, who, it was always revealed, really called the shots. There can be no denying that being an "ad man" in these heady times garnered a level of both admiration and vilification that law, finance, or other forms of business did not. "Advertising men became the new heroes, or antiheroes, of American life," observed Halberstam. Advertising remained an elite career destination, attracting many of the "best and brightest" from Ivy League schools, other businesses, and the Anglo-Saxon Protestant "old boy" network. It was television, with its promise of being a part of something new, unproven, and exciting, that drew a new breed of professionals to advertising after the war. Just as many of today's best and brightest are foregoing traditional professions in order to be a part of the information revolution because it is history (and potential fortune) in the making, so trailblazers of a half century ago passed on the "old media" of print and radio to break new ground in the new medium of commercial television.[15]

Despite the pull of some of yesterday's best and brightest, it was this first era of television advertising that made us skeptical and cynical toward those responsible for commercials (current surveys show that we still trust people in the ad business just a little less than used car salespeople). As a symbol of lowest common denominator thought and a key target of FCC chair Newton Minow's 1961 "vast wasteland" speech, television commercials emerged as a passion point in this country as soon as they appeared on screens no bigger than a bread box. The commercialization of radio was much more gradual than that of television and was, of course, limited to sound. Most Americans were not quite prepared for the parade of talking cigars, dancing cigarettes, and marching beers that immediately populated their television screens. Often intrusive, loud, and inane, television commercials were viewed by many as the end of the world as we knew it. Advertisers routinely resorted to what was known in the trade as "puffery," the tweaking of reality to overcome the technical obstacles of the medium. Until the government agencies slapped their collective hand, advertisers and their agencies were not above sticking lit cigarettes in chickens, rubbing Vaseline on raw meat, or dropping Alka-Seltzers into glasses of cola to enhance the appearance of their products. Slowly, however, television commercials improved until they evolved into what some critics believed to be a legitimate art form, leading to the creation of a new industry award—the Clio—handed out to the cream of the crop. A decade and a half after the birth of television advertising, a true creative revolution began to bubble up, led by Doyle Dane Bernbach through the renegade agency's work for Volkswagen, Cracker Jack, and other lucky marketers. Other agencies would soon join Doyle Dane Bernbach in the creative revolution, ending the postwar age of television advertising but sparking the beginning of a new, radically different era in the history of commercials.

Brought to You By is organized chronologically, beginning with the rise of commercial television immediately after World War II and ending in the final year of the baby boom, 1964. This approach reveals the cultural arc of the formative years of television advertising and offers a trajectory by which to view the subject in historical context. Segments within each of the book's six chapters address the events, issues, people, and organizations and institutions that made television advertising such a compelling part of postwar American life. Part 1, "Home Sweet Home," traces the rise and development of television advertising over the decade following the war, showing how the new medium was instrumental in jumpstarting the American Dream grounded in domestic and family life. Part 2, "Keeping Up With the Joneses," equates competitive pressures within the television and advertising industries in the latter half of the 1950s with those of the proverbial average American trying to stay one socioeconomic step ahead of his or her neighbor. Part 3, "The New Society," examines the shifting dynamics of both television advertising and the American Dream as the nation became more youth oriented in the first half of the 1960s.

In terms of sources, much of this book relies on the accounts of journalists documenting the development of television advertising as it happened. Writers such as Goodman Ace of the *Saturday Review* and Hal Humphrey of the Los Angeles *Mirror* were keen observers of commercial culture, directing their take on the sights and sounds of television advertising to a broad, general audience. Although occasionally sensationalist, these contemporary sources offer a fresh, vibrant, and generally objective, unbiased picture of the television advertising scene (far more unbiased, I believe, than agency, corporate, and network sources). Accounts from trade journals such as *Printer's Ink* and *Advertising Age* add an inside-the-industry perspective, highlighting the key issues of the day.

In addition to these secondary sources, my own readings of television advertising gleaned from hours (days? weeks? months?) viewing seminal commercials and programs of the era add a vital textural element to the work. Still, these readings represent just an inkling of the millions of images that were beamed coast to coast in the 1950s and early 1960s. Luckily, many of these trailblazers' efforts still survive, documented on film and videotape. Nick at Night's *TV Land* even broadcasts golden oldies as entertainment, resurrecting the White Tornado, Bert and Harry Piel, and Josephine the Plumber from their advertising graves. Taking a look back confirms that we have come a long way from the pre-cable, pre-VCR, pre-TiVo days, but maybe not as far as we may think. Is the "Got Milk?" campaign truly better than the "Let Hertz Put You in the Driver's Seat" spots? You decide. For the devoted fan or student of television advertising, I heartily recommend a visit to the Museum of Television and Radio in New York and Beverly Hills for full immersion in commercial heaven (and hell). The book's notes provide a guide to some of the many other works that address specific dimensions of televisual life in postwar America.

Finally, the story of the evolution of television advertising will no doubt bring to mind some very interesting parallels with the rise of the medium du jour, online technology. The current gold rush to cyberspace is in many ways repeating the developments of a bit more than half a century ago, as the infrastructure forms around a new system of communicating and advertising. People today are asking the same questions people asked fifty some years ago with regard to a relatively unknown medium. What is its commercial potential? How large is the audience? How long will it take to develop and how much will it cost? What are the legal and ethical implications? Who will be in control? As we plunge headfirst into the twenty-first century, looking back at the birth, adolescence, and maturity of the last "ultimate" commercial medium helps provide answers to these questions, and helps us envision the American Dream of our future.

PART ONE

Home Sweet Home

✻

Chapter One

The Precocious Prodigy,
1946–1952

Why don't you pick me up and smoke me sometime?
Muriel the talking cigar, 1951

This is the story of the birth of the most powerful advertising medium in history, a story that has never been fully told. In the seven or so years following the end of World War II, the fledgling upstart medium of television advertising would irrevocably alter the social, economic, and political landscape of the United States. Over the course of the latter 1940s and early 1950s, television advertising emerged as a lightning rod of passion and conflict, electrifying politics, the legal system, and of course, everyday life in America. Like the beginnings of most new technologies, the first era of commercial television was a wild and wooly period fueled by an entrepreneurial spirit, gold rush mentality, and corporate interests. Its frontier orientation recast the trajectory of advertising, broadcasting, and marketing, and the careers of those working in those fields. Within this relatively short period of time, a new, original culture would form and be canonized in literature, film, and television itself. Most important, television advertising emerged as a loud, and I believe the loudest, voice of the American Dream, promoting the values of consumption and leisure grounded in a domestic, family-oriented lifestyle. After the Depression and the war, television advertising took on the important responsibility of assuring Americans that it was acceptable, even beneficial to be consumers. A vigorous consumer culture, largely suspended for the previous decade and a half, was about to be primed by the biggest thing to hit advertising since the commercialization of radio in the 1920s.

As in the case of many key sites of twentieth-century American social history, the creation of television advertising was dependent upon a series of technological advances and regulatory decisions. Commercial television began in earnest in the mid-1930s when RCA, Philco, Allen B. Du Mont, and others started testing the medium. NBC and CBS began broadcasting in 1939, with RCA offering sets for $200–$600. Television made its grand debut at the 1939 World's Fair, and by May 1940, twenty-three stations had begun telecasting in the United States. As America shifted to a wartime economy, however, the FCC soon put limits on commercial operations, which slowed growth of the new medium and made new sets impossible to find in the marketplace. No sets were allowed to be manufactured or stations to be licensed during World War II, postponing commercial television despite technological readiness.[1]

Months before America's entry into the war, however, a handful of brave advertisers gained their first experience with the medium. The first television commercial was for Bulova watches, aired during a July 1, 1941, broadcast of a Brooklyn Dodgers versus Philadelphia Phillies baseball game. The history-making event was inauspicious at best, made possible when the FCC authorized WNBT, the New York City NBC affiliate later called WNBC, to allow its broadcasts to be sponsored by advertisers. At precisely 2:29:50 P.M., a Bulova clock showing the time replaced a test pattern, while an announcer told baseball fans it was three o'clock. Bulova paid a total of $9 for the twenty-second spot—$4 for the time and $5 for "facilities and handling." Later that same day, Sunoco Oil, Lever Brothers, and Procter and Gamble sponsored broadcasts on the station, each paying $100 to reach what was estimated as 4,500 viewers. WNBT's rate card (the price list given to advertising agencies and sponsors) was, from today's standards, ridiculously basic, offering media buyers the simple choice of "night" or "day" rates.[2]

Despite the wartime moratorium on new stations, some existing ones were permitted to test the waters of commercial television. In March 1943, for example, WABD, the New York television station owned by Du Mont Laboratories, offered free time to advertising agencies to experiment with the medium. Ruthrauff & Ryan was the first agency to take Du Mont up on its offer, producing a weekly half-hour show called *Wednesdays at Nine Is Lever Brothers Time*. The variety show was a vehicle to promote three Lever brands—Rinso detergent, Spry baking ingredients, and Lifebuoy soap and shaving cream. Lever's commercials were surprisingly sophisticated, using dissolves, superimposed images, and even identical twins to create special effects. Most impressive, however, were commercials that were integrated within the program itself. In one skit, for example, the master of ceremonies led a game of charades, with the correct answer one of the sponsor's slogans, "A daily bath with Lifebuoy stops B.O." In another show, a lost puppet character is found in a giant Rinso box, and told he will win over a girl puppet by offering her

A 1944 commercial for Chesterfield cigarettes on the Du Mont network not surprisingly depicted a military scene. (NMAH Archives Center, Smithsonian Institution)

"a life free of household drudgery" by using Rinso. These early commercials laid the groundwork for advertisers' use of television to sell products under the guise of entertainment, a strategy advertisers had used since the early days of radio and before in newspapers and magazines.[3]

Radio Days

Indeed, much of the unapologetic commercialism of early television was predicated on the structural familiarity of radio. Karen S. Buzzard has noted that radio shows were "conceived, more or less, as one continuous commercial," best evidenced by the fact that the shows often carried the sponsor's name, for example, "Lux Radio Theater." In her book *Selling Radio,* Susan Smulyan wrote that sponsors' ultimate goal in radio was to create a "program [which] personifies the product." Clicquot Club was perhaps the best example of this pursuit, as the beverage marketer and its agency designed their radio program around the physical attributes of the product, specifically peppiness and effervescence. With snappy music and lively chatter, Clicquot Club's radio program was an audible metaphor for the bubbly tonic. J. Walter Thompson was recognized as the master of the radio program as advertisement, its goal to, in one advertising executive's words, "get radio shows that would work as advertising."[4]

In his definitive book on advertising in the 1920s and 1930s, *Advertising the American Dream,* Roland Marchand too has noted radio's "dovetailing of entertainment with advertisement." Radio commercials often resembled the tone, locale, and pace of their host programs or, better yet, used the programs themselves as the advertising delivery vehicle. A barber on the Chesebrough "Real Folks" radio show was known to casually praise the value of Vaseline while shaving a customer, while characters on the Maxwell House Program chatted up the merits of the coffee. This interweaving of entertainment and

Another 1944 commercial on Du Mont for Rinso White detergent featured this scene right out of a Norman Rockwell painting. (NMAH Archives Center, Smithsonian Institution)

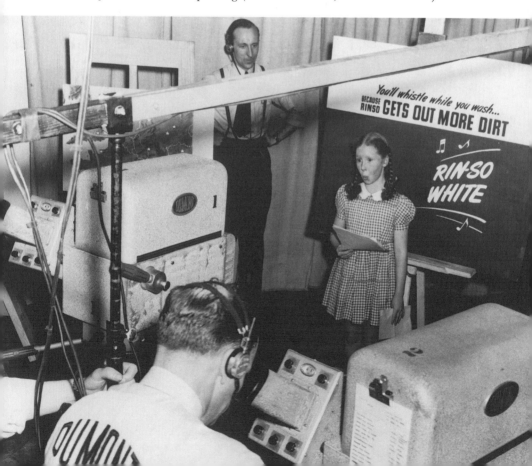

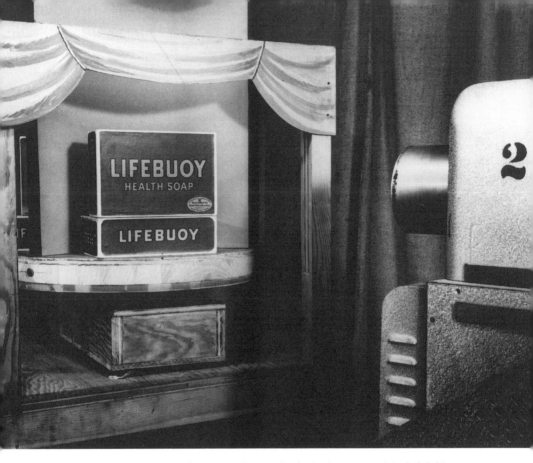

State-of the-art production techniques in the 1940s by the Du Mont network included this lazy Susan turntable which was swiveled around to reveal an oversized box of Lifebuoy soap and other products. (NMAH Archives Center, Smithsonian Institution)

advertising, Marchand points out, was in fact not original to broadcasting but had its origins in print. Advertising agencies had long practiced the art of "editorial copy," in which newspaper and magazine ads were blended into articles through similar type fonts and writing style. With their presentation of entertainment-as-advertising (or advertisement-as-entertainment), television advertisers were carrying on an established industry tradition known to be an effective technique to sell products and services. Advertisers and their agencies exploited this successful formula in television by producing most of the programs and simply buying blocks of airtime from the networks. This system would serve the advertising community well during this first decade of commercial television, until a series of events irrevocably altered the industry's underpinnings.[5]

The Race Is On

With the invention of the Image Orthicon tube during the war, making possible a cheaper yet better product, television was now ready to be much more than what Miller and Nowak called a "clumsy and expensive toy." Television began to earn true legitimacy in 1945 when an allied victory in World War II seemed assured, part of the "guns-to-butter" transition from a military-based economy to a consumer-based one. As factories retooled in the months following the end of the war, advertising agencies and their sponsors moved quickly. Immediately after the FCC announced in June 1945 that prewar spectrum standards would be resumed, in fact, many advertising agencies rushed to create television departments, just as they had quickly created radio departments a generation earlier when they saw opportunity. Marchand has observed that once advertisers fully realized the power of radio shows to function as extended commercials, radio departments within ad agencies grew significantly in both number and importance. In mid-1945, about thirty ad agencies already had television departments, although "department" perhaps overstates the resources agencies were allocating to the new medium. Many of these departments consisted of a single person or were small groups within existing radio departments (not unlike the interactive or "new media" departments of agencies circa mid-1990s). Some departments were assigned the exclusive task of monitoring industry events, while others were given the charge to jump into the cutting edge technology. In addition to Ruthrauff & Ryan, the first agencies to make a commitment to television included Batten, Barton, Durstine & Osborne (BBDO), J. Walter Thompson, Young & Rubicam, N. W. Ayer, Compton Advertising, and Kenyon & Eckhardt.[6]

Given the extremely limited size and scope of television immediately after the war, the advertising business was already taking the medium fairly seriously. According to the Television Broadcasters Association, in the summer of 1945 the country's nine television transmitters were reaching a total of fewer than 10,000 sets, all of course in large cities. Of these 5,000–6,000 sets were located in the New York City-New Jersey-Philadelphia area, 800 to 1,000 in the Chicago area, and 500–700 in or around Los Angeles. Set ownership in the early years of television was generally limited to the wealthy, what one publication termed "the mink coat and luxury car class." Most agencies active in television were producing their own shows (commercials as we know them were still about a year away), although a handful of independent production companies had already sprung up. Despite the rumblings in the advertising world and interest among the more curious to own a television set, few people in 1945 recognized the potential commercial applications of the medium. Some believed that television would be most effective as an internal selling device within department stores. In October and November 1945, Gimbel's in Philadelphia tested the effectiveness of "intrastore" (what would be later called closed-circuit) advertising, telecasting sales pitches shot live from the central auditorium to twenty receivers scattered around the store. The telecasts did prove to boost sales, although the cost of such a project on a large-scale basis would have been prohibitive.[7]

On the basis of Gimbel's test and other localized efforts, it soon became apparent that advertising on a mass scale represented the greatest chances of making television a viable medium. In 1945, $3 billion in advertising was spent in the United States, and the neophyte television industry firmly believed it could grab a share of these dollars. At its annual convention, held in Washington, D.C. on January 29, 1946, the Television Institute trade group focused on the looming opportunity of advertising, addressing questions such as, how much would the process cost the industry? How fast would the audience develop? What technical improvements were necessary? What role would the FCC play? The group boldly assumed that even with production and media costs three to ten times those of radio, television could effectively compete for advertisers' money. The Institute's research had indicated that television could "pull" (generate sales) ten times that of radio, a function of the former's ability to offer both sight and sound. "Action plus animation," the Institute argued, "create a stepped-up emotional drive lacking in all other forms of advertising art." Television programming, and its advertising stepchild, were envisioned as drawing from a variety of arts, a powerful fusion of movies, radio, music, writing, and theater. Experts, however, advised sponsors-to-be to purchase a television set so "you can really see whether your program is laying eggs."[8]

By the spring of 1946, industry experts were predicting that television advertising would take the form of commercials, or what was described by *Sales Management* as "one-minute movie shorts." "Video sales messages," the trade publication forecast, "are going to be something new in advertising and selling, because television commercials are pretty certain to be 16 mm. film episodes, one minute in length, or less." Believing commercials would be much like movie trailers (or perhaps bad lovers), the magazine accurately predicted that they would be "something that moves fast, with abundant noise, holds your attention for two or three minutes . . . , and leaves you [with a] promis[e]." Suggestions regarding the kind of commercials current print and radio advertisers should make were even made. For Campbell Soup, advice was offered that "stress [be] laid on quickness of preparation"; for Arrow shirts, that "comic misfits" and "hints to the bachelor" be employed; and for Mennen, the casting of "a girl say[ing] 'I like smooth men.'"[9]

Despite a few naysayers, such as E. F. McDonald, president of the Zenith Radio Corporation, who stated in February 1947 that "advertising will *never* support large-scale television," most agency, corporate, and broadcast executives believed that the television advertising train had by then already left the station. Agencies were holding symposiums to learn more about the medium, continuing to build television departments, and urging clients to experiment with commercials while it was inexpensive. With a vested interest in a full revival of a consumer-driven economy, companies such as U.S. Rubber, General Mills, Chevrolet, Ford, Standard Brands, and Standard Oil had all invested in television advertising by the beginning of 1947. These were, not coincidentally, some of the flagship accounts of ad agencies blazing the televisual trail. Helping the industry's confidence were the long lines of shoppers at Macy's, pushing and shoving to purchase one of the limited number of ten-inch screen television sets selling for $350. Long lines also formed at retail stores in Chicago, with thousands of customers put on waiting lists to purchase a set when more came in. The frenzy over television was even more remarkable given the fact that most Americans wanting to own a television set had actually never seen one in use. A study completed in summer 1946 by Sylvania Electric Products found that less than one in six consumers who were in the market for a set had ever watched a television show. "Television is going to move very soon and very fast," *Printer's Ink* accurately forecasted in March 1947. Even before most Americans had personally experienced the medium, television was being considered an integral part of postwar domestic life.[10]

General Foods, an avid radio advertiser, was particularly eager to get in on the ground floor of commercial television. The company set up an advertising committee in 1946 to provide reports of industry goings-on and recommend what steps to take. By May 1947, Howard M. Chapin, sales and advertising manager of the company's Jell-O division and chair of the committee, was able to report that General Foods was at the "'getting our feet wet' stage." The company was actively purchasing time on all three New York City area stations, including co-sponsorship (with Ford Motor Company) of the Brooklyn Dodgers' seventy-seven home games to be aired on WCBS-TV. Television advertising was viewed, over the long term, as an ideal means to efficiently promote the company's national brands. To reach a mass audience, General Foods and other big marketers had to advertise on many radio stations and in many magazines and newspapers, a cost- and time-intensive way to do business. Television advertising was the stuff of dreams for companies like General Foods, offering potential unprecedented economies of scale and, ultimately, tremendous profits. Beyond its role as an advertising medium, television advertising could and would act as a catalyst for selling the idea of consumption in general, a critical function in the first years after the war. As Lipsitz described it, television "irreparably inscribe[d] consumer desire and commercialism into the fabric of entertainment, news, and sports."[11]

The Medium of Mediums

By late 1947, the cultural implications of the new medium were becoming quite clear, given the way that television was impacting Americans' relationship to sports. Television was turning out to be as communitarian a broadcasting medium as radio, with family members routinely watching sports broadcasts together. When it came to advertising on sports broadcasts, early research was suggesting that TV also had tremendous "recall" potential. Three out of four viewers could name Ford as one of the sponsors of the Brooklyn Dodgers games, for example, as high a percentage as any advertiser could hope for. As important if not more important was the effect the new medium was having on who watched sports broadcasts. Many women who had never attended a major sports event in person in their entire life were now watching and enjoying baseball and basketball games, horse races, and tennis matches on television. Excited about the recall levels and new audiences that television appeared to be responsible for, sponsors of sports broadcasts quickly found opportunities to raise the level of corporate or brand identification among viewers. One strategy was for commentators to make "ad-lib" comments referring to sponsors and their products. "When the comment is clever and correctly timed," Donald Horton and Halsey V. Barrett of CBS Television advised, "it serves not only as an advertisement but as supplementary entertainment." Advertisers also integrated their products into televised sporting events, such as when the presentation of a pair of silver spurs to the winner of a rodeo contest was made from a Ford station wagon. Placing billboards with the sponsor's name in full view of the television camera, of course, became standard operating procedure for advertisers wanting to get the most for their media buck.[12]

Years later, television advertising would also be responsible for the "television time-out" in sports, although initially commercials were run only when the teams themselves called the time-out. During football games, teams had the option of not using the full two minutes per time-out allowed, a complicating factor in a business where time was of the essence. Television advertising executives, however, were somehow able to solve the problem by pressuring game referees to delay starting the game even though the teams were ready to play. "The officials," one network football game announcer stated, "have been most cooperative in inducing team captains to take the full two minutes." Television advertising was well on the way toward assuming control of the "natural" pace of professional sports, in effect dictating the ground rules of one of America's central institutions.[13]

More important than attracting viewers, television advertising appeared to be motivating consumers to take action. When makers of Bab-O, a surface cleanser, offered a premium during its commercial, 6 percent of the total viewing audience responded to the offer. This was, according to the Bab-O account executive, "an unheard-of thing in ordinary radio." Mueller Macaroni generated 642 telephone calls in the first forty-five minutes by offering $25 for the best name for a salad featured in its commercial. (The prize was won by a Mr. Reubens with his entry, Mueller's Pin Money Salad.) And, $800 worth of silverware and pillows were reportedly sold by one $65 commercial announcement, and 265 toy trains by a single demonstration. "This thing is so big we don't know what do with it," one executive gleefully declared. Despite their enthusiasm, advertising executives were generally confused as to the role television would or should play within their clients' marketing plans. "Television provides advertising with a new tool," declared Kenneth W. Hinks of J. Walter Thompson at the 1948 American Association of Advertising Agencies (AAAA) convention, but neither he nor other industry experts could say exactly how the tool should be used. Between October 1947 and April 1948, according to Young & Rubicam research, the number of television advertisers grew from 89 to 211, but this was still a fraction of radio's 1,150 national advertisers. Sixty percent of television's 1 million viewers in the U.S. (and thus the world) were concentrated in the New York City metropolitan area, deterring advertisers in other parts of the country to invest in the medium. A lack of understanding about the effects of television upon the viewer also contributed to the reluctance among some advertisers to jump into the new medium. Television "induces fatigue at a much greater rate than . . . radio, and possibly encourages sly drooping of the eyelids during the duller portions of a program," claimed Peter Langhoff, research chief of Young & Rubicam.[14]

Perhaps to avoid viewer "fatigue," early television advertisers often made full use of the medium's visual power, particularly when it came to the long, intimate relationship between advertising and sex. Sweetheart Soap, for example, employed women models in commercials for its bathing suits in 1947 because, as a company executive described it, "the women like the fashions but the men look because it's cheesecake." With few regulations or standards, early television advertisers also took full advantage of the deception inherent in the medium, if only to eliminate as much risk as possible from airing live commercials. In a 1947 dog food commercial, for example, a dog galloped toward a bowl of the competitor's brand, sniffed and shuddered, and made a beeline for the sponsor's bowl, which he happily gobbled down. "It went over beautifully," claimed the producer, admitting that "we filled the competitor's bowl with ammonia." Because of the visual nature of the medium delivered to viewers in real time, advertisers were quickly recognizing the perceived need to adjust reality to their advantage. Selling the American Dream to viewers simply could not accommodate advertisers' products coming off as less than wonderful, even if dogs were the ultimate consumers.[15]

It is difficult now to appreciate how bizarre the new world of television advertising seemed to viewers and critics in the late 1940s. No amount of print or radio advertising or moviegoing had prepared audiences for such images as square dancing Lucky Strike cigarettes and marching Rheingold beer bottles. Advertising of this era was truly a theater of the absurd, as when New York's Chevrolet dealers cast six dwarves as garage repairmen, naming them Howdy, Quickie, Tidy, Thrifty, Brainy, and Brawny. Observers found disembodied hands in commercials particularly disturbing, snapping on Ronson lighters or pouring Ivory Snow detergent independently from the remainder of the human body. The types of commercial vignettes or dramas that are so familiar to us now were often perceived as having little or nothing to do with the product being advertised because the genres were new, at least in a visual sense. The length of television commercials was an especially sore issue, with some spots (such as those run by Kelvinator kitchen appliances) running for a full fifteen minutes. Americans were being introduced to, perhaps indoctrinated in, a new language of consumerism, a language which was increasingly becoming a form of public discourse.[16]

In addition to television being the least proven advertising medium, it was also the most expensive. The cost of producing a television show was, by radio standards, enormous. Five times as many technicians were needed in television than in radio, with a high-budget show costing a sponsor $15,000

A home economist for Kraft making sandwiches with Miracle Whip on live television for station WRCA. (NMAH Archives Center, Smithsonian Institution)

a week to produce and air. Maxwell House paid this much money to sponsor *The Lambs Gambol,* a variety program that reached an audience of about a million people in 1949. With the "cost per viewer" estimated as one and a half cents, only sponsors with deep pockets could afford to create programs on a weekly basis. Top radio shows reached about 20 million people at less expense, with the cost per listener as low as one-fifth of a cent. Despite the higher cost, almost all large agencies had or were creating television departments in the late 1940s in order to retain existing and attract new clients. Rather than representing a new profit center, however, television was proving to be a necessary evil for many agencies. "When we get into television," one advertising executive complained in 1948, "we lose our shirts." Television stations were also losing money, luring advertisers with cut rates just to fill air time. Attracted by discounted media time and the occasional success story (such as Kraft Foods causing a run on a previously little known brand of cheese in Philadelphia), however, the number of television advertisers continued to rise. Between June and October 1948, the total number of television advertisers increased from 243 to 495. Many advertisers were "investment spending," building equity with viewers as the number of television sets in households and number of stations gradually grew. Larger advertisers were in television for the long run, willing to take short-term losses for the future dividends that they correctly believed lay around the corner.[17]

Some advertisers found ways to justify the high price of television through alternative measures of return on investment. General Foods, which soon became one of the heaviest advertisers of the late 1940s, adopted this philosophy on the basis of research published in January 1948. The report revealed that most television viewers had higher-than-average-incomes, could identify program sponsors, and remembered commercial selling points. The study also showed that the average evening audience per television set was 3.54 persons versus 2.37 per radio set, further adding to the attractiveness of the new medium. The fact that television combined sight with sound would, as the Television Institute predicted, prove to be a compelling factor in convincing large advertisers like General Foods to devote dollars to the medium despite its high cost and lack of a track record.[18]

Even with its relative higher cost, television advertising grew over the course of the late 1940s at a truly staggering rate, helped along by the growing number of broadcasting hours in a day. From 1947 to 1948, total expenditures on television advertising skyrocketed from $1 million to $10 million. Sixty advertisers sponsored network television shows in 1949, three times the number of the previous year. The number of national and regional advertisers increased from 119 in 1948 to 337 in 1949, while the number of local retailers using television jumped from 236 to 1,141 (virtually all of the latter in major cities where set ownership was still concentrated). About 200 advertising agencies across the country had television departments by February 1949. "Television is developing with such atomic fury that what is written today is likely to be outdated tomorrow," *Printer's Ink* declared, interestingly using the metaphor of atomic energy to describe another of postwar America's cultural icons. The changes in the geographic landscape of America backed up all the hype in the trade media. Many landlords were backing down from their original stance that they would not allow television antennae to clutter the rooftops of their apartment buildings, for example, a crucial step in the popularization of the medium. With costs still exceeding income resulting from television advertising, however, marketers with large promotion budgets were aggressively securing the best time, talent, and programs before their competitors could do so. Not surprisingly, the largest radio advertisers were also the largest television advertisers in the late 1940s, with marketers of standardized products intended for mass consumption leading the way. Food and beverage marketers accounted for the largest share of television spot (regional) advertising in 1949, while drug and toiletries, food, and tobacco marketers were most likely to be network sponsors. Seventy-four percent of all television advertisers used spot commercials, with the remaining 26 percent using network alone.[19]

Although many large advertisers were committed to television by 1949, a good share of those began to look for ways to lower the enormous costs associated with the medium. There were various ways advertisers could do this. First, being the producers of television shows, network sponsors had the power and ability to change program format. Maxwell House did just that in November 1949, dropping its $15,000 a week *The Lambs Gambol* in exchange for a less expensive dramatic show retrofitted from radio, *Mama.* A second way was for network sponsors to pull out of the production end of the business and simply run filmed commercials, an idea that would take an entire decade to fully develop. A third, rather clever, option was termed "simulcasting," airing the audio portion of a network television show (live or taped) over the radio. Through simulcasting, large advertisers using both media would save on virtually all radio production costs, lowering total expenditures. Yet another way to lower costs was for multiple advertisers, often competitors in the same business but located in different geographical markets, to share a sponsorship. Fourteen drug store chains, in fact, each based in a different city, sponsored the *Cavalcade of Stars* show over the Du Mont television network during the 1949–1950 season, although a viewer would think that the chain in his or her local market was the sole sponsor.[20]

Even without cost-cutting measures, television advertising was proving to be a smart, if not necessary, investment for leading marketers of consumer goods. Big advertisers were, in fact, essentially forced to add television to their media mix as it eroded the listening base of radio. In April 1950, A. C. Nielsen research showed that night-time radio listenership dropped from 1 hour, 39 minutes to 27 minutes after a household purchased a television set. Although daytime radio listening fell off only 20 minutes, advertisers still had to add television to their media schedules to reach the same number of listeners with the same frequency. Because television was still in its formative period, however, it could not by itself offer advertisers the reach and frequency levels that radio used to. Thus advertisers found themselves in the sometimes uncomfortable position of having to be a television advertiser and enduring the financial and technical headaches of the new medium until it achieved its full potential.[21]

Gray Flannel Suits

As more marketers included television in their media mix, television advertising naturally increased its presence within the discourse of everyday life in America. The culture of television advertising had, in fact, already become an archetype by the early 1950s, well-documented in films, literature, and even television advertising itself. On a June 1950 episode of *Cavalcade of Stars,* for example, a pompous man in a tuxedo identified only as a "representative of the sponsor" bossily demanded that host Jerry Lester sing the "Quality Drug Stores" song at the party after the broadcast. As the payer of the bills, the sponsor or corporate executive was unarguably on the top rung of the television advertising ladder. Next in the hierarchy were the network and agency account executives, the latter characterized by Gilbert Millstein of *The New York Times* as "a thin, dynamic man in the middle forties with a deceptive boyish complexion, an ulcer, hypertension, and a palpitating heart." He unfailingly had a crew cut and wore gray flannel suits. Last in the pecking order were actors and writers, although there was some dispute regarding which of these professions was the bottom rung of the ladder. The relationship between the television industry and the advertising business was a symbiotic one, reflected by their physical closeness in New York City. CBS was headquartered at Madison Avenue and 52nd Street, within the very epicenter of the advertising agency world, with NBC and ABC located a block and a half away at 30 Rockefeller Plaza. "The proximity of the agencies to the networks," Millstein observed, "deeply affects the folkways of both." [22]

Television, like radio in the past and the Internet in the future, had a major impact on the advertising business by being a revolutionary medium in which many of the old rules no longer applied. An escalated amount of account switching occurred in the industry in the early 1950s, a function in large part of the relative willingness among agencies to confront the challenges of creating television commercials. When the Gruen Watch Company announced it wanted to spend 90 percent of its advertising budget on television, for example, many agencies declined to bid for the account, believing the company's plan too ambitious (and unprofitable). Advertisers naturally expected a return on their costly investment, pressuring agencies to provide unusual levels of service to television-based accounts. With the opportunities for production errors great, advertising agencies ran the fair chance of exceeding their clients' budgets and appearing incompetent with each television commercial venture. The dynamics of television had the net effect of significantly improving the reputation of some agencies and destroying that of some others, not unlike that which occurred a generation earlier when advertising agencies either dipped their toes in radio or stayed close to the tried-and-true tradition of print.[23]

Until television networks took control over programming in the latter half of the 1950s, advertising agencies continued to create shows for their clients through on-staff directors and producers, or else farmed them out through independent production companies. After the war, executives at the television networks saw a window of opportunity for their industry, rather than advertising agencies, to take control of the new broadcasting medium by producing and owning programming. It soon became clear, however, that the same pattern would emerge as in radio, where ad agencies retained primary power by producing shows on behalf of their clients. Advertising agency culture thrived in the postwar years largely because of its being in the televisual catbird's seat, and as many of the so-called best and brightest opted to get on the ground floor of a new, mushrooming industry. "Everything you do in television is new," exclaimed one agency executive. "No matter what you try, it's never been done before." [24]

With television now an important component of large advertisers' media plans, many ad agencies seized the opportunity with zeal. After the hard times of the Depression and four war years of "investing in the future while the present was out of stock," advertising executives looked at the new medium as a problematic but vital vehicle by which to deliver the American Dream literally door to door. By June 1950, BBDO had put forty of its clients into television and was turning out commercials at the rate of one a day. Half of BBDO's commercials were presented live, half on film. A one-minute live commercial typically cost about $750 to produce, not including talent, while a one-minute filmed commercial cost about $1,000. Many advertising people felt the extra cost of film was well worth it. "If an actor makes a fluff, you can reshoot the scene," stated Jack Denove, account executive at BBDO. "If he makes a boner on a live commercial, there's nothing you can do about it." [25]

BBDO was agency of record for Lucky Strike cigarettes, and helped produce *Your Lucky Strike Theater,* a one-hour drama in which six minutes of commercial time were devoted to promoting the sponsor's brand. The show generated a 35 audience rating (meaning 35 out of every hundred people viewing television watched the show), an unheard of share in today's 100-plus channel world. "Smoking looks wonderful on television," exclaimed Denove, believing that "smoking is an instantaneous act." A key criterion for being an announcer on this show was being an "inveterate" smoker, evidenced by the ability to simultaneously talk and exhale. Aptitude in producing multiple smoke rings was a particularly valuable skill, although studio lights and air conditioning played havoc with "ring integrity." Cigarette companies were of course avid television advertisers in these days, with Chesterfield sponsoring *Arthur Godfrey and His Friends* and the *Chesterfield Supper Club,* with Perry Como. Camel sponsored the *Camel News Caravan, The Ed Wynn Show,* and a drama, *Man against Crime.* Old Gold sponsored the popular *Original Amateur Hour* and half of *Stop the Music,* while Pall Mall sponsored *The Big Story,* and Philip Morris sponsored *Candid Camera.* As a basic commodity relying on the creation of a compelling brand identity, cigarettes had by necessity become an immediate staple of television advertising's diet. For ad agencies, having a tobacco client on its client roster was a key signifier of industry status and a vital source of revenue and profits.[26]

Technical Difficulties

Although concerns such as "ring integrity" might seem trivial, technical issues such as this one were hardly insignificant matters to producers of commercials at mid-century. Filmmakers had successfully brought sight and sound together for a generation, but a variety of problems plagued television advertising throughout its early years. Commercials, *Time* reported in February 1948, were "causing deep furrows in admen's brows," as the industry struggled with the peculiarities of the new medium and its often live nature. Cameras often dwelled seemingly interminably on static objects like a bar of soap, or bloopers would occur as when an electric razor refused to turn off or the cover of a manual one wouldn't budge. The human factor was always an unknown variable in live television advertising, as when a model mistakenly lauded the praises of Lipton Tea while brewing a pot of the clearly labeled sponsor's brand, Tender Leaf. The opportunities for bungles were many and, from our vantage point today when everything on television is carefully planned, predictable. Praising the reliability of a sponsor's lighters, for example, a spokesperson futilely flicked the lighter with no response. Proudly holding a sponsor's loaf of bread aloft, another announcer urged viewers to buy a competitor's brand. Immediately after saying "Never an irritation," a cigarette pitchman coughed apoplectically. In a live beer commercial, the camera was supposed to momentarily break away from a shot of the drinker bringing a beer to his lips to his smile of satisfaction. In a less than perfectly choreographed instance of this technique, however, the camera returned not to a smile but to the drinker sloshing the beer into a pail at his side. Early commercial television was, as Halberstam put it, "all on the job training and, at first, almost everyone was getting it wrong."[27]

A single evening of television watching could reveal any number of the technical nightmares that pioneering producers of television commercials faced. Shiny surfaces and the color white caused "halation" on television screens, a technical term for glare. Advertisers found white cows to be not at all fit for broadcast, as the medium had the unpleasant effect of turning the creatures into supernatural masses of bright light. Orthicon pickup tubes in some early television cameras were also red sensitive, turning all things crimson into unrecognizable blurs of white. Visual problems were often complemented by awkward, unnatural copy created by writers struggling within the unknown territory of television. Copywriters of radio commercials often suddenly found themselves writers of television spots, and typically had difficulty adapting to the new medium. The phenomenon was similar to what occurred in the film industry with the introduction of sound, when scenes were "overwritten" to feature the new technology. Actors in commercials unnecessarily indicated numbers with their fingers, or spelled out words agonizingly slowly, a habit inherited from radio. Writers imported from the film industry also overestimated the capabilities of the medium, such as by calling for crowd scenes of a dozen or more people, not realizing that on television just four or five people would constitute a crowd. Refugees from the movie business, who were attracted to advertising by its frontier orientation as the studio system fell apart, would also call for long camera shots to depict huge props, making people appear Lilliputian. Television writers quickly learned to focus action in the center of the screen, away from the periphery where images got fuzzy. (It was normal to lose 8 percent of the vertical image and 13 percent of the horizontal in any shot.) Writers previously employed at Walt Disney Studios were also startled by the pace of television, no longer afforded the luxury of having three months or so to write and produce a scene.[28]

Additional, nontechnical concerns plagued advertising executives and their clients during the nascent years of commercial television. Broadcast-

Early television advertising snafus, such as when the cover of a razor stuck during a live spot, were considered newsworthy events. "It took a display of brute strength to get the thing to work," observed one reporter. (Library of Congress)

ing baseball games, for example, as done by Chesterfield in its sponsorship of New York Giants home games over the 1948 season, brought unanticipated risks. Crowd shots occasionally caught married men at the games accompanied by women other than their wives, eventually forcing advertisers to avoid televising scenes of fans over which they would superimpose their logo. Music was an especially tricky area. In 1944, James C. Petrillo, head of the American Federation of Musicians, forbade all members of the union to record music on film for television, afraid perhaps of what effects the unknown medium might have on live music performance. Most early television jingles were thus sung a cappella or accompanied by a musical instrument not officially recognized by the union. An inordinate amount of ukulele music was thus recorded under television commercials of this era, as were the sounds of other "non-official" instruments such as tipples (a steel-stringed ukulele), Jew's harps, kazoos, children's xylophones, toy pianos, and sand blocks. Human voices were also used to simulate the sounds produced by standard musical instruments, creating a cottage industry consisting of people able to replicate bass fiddles, snare drums, trumpets, and saxophones through their mouths and noses.[29]

Not surprisingly, higher brow critics were generally appalled by the sights and sounds of television advertising at mid-century, offended by the medium's clumsiness and carnivalesque qualities. Compared to some other art forms of the era—abstract expressionism in painting, bebop in music, the International Style in architecture—television advertising did indeed seem downright prehistoric. Evangeline Davis, a freelance writer, considered it to be "the spectacle of the crack-up of the Atomic Age," another journalistic coupling of television advertising and atomic energy.[30] In September 1950, Charles W. Morton, a writer for *Atlantic* magazine, attacked the medium for its overt crudity:

Radio's ten-word advertising vocabulary (richer, bigger, easier, finer, newer, smoother, better, milder, safer, brighter) still bounds the chatter of TV's spellbinders, while the accompanying pictorial techniques are largely based on the kind of trick photography that once animated cartoon advertising in the old-time movie house. . . . Messages by smoke signals are about the only stunt that TV has not carried over from more primitive days.[31]

Critics such as Morton were also amazed by television advertisers' penchant for condescending to viewers and overstating the obvious. A commercial for the Lincoln Cosmopolitan, for example, featured a woman pushing a button to lower a window and closing a door, as if these acts in themselves were new and impressive to viewers. Overcome with the ability to show moving pictures of a product, advertisers were acting as if viewers had never seen an automobile, sometimes believing they had to offer proof that the car would actually run. After deconstructing commercials for Chevrolet and Oldsmobile, Morton concluded his critique of the state of automobile television advertising by stating that "most of the motor makers had incomparably better exhibits at the New York World's Fair in 1939 than anything they have shown the growing millions of TV customers."[32]

A stage set for a commercial for Chevrolet in the late 1940s. The studio audience can be seen in the foreground.

By drawing upon scientific and technological themes, however, some automobile manufacturers were able to position their products as symbols of the future versus remnants of the past. Oldsmobile, in fact, advertised its 1949 88 model as "futuramic through and through," the least expensive automobile to have a "high compression rocket engine." (The "Rocket 88" would indeed point the way to the future, becoming the subject for what many argue is the first rock'n'roll song.) Commercials for Studebaker's 1950 Champion emphasized the car's progressive marriage of form and function, referring to the automobile as a "melody in metal" and "symphony in steel." Through such commercials, television advertising shared and promulgated the forward-looking, utopian vision of the postwar years, portraying the American Dream as a technological wonderland.[33]

Arts and Crafts

Postwar themes such as the future, outer space, or industrial design illustrated the range of conceptual elements advertisers had at their disposal. In addition to having a palette of culturally charged references to draw from, advertisers had an array of different creative genres to choose from, resulting in some commercials which could be considered excellent even by today's standards. The musical extravaganza was by and large considered the most popular, with singers, dancers, clowns, and announcers collaborating to create a Broadway-like production number. Commercial presentations on *Lucky Strike Theater* best exemplified this approach, as some 150 people performed 214 separate jobs to present Luckies as Cecil B. DeMille might have. Cartoons or animated commercials were a second major genre, allowing advertisers to enter the realm of fantasy and imagination. Documentaries were another form of presentation, applied most effectively when advertisers showed consumers the makings of their product in a factory or on an assembly line. The slice-of-

A commercial for Shell gasoline from the late 1940s, complete with a mock service station in a television studio.

life drama or morality play borrowed from radio was, of course, a common genre, with advertisers featuring their products as the solution to everyday problems. Hair tonic became the key to instant popularity, breakfast cereal the deliverer of superhuman energy. All of these genres had deep roots in American popular culture, which helped cloak television commercials as a form of entertainment. There was no doubt that early television advertising had some very rough edges, but its appropriation of popular culture was as powerful a propaganda technique as any.[34]

At the local level, the production of commercials was a significantly less sophisticated affair. In fact, sponsors were known to tell television station owners "not to worry about talent," that is, professional announcers or actors, with many owners agreeing to sponsors' requests that the former personally deliver the commercials. Likewise, it was not unusual for station owners to encourage sponsors to act as commercial talent, believing that the medium was too new for viewers to tell a good spokesperson from a bad one. Sponsors sometimes wanted to appear in their own ads on the premise that a professional announcer's lack of knowledge and sincerity about the product being sold would not come across visually. At the network level, many sponsors believed that they knew more about the formula for a winning television show than the writers and directors. Sponsors with their wives and friends were known to watch "their" show at dinner parties, often leading to suggestions on how to improve it. After a sponsor insisted on tinkering with the production elements, however, the show's ratings almost always fell, puzzling the sponsor but not at all the show's producers.[35]

Despite sponsors' misguided leanings toward the creative side of the business, television was immeasurably advancing the evolution of advertising, making possible a quantum leap in the industry's development. As uni-dimensional media, both radio and print placed severe constraints on advertising technique. As a bi-dimensional medium, television exponentially added to the ways in which advertising could be presented to the consumer. After initially borrowing radio's format of simply reading a sales message into a microphone, television advertisers quickly incorporated visual devices— demonstrations, optical slides, flap cards—into commercials. Filmmaking techniques were next applied to television advertising, as alumni from cinema brought animation, stop motion, and live action to the medium. Afforded the ability to make their products march, skip, and jump, advertisers were now pressuring directors to pack every technique of a Hollywood film into a one-minute commercial. When professional actors were not cast as talent, advertisers looked to the infinite possibilities of animation and special effects to make their products seem truly fantastic. A menagerie of waddling polar bears, skating penguins, magic rabbits, and talking dogs, for example, populated television screens at mid-century, descendents of the workings of Walt Disney's and the Warner Brothers' imagination. Dazzled or perhaps dazed by the creative possibilities in television advertising, *Time* magazine viewed the medium in June 1951 as "a precocious prodigy," with "a dozen different ways of huckstering its products and dizzying its audience."[36]

One of the more popular special effects advertisers used to "huckster" was combining animation with live action. Young & Rubicam, for example, used the technique notably well in a 1952 spot called "Swinging Apples" for Mott's Apple Cider, also suggesting that craft-obsessed 1950s homemakers save the jug and make a lamp out of it by using a "handy converter kit available from Mott's." Through the wonders of technology, agencies also had the ability to ensure their clients' products would be in fashion months after a commercial was shot. For a commercial for a home permanent kit called Shadow Wave, made by the Pepsodent Company, for example, McCann-Erickson styled and filmed model Barbara Britton's hair seven different ways. With the commercial scheduled to air six months after the shooting, the agency planned to air the version with the most up-to-date hair style.[37]

Dodge was an avid supporter of the fauna-inspired school of television advertising, in one spot using a family of talking rabbits as a metaphor for the viewing audience (many of whom were breeding just as prolifically). The company's new 1951 model was filled entirely with real rabbits to illustrate how much room the new car held. "If you're a big family man like me," the daddy bunny advised via a human voice-over, "better get a Dodge." The automobile maker's penchant for using vocally gifted animals was apparent in another commercial for the 1951 model. After an announcer wondered aloud what could be more beautiful than a peacock, such a bird miraculously appeared to suggest that he "step inside a new Dodge" to find out. Viewers were then treated to the "pleasing color combinations and new ideas in fabric and design" which made up the car's interior, a legitimate reference to the amazing advances being made at the time in synthetic textiles. Dodge's emphasis on the roominess and aesthetics of its 1951 model was complemented by commercials featuring the car's safety features. In yet another talking animal spot for Dodge which employed a "wise old owl," viewers were encouraged to "play it safe and buy a Dodge." The bird proceeded to list the many safety features of the 1951 model, which included rugged all-steel body construction, wraparound windshields for greater visibility, wider rearview mirrors, improved handling, "safety rim" wheels, and "safe-guard" brakes. Although Americans in fact put style over safety when it came to automobile priorities, Dodge's owl hootingly concluded that "for safety first, it's Dodge." Dodge's commercials clearly borrowed from Hollywood's anthropomorphic animals so pervasive in family entertainment, a smart co-opting of popular culture.[38]

In addition to special effects, testimonials from celebrities represented a tried-and-true means of attracting viewer attention. Themselves new to the medium, stars almost always tempered their fame by speaking with unusual sincerity and conviction. Stars also began to incorporate plugs into their acts, regularly pitching products for sponsors before, in between, or after their television performances. In 1949, Gertrude Berg, star of the popular situation comedy *The Goldbergs,* stayed in character on behalf of Sanka decaffeinated coffee. "You can drink as much as you want, as often as you want," she explained, "because the sleep is left in." Lipsitz has acutely noted the semiotics of coffee in *Mama,* arguing that the integration of Maxwell House into the narrative of that show linked the powerful concept of family to "an entire attitude about consumption." Other stars used their talent to deliver advertising as entertainment. Television's first big star, Milton Berle, bravely sang the "Pepsi-Cola Hits the Spot" jingle on a June 1949 episode of *The Texaco Star Theater,* while Dinah Shore, of course, regularly sang "See the U.S.A. in Your Chevrolet" on her own NBC show. Such techniques, what Marchand called "dramatized commercials," were lifted from radio days when, in the early 1930s, radio talent were known to pitch sponsors' products while in character in a separate segment of the program. Although some in the radio industry believed this sort of advertising strayed too far into commercial crassness, it soon became standard practice, and ultimately applied to and expanded in the new medium of television.[39]

Advertainment

The most effective kind of commercials, however, were those which did not appear to be commercials at all, a tenet that stemmed from radio. Most advertisers rightfully believed that any form of overt selling caused a certain level of skepticism among consumers, the underlying premise being to disguise advertising as entertainment. The "pitchman" on *The Texaco Star Theater,* for example, was presented as simply one of the show's characters. Studio audiences actually applauded his readings of Havoline oil and gas commercials, considering the ads just another part of the show. For the millions viewing at home, commercials were designed to act as surrogate personal salespeople, able to make more calls than an army of Willy Lomans. Communicating with viewers was most effectively achieved, advertising theory went, when commercials were perceived as an integral part of shows. "A truly good commercial is the well integrated one," said Norman Nash, assistant copy chief of the Kudner Agency, "one that does not break the mood of the entertainment vehicle." On *Private Eye,* a detective drama sponsored by U.S. Tobacco, commercials were regularly woven into shows. The hero of the series regularly "dropped in" on his favorite smoke shop, bantering with other characters about the merits of different types of tobacco. Counter and shelf displays of the sponsor's brands visually complemented the audio, multiplying the number of advertising impressions or exposures.[40] Scripted commercials often ran as long as six minutes, the same amount of time the industry code allowed for advertising in an hour. Because integrated commercials were "off the clock," however, sponsors theoretically had unlimited time in which to sell their products. Hal Humphrey, noted television and radio critic for the Los Angeles *Mirror,* half-seriously feared that

some sponsor will come up with the brainy idea that he can build an entire thirty-minute plot around his product. The hero will be floundering around in the Sahara Desert, ready to die of hunger, exposure and thirst, when suddenly he will come upon a cache of food, clothing and beer upon which will be the brand names of all the participating sponsors.[41]

Integrated advertising was also used to counter sponsors' and ad agencies' worst fear—that viewers were using commercial breaks to prepare snacks or visit the restroom. In order to avoid spending good money on temporarily absent viewers, sponsors had performers extol the wonders of their product as part of the program. One of the better interpretations of integrated television advertising took place during *The Burns and Allen Show,* when Bill Goodwin, the announcer, would chat with Gracie about the joys of Carnation Milk. The technique was successful in holding onto viewers, as it was unclear when the interchange would segue back into the main part of the show. In radio, Jack Benny, Arthur Godfrey, and others had proved that commercials could be made entertaining, perhaps as much so as the rest of the program. In their radio careers, Marchand has noted, Benny, Godfrey, and other stars such as Ed Wynn were encouraged by sponsors to mention ("kid" in showbiz lingo) brand names into their skits and routines as a means to link the star's personality to the product. When these stars entered tele-

Paul M. Hahn, president of the American Tobacco Company, accepting TV Guide*'s Gold Medal from publisher Lee Wagner, as A. R. Stevens, American Tobacco's advertising manager, looks on in January 1951. The company received the award for its "Be Happy, Go Lucky" campaign, which the magazine cited for "delivering the sales message in the most beguiling and painless way, with deftness, freshness and originality that make it a fine little entertainment on its own." (Library of Congress)*

vision, they continued to personalize commercials by blending them into their schtick, often to critical acclaim. "Some of [Benny's] 'Be Happy, Go Lucky' plugs [for Lucky Strike]," Humphrey, wrote, "are more entertaining than the programs." [42]

Over the course of *The Jack Benny Program*'s long history, advertising was woven into sketches and character personalities to the point where it could hardly be distinguished from other elements of the show. Both regular cast members and guest stars sang commercial jingles and endorsed products for the show's principal sponsors, Lucky Strike, Lux, State Farm Insurance, and Jell-O, a direct lift from radio days. As announcer, Don Wilson usually delivered the commercial, but was often joined by Benny, Dennis Day, Rochester (played by Eddie Anderson), and Harlow, Don's teenage son. The Sportmen

Quartet regularly sang the sponsor's jingle in a style accordant with a particular show's theme, occasionally joined or replaced by a guest singer. Made perfectly clear by the opening words "brought to you by," *The Jack Benny Program* was as pure a commercial vehicle as television could possibly get. In 1952, for example, plugs for Lucky Strike were directly integrated into the scripts of shows, a practice that continued through the life of the program. In a January episode, Don refused to read the Lucky Strike commercial, believing it too silly, but Jack forced him to do it. In a March show, the Sportmen Quartet performed the sponsor's jingle ("Any Time You Light a Lucky") in Benny's crowded dressing room, while in June they sang "Bye Bye Benny" as part of the Lucky commercial (Benny was purportedly off to England for a concert tour). In an October show, Don read the Lucky Strike spot while new cast member Bob Crosby and Benny discussed contract terms, while four weeks later, Dinah Shore joined the Sportmen Quartet for the Lucky jingle. The product and jingle appeared to be infinitely malleable, able to fit into virtually any scenario or plotline.[43]

Like *The Jack Benny Program*, Arthur Godfrey's show represented state-of-the-art integrated advertising and raised the bar of "commercialness" in commercial broadcasting. Godfrey was a master at the "impromptu" commercial, weaving announcements for Lipton, Pillsbury, and Chesterfield products into his *Talent Scouts* show. Godfrey effortlessly transferred his relaxed, folksy style from radio to television, furthering his reputation as a master in subtle persuasion (Godfrey is credited with popularizing air travel because the star said it was safe). On his radio show, Godfrey was known to surprise both listener and sponsor, as in the time he audibly ate Peter Pan peanut butter on the air. On television, Godfrey came off as equally spontaneous, although his pitches were in fact more carefully orchestrated. In a classic 1950 plug, Godfrey said he wished that all the seats in the theater were equipped with fountains flowing with Lipton tea. With observations like these, Godfrey defied another staple of postwar advertising, the rational approach calling for facts, figures, and diagrams.[44]

Stars were not also above shameless self-promotion, using television guest spots as vehicles to advertise their own "products." On a May 1950 episode of NBC's *Star-Spangled Revue,* for example, Bob Hope cleverly substituted the name of the show's sponsor to spoof (and promote) his road movies. In the sketch called "The Road to Frigidaire," Hope played himself opposite Frank Sinatra (in his television debut), the latter playing Bing Crosby's role in "The Road to" film series. Milton Berle appeared briefly at the end of the sketch, adding to the mayhem. The idea was a win-win situation for both Hope, who received free (actually paid) publicity for his movies, and Frigidaire, which gained significantly greater brand recognition than via the General Motors division's regular commercials for automatic washers running during the show. On *The Jack Benny Program* in January 1951, Sinatra conveniently dropped the name of his own music and variety show (also on CBS), as well as the show's sponsor (Timex). The next month on *The Colgate Comedy Hour,* Jerry Lewis somehow managed to plug not only the sponsor but also a number of his friends in a single, frenetic outburst. Literally combining the language of entertainment with that of commerce created a powerful synergy of "advertainment," endorsed by the biggest stars of the day.[45]

In its earliest, most innocent incarnation, which also dated back to radio, plugging a sponsor's product (referred to in slang as "plugola," after "payola," paying disk jockeys to play a record company's songs) typically involved rewarding a comic or writer with a free product sample for a mention during an act. Entrepreneurs in plugola, known as "schlockmeisters" in the trade, facilitated the process by sending requests to writing teams for product plugs. Although some writers and producers objected to the practice, others believed that brand names were a legitimate part of the vernacular, thus warranting inclusion in entertainment programs. Receiving some sort of gift, ranging from a case of scotch to a lifetime supply of fertilizer, was viewed simply as fair compensation, an expression of American free enterprise.[46]

Although plugola certainly gave the appearance of excessive greed among stars, some hosts of popular shows used their fame to also plug their favorite charities on air. On the *Cavalcade of Stars* in December 1951, for example, Jackie Gleason solicited viewers' contributions to the National Amputation Foundation. In April 1952 on *The Colgate Comedy Hour,* Jerry Lewis requested donations to the Muscular Dystrophy Association, a foreshadowing of his later telethon work. Such appeals—half genuine goodwill and half smart public relations—were not unusual. Critics such as Humphrey nonetheless believed that it was a mistake for stars to be television spokespeople, accusing Dean Martin, Jerry Lewis, and Danny Thomas of pure greed for endorsing Bulova watches. "Our admiration for the talents of many video names drops sharply as soon as they shed their role as actor to give a sales talk on soap or automobiles," he thought. By September 1952, Humphrey had completely tired of any form of celebrity endorsements on television, believing them to "smack of the old carnival practice which lured the hicks into the tent with dancing girls, but you didn't get to see them until you shelled out another 50 cents."[47]

Undaunted by such criticism, sponsors continued the practices of integrated advertising, testimonials, and plugola. Additionally, advertisers who could not afford expensive sponsorships found other ways to get their products seen on national television. "Hidden" commercials were those in which an advertiser's product was inserted into a scene of a television program. On an episode of *Philco Television Playhouse* in June 1951, for example, a bottle of Johnson's Baby Oil was shown on a night table as a mother was about to change her baby. On a *Garroway at Large* program that same month, Connie Russell poured herself a cup of coffee with a can of Pet Milk in full view. In each case, the marketer of the product shown was not a sponsor of the program; the placement was simply an arrangement made with a propmaster or producer in exchange for an under-the-table payment of some kind. This form of visual, silent plugola had been common in films before the industry temporarily banned it. A more legitimate form of placement was that in which sponsors' products were given away as prizes on shows. On *This Is Your Life,* for example, honored guests received not only a movie camera, television, and range, but also some of sponsor Hazel Bishop's Lipstick as well. The gift-awarding portion of shows was, of course, free incremental advertising, a means to extend sponsors' product exposure and time on the air.[48]

Kid Stuff

Disturbingly, advertisers had no qualms about using such techniques to promote products to children, drawn to the huge and still growing target market of "junior consumers." Ellen Seiter has observed that marketers of children's products have always relied on television advertising simply because younger kids cannot read, which automatically eliminates newspapers, magazines, outdoor, and direct marketing as media options. This fact was not lost on radio advertisers either, who recognized that kids could listen to shows (and commercials) without adult supervision. Early television advertisers exploited this advantage by creating programs that were essentially extended commercials. On NBC's *The Magic Clown* in 1951, for example, sponsor Bonomo Turkish Taffy made the confectionery product a major component of the show's plots. On one such program, a particularly excited harlequin (in the title role) performed magic while passing out the taffy to the studio audience of children (who, strangely, happen to be wearing fezzes). The sponsor found another way to blend the show with its product, employing another character, Laffy the puppet, to cast a spell that dissolved into a commercial for the taffy. After urging viewers to buy all three flavors of Bonomo Turkish Taffy, Laffy recited a poem that segued into a commercial for yet another sponsor product, Bonomo's Peanut Brittle. At the end of the show, The Magic Clown fittingly returned to remind viewers to buy lots of taffy. Since its premier in late 1947, the NBC children's show *Howdy Doody* had also been used as a platform for sponsors to sell products to kids. By using the show's characters to endorse products, sponsors were exploiting children's relative inability to distinguish commercials from entertainment. On a July 1952 show, Buffalo Bob, Clarabell, and Oil Well Willie pitched Kellogg's Rice Krispies and Colgate's Toothpaste, while the very next day Howdy Doody and Buffalo Bob conversed about the wonders of Wonder Bread. Buffalo Bob and his wooden friend also occasionally made appeals for products targeted to adults, as when they used the Doodyville Clubhouse to do a commercial spot for *TV Guide.* Because both moms and kids often watched children's television shows together, they were an ideal means of selling the American Dream to the entire family.[49]

As Lynn Spigel discussed extensively in *Make Room for TV: Television and the Family Ideal in Postwar America,* children were also considered an important target audience by the television manufacturing industry itself. Late in 1950, television manufacturers led a newspaper and radio advertising campaign in the attempt to sell more sets, focusing on the kid market. The industry's campaign used scare tactics, telling parents that their children would become social misfits if they didn't have television sets at home. "Your daughter won't ever tell you the humiliation she's felt in begging those precious hours of television from a neighbor," one ad read, while another claimed that "it is practically impossible for boys and girls to 'hold their own' with friends and schoolmates unless television is available to them." Hal Humphrey noted that marketers of consumer goods were also targeting children through questionable advertising techniques, reprising some less than proud moments of radio's past. More advertisers are "borrow[ing] a page from radio and direct[ing] their sales pitches at the small fry, asking them to 'tell your daddy and mommy to buy you one, like all the rest of the children have,'" Humphrey observed. A survey conducted by Advertest Research of New Brunswick, New Jersey in 1951 confirmed Humphrey's observation that advertisers were aggressively targeting kids, finding that 60 percent of mothers said their children asked for products they saw advertised on television. Humphrey believed that it was not children who were at emotional risk but rather "the parents who will have to look up a psychiatrist" if kids continued to be targeted as consumers.[50]

As marketers flocked to television to reach a mass audience of all family members, other interesting ethical issues arose. One particularly interesting site of commercial television's intersection with ethics took place in November 1951 when executives at KSL-TV, a station owned by the Mormon church in Salt Lake City, decided to put aside their religious scruples to run beer-sponsored shows on CBS. Although the station claimed that "the audience building motivation rather than money" was the deciding factor, the network was likely pressuring KSL to carry the programs, losing patience with having to divert the shows to competing stations. Beer ads thus joined the cigarette-sponsored programs and commercials the station was already airing to a largely Mormon audience. Church officials, however, quickly found a way to ease their lingering guilty consciences. The station developed a series of shorts depicting the evils associated with smoking, sometimes airing them shortly after the cigarette-sponsored shows. In one such short, a policeman examining a car wreck somehow determined that the motorist had taken his eyes off the road to light a cigarette. Such counterproductive, schizophrenic efforts could be expected in those pockets of the country not quite ready to embrace unrequited consumerism involving the vices of tobacco and alcohol.[51]

Public Affairs

As television advertising became a louder voice in the public arena, it was inevitable that politics would soon cross its path, creating quite a stir in journalistic circles. The 1948 political conventions were televised, but the 1952 conventions were the first to be sponsored by advertisers. As a public service, Westinghouse offered to sponsor the Republican convention on CBS while Philco offered to sponsor the Democratic convention on NBC. Newspaper editors were suspicious of the plan, believing that corporate sponsorship and politics did not mix, and that such an approach would somehow affect the objectivity of the telecasts. Their wariness toward television, and particularly television advertising, was in part being driven by the realities of competition. With advertising dollars (and perhaps their jobs) at stake, newspaper publishers and editors had been openly critical of the television industry for running too many commercials. The subtext of these claims was, of course, that the precocious prodigy of television advertising represented a real threat to the fiscal health of newspapers across the country. The claims of television

Home Team

There is great happiness in television...great happiness in the home
where the family is held together by this new common bond – television. And for those
who would know the fullest measure of television enjoyment, and see its stirring pageant
in thrilling clarity, Du Mont laboratories build television's finest instruments...the Du Mont receivers.
Everything a television set can be, everything it can offer, is yours in a Du Mont.
Console, combinations, table models.

*Du Mont built the first commercial home television receiver –
Du Mont builds the finest.*

DU MONT

First with the finest in Television

THE TARRYTOWN BY DU MONT,
with 17-inch Lifetone* picture.

Ad No. 280B
Look Magazine—October 10, 1950
Colliers (Roto)—October 14, 1950

This ad for Du Mont television sets, which ran in Look *and* Collier's *magazines in October 1950, positioned the medium as an agent of family togetherness and home sweet home. With its own network, Du Mont (like NBC with its parent RCA) delivered the American Dream through both consumerism (TV sets) and entertainment (TV shows). (NMAH Archives Center, Smithsonian Institution)* being overcommercialized relative to newspapers were, in fact, unwarranted. One independent analysis revealed that an average newspaper contained far more column inches of advertising than news, a proportion much greater than the commercial-to-program ratio in television.[52]

Presidential candidates themselves used television advertising for the 1952 campaign, perhaps the first real packaging of political figures for American consumption. With Cold War paranoia running rampant, candidate Dwight Eisenhower adeptly used television commercials to tap into Americans' fears of a Russian attack. The visual portion of his campaign, themed "Eisenhower Answers America," employed a montage of photographs of the general in military action, World War II film footage, and Ike answering questions from "ordinary" Americans. The spots were created by Rosser Reeves of the Ted Bates Agency, which filmed Eisenhower giving answers to a set of preset questions that were only later posed by "ordinary" people such as a housewife and veteran. In one spot, Eisenhower (billed as "the man from Abilene") was asked, "General, if war comes, is this country ready?" Eisenhower's rehearsed answer:

It is not. The administration has spent many billions of dollars for national defense, yet today we haven't enough tanks for the fighting in Korea. It is time for a change.[53]

Viewers were then ordered to "put out a sturdy lifeboat in November" by making the war hero president. Ike's boat did indeed come in to shore, despite the fact that agency executives thought their client consistently came off on television as rather clumsy.[54]

Betty Furness, an ex-screen actress, played a prominent role during the 1952 political convention telecast, actually getting more screen time (four and a half hours) than any of the candidates or reporters. Equipped with a wardrobe of twenty dresses, Ms. Furness went on the air on behalf of Westinghouse appliances a total of 158 times. By the end of the conventions, she had opened 49 refrigerator doors, looked into 12 ovens, demonstrated 23 washing machines and dishwashers, and turned on 42 television sets. Furness's career was rejuvenated by commercial work, as she became more famous than ever by demonstrating Westinghouse products on the show *Studio One*. Westinghouse chose Ms. Furness not only because she was "an excellent actress who didn't look as if she was acting," but also because she "looks a little older than a woman who will steal your husband." (Betty was a ripe old thirty-six.) Furness was a perfect choice for Westinghouse, as was the company's sponsorship of the political convention. It would be a full decade, in fact, before most advertisers recognized the prestige to be gained by sponsoring public affairs programming.[55]

Television advertising's venture into the political arena was just one way civic events were becoming, literally, commercial affairs. Many viewers were surprised if not shocked by the encroachment of advertising into broadcasts considered to be "public service." In the spring of 1952, blouse and hat manufacturers sponsored the national broadcast of the Fifth Avenue Easter Parade, considered by some to be an inappropriate coupling of public and private interests. In fall 1952, NBC sold the upcoming broadcast of the Eisenhower inauguration to General Motors, while the Du Mont network sold a series of Bishop Fulton Sheen sermons to the Admiral Corporation for $1 million. These too were interpreted by some to be signs that the American broadcasting system had become overcommercialized, and that television stations were no longer dedicated to serving the public's interest as stated in their license agreements. Further blurring the lines between information and commercialism were the first "advertorials," termed "educational films" when they first appeared in the early 1950. The Aluminum Company of America (Alcoa) was one of the initial advocates of this form of television advertising, recognizing its power to influence public opinion in a subtle manner. Alcoa sponsored Edward R. Murrow's *See It Now,* a good fit for public relations-style advertising given the show's journalistic bent. On an April 1952 show, Murrow discussed fan mail about an Alcoa advertorial concerning an aluminum PT boat, thereby effectively promoting his sponsor during the "news" part of the show. The lines between journalism and commerce would become increasingly fuzzy in the years ahead as corporate interests looked to the public domain as advertising fodder, extending the reach and hegemony of consumer capitalism.[56]

Growing Pains

Via its gradual appropriation of public events and its consistently increasing number of viewers, television advertising's status as a media vehicle continued to grow. With the rush to television advertising on, and the cost of producing shows still rising, network sponsorship fees reached all-time highs. For the 1952 television season beginning in the fall, CBS priced sponsorship of *The Jackie Gleason Show* at $90,000 a week, considered a huge amount of money at the time. A seasonal contract for the show, which consisted of thirty-nine weeks, was available for the startling figure of $3,510,000. For its ninety-minute *Your Show of Shows* starring Sid Caesar and Imogene Coca,

NBC priced a half-hour sponsorship somewhat more reasonably at $55,000. One-minute commercials placed after each half-hour segment of the show were priced at $17,600, or a cool $1 million for the full fifty-two-week season. Holding basically all the cards for companies wishing to tell their message to a national audience in a single evening, networks knew they could command such prices. The Sunday night *Colgate Comedy Hour,* which cost a sponsor $60,000 for the hour, was sold out, as was the Saturday night *All-Star Revue,* the most expensive of television shows at $110,000 for the hour.[57]

Despite the rising cost of television, marketers continued to allocate more of their advertising dollars to the medium and less to radio. According to *Advertising Age,* in 1951 radio advertising billings were down 5 percent from 1950 and down over 12 percent from 1948, with most of this money shifted into television advertising. For the first time in their history, networks were beginning to make more money from their television operations than from radio. Recognizing an opportunity to save some money, Procter and Gamble, radio's largest advertiser, told CBS it would cancel some of its programs unless the network dropped radio advertising rates (which CBS and the three other radio networks promptly did). Even with these lower rates, Procter and Gamble and other big marketers began a major defection from radio advertising in 1952, putting more and more money into television. As Lynn Spigel found in her research, daytime television, often a test pattern in the late 1940s, became a hot commodity during the 1950–1951 season, as "A" (later, prime) time sold out.[58]

Because of its high cost, however, the traditional single sponsorship (which had also been standard in radio) was showing the first real signs of breaking down in commercial television. The number of single sponsorship shows was beginning to fall as networks began to offer alternate or shared sponsorships as a means for advertisers to cover production costs. According to Edward Madden, sales and operations vice president at NBC, splitting costs was the only way that many advertisers could afford network television. During the 1952 season, in fact, *Your Show of Shows* had six sponsors, while *All-Star Revue* had three. For marketers who could afford it, however, television advertising was clearly worth the price. Half of the nation's 16 million television sets were usually tuned to the most popular show at any given time, with an average of about three viewers per set. How else could advertisers literally speak to 24 million Americans scattered across the country at once?[59]

The huge profit to be made in television broadcasting was reflected by the temptation among both network and local television stations to crowd more commercials into their shows. In June 1952, the National Association of Educational Broadcasters found that 19 percent of the total content on New York and Los Angeles television consisted of advertising. It was not unusual for nine minutes of a half-hour show to be devoted to commercials, with another twelve minutes of the show prominently featuring the name of the sponsor on a backdrop during the program itself (meaning some shows were 70 percent advertising!). Although the FCC had no jurisdiction over the length or number of commercials, the National Association of Radio and Television Broadcasters (NARTB) employed a voluntary code or set of standards to which all four networks subscribed. For "A," or prime viewing periods, a maximum of three minutes of commercial time was recommended for a half-hour show. It was clear that television broadcasters were regularly exceeding the code's guidelines regarding the amount of commercial time, as they were with respect to sponsor backdrops; the NARTB code stated that "stationary backdrops or properties in television presentations showing the sponsor's name or product . . . may be used only incidentally." The NARTB was more firm regarding what could or should be depicted in commercials, apparently more concerned with the content of advertising than its quantity. "Profanity, obscenity, smut, and vulgarity are forbidden," the code stated, adding that "suicide as an acceptable solution for human problems is prohibited." The industry association's priorities were not surprising given that more advertising meant happier members with fatter wallets from higher sales.[60]

George Washington Hill's Ghost

Operating with a set of purely voluntary guidelines, the NARTB could and would do little to stop broadcasters choosing to look the other way when it came to infraction. Some advertisers, such as Charles Antell Inc., a maker of hair tonic, completely violated the NARTB's suggestions, producing and airing fifteen-minute—and sometimes half-hour—commercials not unlike today's infomercials. Radio networks and stations refused to air Antell's commercials, but some local profit-hungry television stations willingly took the business. Although Charles Kasher, the president of the company, positioned his commercials as a form of education and entertainment, viewers did not mistake the voice and gestures of the spots' carnival barker-like spokesperson as anything but an extended advertising pitch. Additionally, with no enforcement of the sound volume of commercials, many advertisers turned up their audio to obnoxiously high levels. Some advertisers appeared to be heeding the famous advice of the late George Washington Hill, founder of American Tobacco, who believed that the most effective advertising was that which irritated people into buying products through insistent, unrelenting clamor.[61]

With their hard-sell approach, marketers of beauty aids and over-the-counter health remedies were considered by most critics and lay people alike to be carrying on the tradition of George Washington Hill. Manufacturers in these product categories were almost always firm believers that when it came to television advertising, more was definitely more. For a 1952 commercial for Bufferin, "The A & B Race," for example, Young & Rubicam used a combination of sound effects, visual aids, and an authoritative voice-over to get and keep viewers' attention. The mnemonic device of a beating drum was used to represent the pain associated with a headache, supported by an equally disturbing diagram simulating the condition. Against this "scientific" audio-visual backdrop, viewers were told that Bufferin was "the modern way to get fast relief from headaches, neuralgia, or ordinary muscle aches and pains." With the combination of music, art, and rational argument, popular advertising theory went, all dimensions of viewers' thinking processes were activated, the key to effective persuasion. Despite or perhaps because the commercial is a masterpiece in annoyance, it is enshrined in the Clio Hall of Fame, the industry's central repository of what it has deemed the greatest commercials of all time.[62]

With scientific research a ubiquitous presence in postwar America, all things scientific invaded television advertising with a vengeance. Actors playing doctors or researchers, almost always in white laboratory jackets, routinely provided facts and figures definitively "proving" their sponsor's product was superior to the competition, at least until a competitor's commercial would offer directly opposite "proof." More critical viewers quickly tired of the contradictory tests, charts, and graphs, recognizing that the offered evidence was generated by a distant cousin of science created especially for the medium. Both the *Southern California Dental Association's Journal* and the *Los Angeles County Medical Association Bulletin* took issue with such science for advertising's sake, calling for the banning of doctor and dentist "imposters" in television commercials. Not only did those in the health care field believe that their professional reputations could be damaged by such representations, but they feared that the public's health was endangered by such advertising. "Medical analysis of the 'T-zone,' physiological effectiveness of deodorants, means of ending vitamin deficiencies and causes of hair disorders belong in the competent hands of an authorized doctor," wrote Dr. Paul D. Foster of the County Medical Association, "not in the hands of an advertising agency searching for the most effective method of bringing the public into their client's fold."[63]

Largely because of health and beauty aid and some other marketers' reliance on the hard-sell approach, television advertising's public image was already suffering. A study completed by Social Research found in May 1951 that it was "very common in our society to dislike [television] advertising" and that viewers generally regarded commercials with "the stoical air appropriate to a necessary evil." More specifically, viewers disliked noisy and clichéd commercials, when too many spots were stacked together, and when commercials suddenly interrupted programs. Viewers considered the best commercials those in which a star (such as Benny, Godfrey, or Dennis James of *Stop the Music*) inspired or amused them and those in which they learned something through a demonstration. Interestingly, opinions in this study differed significantly by class. The upper middle class (12 percent of viewers) was most critical of commercials, the middle class (65 percent of viewers) somewhat tolerant, and the lower middle class (23 percent of viewers) generally receptive, the latter feeling a sense of duty to pay attention to the sales message "because the advertiser pays for the program." This class dynamic seemed to reflect the economics of early television ownership, when a set was considered a relative luxury. Less affluent viewers were likely more tolerant of commercials because they were more likely to consider watching television a privilege, and to appreciate being invited by advertisers to the American Dream party.[64]

Other research studies confirmed that many if not most viewers found the number, length, and some techniques of television advertising to be irritating. In a joint NBC-Hofstra College study, researcher Horace Schwerin found that disliked messages were remembered better and longer than "neutral" ones, but well-liked commercials sold twice as many products as hated ones. This fortunate finding was perhaps the only thing preventing more advertisers to adopt the George Washington Hill school of advertising by intentionally and continually annoying viewers. Findings published by Daniel Starch, a leading audience research firm, also indicated that "attention-getting devices are usually a waste of time (and money)" and that "admen must learn that attracting attention is in itself not essential." Television advertising would have to get better not for viewers' sake, but for the marketers' own.[65]

A People's Art

Well-liked commercials not only translated into higher sales, but offered the possibility of bridging social classes and thereby broadening a brand's appeal. Johnny, the diminutive Philip Morris advertising icon, moved effortlessly into television from his previous incarnations in print, radio, and outdoor. Within his persona as a bellhop of a high-class, mythical hotel, Johnny's televisual mission at mid-century was to convince non-Philip Morris smokers that the brand offered "milder, fresher smoke." In one commercial, two construction workers sitting on a skyscraper's steel beam are about to light up a competitive brand when Johnny suddenly appears. "Did I hear a call for Philip Morris?" he famously asks, subsequently persuading the working-class men to come to their senses by becoming loyal Philip Morris smokers. Although a symbol of the elite, the character was intended to transcend class in order to maximize Philip Morris's potential market. "Johnny operates in all levels of society," *Sales Management* succinctly concluded. Lucky Strike also appealed to popular tastes through a series of animated commercials produced by N. W. Ayer. In "Acrobats," a troupe of circus acrobats delivered the brand's slogan of "L.S./M.F.T." (Lucky Strike Means Fine Tobacco), while in "General Leaf," a squad of tobacco leaf soldiers lined up for inspection delivered the slogan. In a third spot of the campaign, an animated Swiss man smoking on a mountaintop served as protagonist. With television no longer an appliance for the wealthy, marketers were using the medium to appeal to the large and still expanding middle class.[66]

There were, indeed, clear signs that television was now one of the most populist of mediums, such as when viewers responded favorably, even passionately, to television commercials by mail. Letters of support poured in to the Schlitz company, for example, after the brewer aired a commercial in complete silence by using pantomime. "Other beer programs usually come out blasting your head off," one viewer wrote. "People will someday wise up and refuse the junky TV advertising, but your type will last." Spokespeople and even fictitious characters were at times similarly praised. Sid Stone, a pitchman for Texaco on *The Milton Berle Show,* reportedly received more fan mail than the star of the show for a period of time. Muriel, the animated lady cigar, was a particularly celebrated icon of television culture throughout the 1950s. In "Sexy Cigar," a 1951 spot produced by Lennen & Newell, the ad agency for Consolidated Cigar, a male and female cigar song-and-dance team performed a "soft-shoe" routine. The spot ended with Muriel asking viewers the famous question, "Why don't you pick me up and smoke me sometime?" which was a somewhat daring double entendre at the time. Not only did Muriel boost sales, but the character entered the vernacular of every-day life by serving as a popular costume for masquerade parties. The cigar company annually received hundreds of requests for the commercial's music and lyrics from viewers wanting to dress up as the sexy cigar. Likewise, the Chiquita Banana was an unusually popular anthropomorphic piece of fruit that served as inspiration for more festive postwar partyers. Perhaps the most memorable and loved symbol of postwar television advertising, however, was the dancing package of Old Gold cigarettes. By June 1952, Floria Vestoff had been dancing inside a large cardboard pack of Old Golds for three years, in the process wearing out twelve of the gray-and-white boxes.[67]

With television advertising now entrenched in postwar American culture, critics argued over whether commercials, as a form of creative expression, qualified as "art." Gilbert Seldes, a renowned journalist now writing for *The Saturday Review,* opined that television advertising represented a unique morphing of art and business, that

the commercial cannot be a pure work of art because it is also a piece of propaganda; it lives in no tower of Ivory Soap; it comes down into the marketplace and fights. Suppose we call it a highly developed, but mixed, form of people's art.[68]

Whether or not it was a true "people's art," it was obvious by the end of 1952 that television advertising had graduated from its initial experimental phase and was well on the way to becoming the most important and influential com-mercial medium in history. "On the whole," *Newsweek* wrote, "advertisers are learning how to use TV more effectively than they did four years ago, when many of them either went 'motion-happy' with their messages or put a cam-era on unphotogenic radio announcers."[69] What began as a trickle of interest soon became a flood, as savvier ad agencies and marketers recognized that television was the ideal promotional medium for the times. Commercial tele-vision tapped into many Americans' desire to sit down, settle in, and enjoy the fruits of victory over our foreign enemies and economic woes of the recent past. Because they had literally never seen or heard anything quite like it, crit-ics and laypeople alike reacted emotionally and viscerally to the language and images that sprang out of and danced across their small, black-and-white tele-visions. Most believed that television advertising would improve even more

A trio of anonymous dancers, each an Old Gold dancing cigarette pack, rehearsing in October 1955. Despite Floria Vestoff's fame, company executives went to extreme measures to try to keep the dancers' names and faces a secret, ushering them to and from a special wing of television studios. The company claimed that from 1948 to 1955 more than a quarter-million viewers had written letters begging for a look at the faces inside the Old Gold dancing packs. It may well have been true that the dancers' legs were, as the company boasted, "probably seen more than any others on television." (Library of Congress)

in the years ahead, a reflection of the era's deterministic belief in progress. With the possible exception of the rocket, television was postwar America's proudest symbol of technology, and advertising the clearest expression of a consumption-based way of life. As its newest, loudest voice of the American Dream, television advertising was being counted on to make the promise of prosperity and abundance for all a reality.

Chapter Two

Shower of Stars,
1953–1955

Can it core a apple? Yes, it can core a apple.

Ralph Kramden (Jackie Gleason) and Ed Norton (Art Carney) on a November 1955 episode of *The Honey-mooners*, "Better Living through TV," pitching their "kitchen appliance of the future" in a self-produced commercial

In April 1953, a group of fashion models gathered at one of New York City's leading drama schools. Sent by the Ford Agency, the models were there to learn how to overplay versus underplay their emotions in order to take advantage of the new opportunities television advertising presented. Specifically, the models were studying the art of "exaggerated sincerity," that is, the over-the-top gestures and facial expressions that were standard acting procedure in commercials at the time. Trained to appear aloof and cool in photographs, these models like many others had to relearn the rules of presenting products to consumers. Classes in correct smoking techniques were held at the school, with models learning to blow smoke over — never into — the camera lens, while simultaneously puckering their lips erotically. Learning such feats were well worth the effort, however, as $25 an hour print photography models suddenly found themselves making $650 for a one-day shoot. Television advertising was having a huge impact on the modeling industry, rooted in the stylistic traditions of print photography, as a much larger audience increased the value of talent services. As television grew at a faster rate in a shorter time than any other medium in history, it was clear that television advertising was redirecting the trajectory of many such industries and, in fact, everyday life in America.[1]

There was no doubt that seven years after its commercial debut, television had become a staple of most Americans' media diet. Both television and television advertising were going through technological puberty, maturing beyond their "prodigy" status. "TV is no longer a freak," declared *Printer's Ink*, "it is a force." The years 1953 through 1955 represented the heart of television's "golden age." It was a period of critically acclaimed programming and one in which TV would become, in George Lipsitz's words, the "central discursive medium in American culture." With the medium now a proven success, many technical problems ironed out, and a national audience developing, advertising on television was a hot — and expensive — commodity. The economics of television advertising was fast becoming a highly contentious issue, as even major marketers were continually being forced to justify increasing time and production costs. Because of these economic factors, the infrastructure upon which both television and its host medium was founded — the sponsor system — would begin to be seriously challenged over the course of these critical years. Television advertising was entering its own golden age; its charge, to turn American citizens into American consumers by reaffirming our national and individual commitment to consumption and leisure.[2]

Commercial Culture

The greater social status of television advertising was directly related to the once again increasing number of television stations around the country, which had remained frozen at 108 since 1948. For four years, the FCC did not accept new applications for licenses, purportedly because of reports of interference between stations. With the engineering problems now said to be solved, the number of television stations grew sharply after the FCC lifted the freeze in July 1952. Cost of time had also risen significantly, increasing from about $45,000 for an average hour of prime time in 1952 to $60,000 in 1953. Increased production and talent costs were further burdens to marketers, who were finding themselves in the difficult position of having to advertise on television simply to stay competitive. Not helping matters was the relatively new practice of distributors pressuring marketers to advertise on television in their sales area, afraid a competitor might do just the same and steal customers. The richest marketers were more eager than ever, however, to put their advertising money into television. Companies such as General Foods gobbled up time on new stations as soon as it became available in the spring of 1953, lining up ninety-five stations for *The Red Buttons Show,* which the company sponsored on CBS (and benefited from airing on Monday nights immediately after *I Love Lucy*). As new stations began carrying network signals in "virgin" markets, residents of towns like Wichita Falls, Texas (population 3,300 television sets) and Little Rock, Arkansas (3,000 sets) became familiar not only with Red Button's antics but also with the televisual wonders of

Jell-O gelatin. Television broadcasting was reaching virtual saturation in the United States, making it possible for advertisers to reach a truly national, and increasingly homogeneous, audience with both sight and sound. "The full emergence and impact of mass media after mid-century diminished regionalism and increased the simultaneity with which products (ranging from goods to entertainment) could be exposed to a nationwide audience," Michael Kammen has observed. Although total television revenue in 1952 was still lower than that of radio ($336 million versus $473 million), *Business Week* was quick to observe that "undoubtedly television, before long, will far surpass anything radio ever dreamed of."[3]

To vie for advertising dollars in a more competitive television environment, the four networks chose somewhat different strategies. With its focus on big-name glamour, best exemplified by its entertainment extravaganza *Your Show of Shows,* NBC spread the cost of each show to several sponsors. Co-sponsors could thus be associated with "premium" shows they otherwise could not afford. A different approach to co-sponsorship was alternate sponsorship, in which advertisers took turns on a daily or weekly basis. NBC's *Philco Television Playhouse* and *Goodyear Playhouse,* for example, were sponsored on alternate weeks by Philco and Goodyear during the 1952–1953 season. CBS, however, was pushing exclusive sponsorships (the way that radio was structured), selling "packaged" shows like *My Friend Irma.* It too offered co-sponsorships such as *The Garry Moore Show,* a daytime program split between C. H. Masland & Sons carpets and Procter and Gamble. ABC was offering economy packages, either through sponsorship of fifteen-minute shows or by cheaper production and talent fees. Du Mont, now the bottom feeder of the network food chain, offered discount sponsorship packages and the option of buying television markets on an a la carte basis.[4]

The flurry of new television stations beginning in the summer of 1952 extended the reach of both the networks and advertisers to smaller markets, but also caused a problem regarding how to fill the airwaves with original programming. By early 1954, 35 percent of shows were broadcast "non-live," a percentage that would increase with the advent of magnetic tape, which was cheaper and more durable than film. Stations were beginning to discover the financial bonanza of running filmed shows, cleverly repackaged and renamed as new. Viewers of some stations across the country tuning into *The Play of the Week* were likely disappointed to find the show an exact version of what originally aired as the *Schlitz Playhouse of Stars. Ford Theater* was suddenly *Your All Star Theater,* while *Dragnet* was recycled as *The Cop.* With production cost savings in hand, stations found they could find new sponsors for the old shows, creating the format for television scheduling that continues today.[5]

As new stations sprang up in small cities across the country, there was some concern among networks that sponsors would be reluctant to buy time in markets some might call cowtowns. Advertisers were quick to buy all the time they could get for the 1953–1954 television season, however, with even stations on the ultra-high-frequency bandwidth selling fast. Networks and local stations raised their rates as the demand for time increased and as more of America tuned in. As the price of television soared, advertisers began to actively seek ways to spread or cut costs, a trend that would accelerate through the decade. Co-sponsorships became increasingly popular, as did regional media buying. Even large advertisers like Lucky Strike chose the co-sponsorship route, giving up every other week of the *Hit Parade* to Crosley appliances, but then deciding to reinvest their savings in a co-sponsorship of *The Danny Thomas Show.* The spreading of advertising dollars across multiple shows made sense from a numbers standpoint by extending sponsors' reach or total number of viewers. Additionally, co-sponsorships lowered the risks involved should a particular show's ratings fall over the course of a season (which even happened to Mr. Television himself, Milton Berle, midway through the 1952–1953 season).[6]

How much an advertiser invested in television advertising largely depended, of course, on the relative health of its sales and profits. Food and drug companies, consistently among television advertising's biggest spenders, typically based ad budgets on a fixed percentage of net sales. As sales grew, television advertising budgets swelled at a proportional rate. Kraft Foods, for example, increased its level of sponsorship as its sales flourished in early 1953. The company was so pleased with its *Kraft Television Theatre,* on the air since May 1947, that it added a Thursday night show on ABC to its normal Wednesday time slot on NBC. Automobile manufacturers also reinvested incremental revenues into television advertising, creating a cycle of heightened sales and sales promotion. Television advertising was typically treated as the core of a marketing program, with multiple opportunities for promotional "topspin." Bardahl oil additive, for example, spent a half-dollar on point-of-sale merchandising for every dollar it spent on advertising. The company even had reprints and blow-ups of scenes from its commercials posted by salespeople in service stations and garages. This tendency for marketers to reinvest money generated from television advertising into additional promotional dollars created a spiral of corporate earning and spending, driving the postwar economy just as government and business leaders hoped it would. Only seven or so years old, television advertising had already become the most powerful, most efficient marketing tool Corporate America had ever had.[7]

Tricks of the Trade

The popularity and success of television advertising as a commercial medium had much to do with its now proven ability to appear as entertainment. With both sight and sound, television was able to integrate commercials with programs in ways that other media could not, sometimes in remarkably innovative ways. In April 1954, for example, General Foods celebrated its twenty-fifth anniversary by sponsoring a television special dedicated to the music of Richard Rodgers and Oscar Hammerstein (who were also celebrating an anniversary, having been together as a team for eleven years). The company assembled a star-studded cast for the hour-and-a-half extravaganza, broadcast on both CBS and NBC, including Rodgers and Hammerstein themselves, Mary Martin, Rosemary Clooney, Yul Brynner, and Gordon McCrea. Special guest appearances were made by Jack Benny, Edgar Bergen (and sidekick Charlie McCarthy), Groucho Marx, and Ed Sullivan. The special was a huge promotional opportunity for General Foods, reaching more than 75 percent of the nation's television households, or some 70 million viewers. Between the music and jokes, hostess Anna Lee enlightened the viewing audience about a bevy of General Foods products, with the special presented as a party the company was purportedly throwing after the show. (Sponsors like General Foods apparently held so much power they could suspend the usually firm rule of linear time.) Viewers were offered the opportunity to eat the same things at home that the stars would be eating after the broadcast, and were shown some of the thematic elements which would make a General Foods-Rodgers and Hammerstein party a truly special affair. Ms. Lee, for example, described some of the table arrangements, which included party favors in the form of surreys with fringes on top, and tablecloths which bore musical score samples from Rodgers and Hammerstein's shows.[8]

The party's food, however, was the focus of Ms. Lee's appearances, which were woven throughout the show. The guests were to be served both fried Birds Eye Chicken and Birds Eye Chicken Pie, despite the latter being, according to Ms. Lee, "a meal in itself." Minute Rice, introduced just three years back, would accompany the chicken, followed by a cake made from Swans

Down Cake Mix topped with icing made with Baker's Premium Chocolate ("just can't be beat for texture, tenderness, and good eating!"). Also on the menu was Jell-O Instant Pudding a la South Pacific, which consisted of "an island of fluffy Baker's Coconut" plunked in the center of the pudding. Guests were to be given the choice of Instant Maxwell House Coffee ("millions of tiny flavor buds of real coffee") or Instant Sanka ("ninety-seven per cent of the caffeine removed"). Finding no opportunity to incorporate the company's many other products into the menu, Ms. Lee simply listed them, providing a stream of General Foods consciousness that included Kool-Aid, Post's Sugar Crisp, Kernel-Fresh Salted Nuts, Baker's 4 in 1 Cocoa Mix, Log Cabin Syrup, Postum, Minute Tapioca, Calumet Baking Powder, Certo, Sure-Jell, La France, Satina, and Gaines Dog Food. The show cost the company nearly $1 million for production and media, but still generated a lower cost-per-thousand viewer ratio than your run-of-the-mill program. A clearer case of television's ability to create a postwar puree of entertainment and consumerism can hardly be imagined.[9]

Rightfully awed by the possibility to pitch their products to one out of every three Americans with a single effort, some advertisers would go to truly astounding lengths to promote their products on television. In May 1954, the most elaborate production effort to date was pulled off by U.S. Steel Homes for broadcast on its parent company's *The U.S. Steel Hour* on ABC. A twenty-person crew assembled one of its new "Westerners"—a "pre-engineered" six-room house—inside a television studio, getting around union issues by claiming that the house was a product, not scenery. The Herculean effort and tremendous cost in building and then immediately tearing down a 40-foot by 24-foot, 20-ton house were considered well worth it, as U.S. Steel and its dealers were delighted to have an audience of 15 million people simultaneously see its Westerner. That same month, viewers in Los Angeles were treated to an equally impressive if less monumental televisual display—their first glimpse of a girdle being modeled. It was forbidden to show someone wearing intimate apparel on television, but makers of the Sarong Girdle figured out a way to pass such a lascivious act past the censors. Because the commercial was shot under a black light with a model wearing a black leotard underneath a white girdle coated with phosphorescent paint, television viewers could only make out the girdle. Even this, however, was considered too risqué to be seen by male viewers, causing KABC-TV to refuse to run the spot after 5 P.M., when men were more likely to be home. Even though the bikini bathing suit was by now a familiar sight on America's beaches (and

Playboy magazine a new sight on newsstands), television advertising was not yet ready to break through the contained sexuality and strict gender codes of postwar America.[10]

For every big-as-a-house technical feat in the early 1950s, there were many more flops in the high-risk game that was live television. Ladders and/or stagehands not infrequently became part of commercial messages. After the announcer on *The Red Buttons Show* poured hot water into a cup of instant coffee, the china fractured into small pieces. Another announcer was caught on camera flinging breakfast cereal over his shoulder. It was easy to understand why advertising was considered such a stressful business for all parties involved. On the show *Martin Kane, Private Eye,* an actor caused major sponsor distress by omitting the emphasized word from his line, "I put a pack of these cigarettes in front of my son at the table the other day and he hasn't smoked anything *else* since." Demonstrating a pastel-colored moth-exterminating stick, actress Kathi Norris announced, "This exterminator comes in pastel stink." When Henry Morgan opened one of his sponsor's refrigerators, the door fell off. Giving a sales pitch for a brand of cheese on *Wuthering Heights,* spokesperson Susan Delmar skidded on "rain" left over from a scene, ending the commercial from the studio floor. One actress never got to deliver her commercial at all, fainting on camera before uttering one word. Most amusing, however, were situations in which the advertised product was nowhere to be seen, having been eaten or drunk by a hungry or thirsty technician.[11]

Although it may be hard to believe, sponsors invested millions of dollars annually to prevent such nightmares from occurring. Some commercials were tested and rehearsed for five days before airing, but some products were inherently fraught with potential hazards. Cakes, for example, were particularly challenging to successfully exhibit on live television. One individual associated with the *Portia Faces Life* show did not exaggerate in saying that "our cakes are treated better than our stars." The cakes were baked in a special six-range kitchen and then chaperoned by two home economists across town in taxis. Each cake had a stand-in for rehearsals. Despite taking every conceivable precaution, however, no one could prevent a determined fly from landing on cakes just as commercials started, which is exactly what happened on more than one occasion.[12]

In addition to exhaustive preparation, advertisers used an array of interesting techniques to portray their products as attractively as possible. The "dirt" that was effortlessly sucked up by vacuum cleaners was sometimes actual dirt but just as often mashed corn flakes or bits of cork. "Whiskers" dropped out of an electric razor were usually ground-up cloves (televised whiskers, oddly, did not resemble whiskers). Coffee looked remarkably like tar when televised, and thus had to be diluted with water or replaced with flat Coca-Cola. Because of the glare problem associated with the color white, white cakes were often tinted green. White rice was sprayed with gray paint or, even more disturbingly, covered with a black netting. Whipped cream was alternatively real whipped cream, cream cheese, or shaving cream. Hamburgers and steaks were nearly always shot raw (with a petroleum jelly glaze), as cooked meat in black and white was about as unattractive as anything imaginable. This posed a problem for the few color television owners in the mid-1950s, who were no doubt puzzled by the images of raw beef sitting prettily on otherwise perfectly set dinner tables. Some sponsors of NBC shows began filming commercials in color in 1954, although the programs themselves remained in black and white. Because of the novelty of color television, advertisers believed viewers would think twice about leaving the room during commercial breaks, although this of course turned out to be just one of many erroneous leaps of televisual faith.[13]

As the broadcasting and agency industries tackled the various challenges of the medium, the magic at commercial producers' disposal seemed limitless. Carpenters bore extra-large holes in American cheese because the holes in real Swiss cheese were not large enough to be seen easily on television. Televised beer was warm because of its superior foaming quality. Conversely, aniline dye (a poison) was added to instant coffee to prevent foaming. Most bizarre, however, was the standard trick of the trade to stuff roast chickens with lit cigarettes to give them that right-out-of-the-oven, lip-smacking appearance. One production house specializing in food commercials was Video Vittles, responsible for prepping Pillsbury baked goods on *Arthur Godfrey and His Friends* and Uncle Ben's Rice on *The Garry Moore Show*. Beating eggs on Mr. Godfrey's show posed a special problem for the Video Vittles crew, as there was no place in the studio safe from sound-sensitive microphones. The crew would have to wait for loud music to play before whipping up the thirteen egg whites that would go into the preparation of various Pillsbury products. Marketers' concerted — some might say manic — efforts in the production end of the business were not only designed to get around the technical peculiarities of television, but necessary to make their products appear as perfect as possible, part of the idyllic consumer paradise that was the American Dream.[14]

The Lowest Common Denominator

Not surprisingly, as much if not even more attention was devoted to program content as to commercial production, as here too marketers wanted to present a utopian world free from the problems of real life. A tacit assumption of the postwar marriage between television entertainment and selling was tight control over what was appropriate broadcast material. In producing shows for their sponsors, advertising agencies were notoriously risk averse, afraid of broaching any subject that could be considered the least bit controversial or had the potential of damaging their clients' reputations. Consistent with postwar America's habit of repressing versus confronting conflict, a host of topics or issues were simply off-limits to writers of television dramas, including politics, sex, adultery, unemployment, poverty, successful criminality, and alcohol. Patriotic stories were acceptable as long as they were historical, but were generally considered too expensive to produce because of the high cost of costumes. Martinis were taboo not for moral reasons but rather in case a beer marketer ended up as sponsor. Automobiles were risky because if a scene featured a Ford, no General Motors dealer in any part of the country would consider running a spot.[15]

Words carried great particular significance to sponsors of television shows, with any direct or indirect reference to competitors considered legitimate grounds for purging. Cigarette company executives seemed especially sensitive to linguistics, a function of the highly competitive nature of their business, where image was everything. Representatives of Philip Morris, for example, reportedly deleted the line "I'm real cool!" from the script of its sponsored show, *My Little Margie,* objecting to the homonym of "Kool." Tennis player Frank Parker, talking with baseball player Russ Hodges on a show sponsored by Chesterfield, repeatedly referred to his "fortunate" hat, avoiding at all costs the word "lucky," slang for a competitive brand. In addition to linguistics, visual symbols of competitive brands were viewed as potential threats to sponsors. An industry rumor was that Pet Milk had turned down sponsorship of *Duffy's Tavern* because Ed Gardner, the star of the show, consistently wore a carnation during the shooting of the pilot. The restrictions led to ridiculous scenarios, as in the case where the agency of a cake marketer rejected a story line in which a fighter goes on a diet to make weight for a boxing match. Because of sponsors' insistence on retaining creative control, it was very rare for any writers in the early 1950s to be given complete freedom to create work for television without sponsor approval. In a rare exception, NBC commissioned three-time Pulitzer Prize winner Robert Sherwood to write

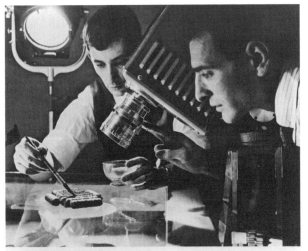

The
J. WALTER THOMPSON COMPANY
Television Workshop

A unique proving ground to insure the quality of television commercials

J. Walter Thompson pitched its Television Workshop to clients and potential clients as state-of-the-art technology in the mid-1950s. Featuring a fully equipped studio with a television camera, 16mm sound motion picture camera, projector, and control booth, the workshop gave the agency the ability to work out technical problems before actual commercial production. (John W. Hartman Center, Duke University)

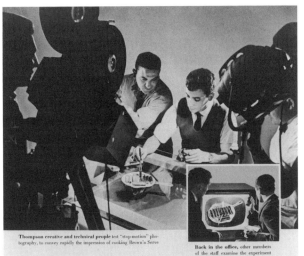

Thompson creative and technical people test "stop-motion" photography, to convey rapidly the impression of cooking Brown'n Serve

Back in the office, other members of the staff examine the experiment under actual telecast conditions

Could cooking that takes 3 minutes be televised in 20 seconds?

● The most effective way to convey the great appetite appeal of Swift's Brown'n Serve was to cook and serve a generous helping before the viewer's eyes.

Yet these sausages take three minutes to cook. What was the best way to give the same impression — and still stay within the limits of a 20-second television commercial?

The Television Workshop explored the problem until exactly the right combination of "stop-motion" and regular photography was achieved.

In this way, many unusual effects have been discovered and perfected with the assistance of the Workshop before making a costly investment in final production.

For Swift's Brown'n Serve sausages, J. Walter Thompson used "stop-motion" photography to shrink the product's three-minute cooking time into a twenty-second spot, deemed an "unusual effect" in 1955. (John W. Hartman Center, Duke University)

The lettering on the famous blue-and-white Lux Flakes box is tested for sharpness and clarity at the Television Workshop

The Dage television camera is used in experiments to discover which background will best set off the yellow Kodak box

Product packages posed a particular challenge to producers of TV commercials in the 1950s, especially those with vivid colors like Lux detergent and Kodak film. (John W. Hartman Center, Duke University)

Might a priceless asset be wasted?

● The blue-and-white Lux box . . . the yellow Kodak box . . . many other famous packages enjoy instant recognition everywhere. But would they get across on television?

Any difference would be costly. It would not only lessen the effectiveness of television — it would waste years of hard work in establishing the identity of these products.

To remove this danger, the Television Workshop has tested products handled by the J. Walter Thompson Company, to make sure that the labels and packaging lose none of their recognition value on television.

Thus a TV-tested package *before* you invest in television is another valuable service you can enjoy through the Workshop.

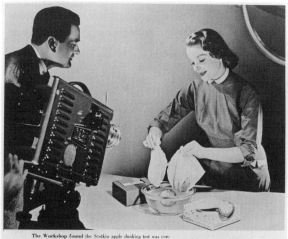

The Workshop found the Scotkin apple dunking test was convincing, easy to see, and familiar enough to appeal to any housewife

J. Walter Thompson developed a memorable "apple dunking" test in its Television Workshop for Scotkins paper napkins, giving the new product a "seeing-is-believing" competitive edge. (John W. Hartman Center, Duke University)

After 25 experiments—the *perfect* demonstration . . .

● Scotkins — the new paper napkins developed by the Scott Paper Company — are strong even when wet. How could this "wet strength" be demonstrated most dramatically on television?

Twenty-five experiments were made on a "live" camera in the Television Workshop — all viewed *under actual telecast condi-*

tions on sets in the office. Finally, the famous "apple dunking" test was selected. Dramatic—but not a stunt—it was the perfect way to demonstrate "wet strength."

Finding the most dramatic way to demonstrate the qualities of your product — *before* investing in costly production time—is another way the Workshop serves you.

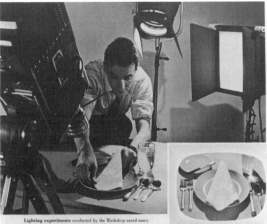

Lighting experiments conducted by the Workshop saved many hours of production time in preparing the Scotkin commercial

Simultaneously, the results were checked on Private Channel 3 — the closed circuit linking the Workshop to sets in the office

But would it look like damask on the table?

• Strong as Scotkins are when wet, at the place setting on the table, they look almost like damask. Naturally, this advantage should be conveyed on television.

But how? Picture definition on most sets isn't sharp enough to pick up such delicate design under *ordinary* conditions.

The Television Workshop devised the method of lighting that would best bring out the damask look…and give just the right effect when televised.

The proper use of lighting to bring out the best in a product is another valuable service provided by the Television Workshop. Here again, production problems are solved without incurring excessive costs.

Lighting too was a major technical concern for television advertisers of the 1950s, compounded by the less-than-crystal-clear picture quality of TV sets of the day. (John W. Hartman Center, Duke University)

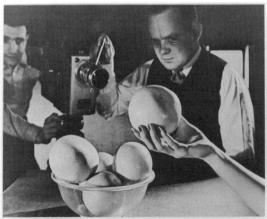

As a double check on casting, the Workshop is especially valuable. Here, *any* mistake can spoil even the best commercial

Wanted: a hand that could hold a grapefruit gracefully

• Even Florida grapefruit looks more enticing when in the hand of a pretty girl.

But a girl's hand is small and a grapefruit is large. So where to find the hand that could do the job easily, gracefully and without any trace of effort?

To find the answer, the Television Workshop auditioned candidates, until the perfect hand for the commercial was found.

Unusual casting problems are solved every day with the TV Workshop's help. Through its closed circuit, Thompson people are able to watch auditions from the office. Guided by actual telecast conditions, they can choose the announcers and models who will convey your sales message.

J. Walter Thompson wouldn't settle for less than "the perfect hand" to hold a Florida grapefruit, a good example of the sometimes extreme measures leading agencies took in casting television commercials. (John W. Hartman Center, Duke University)

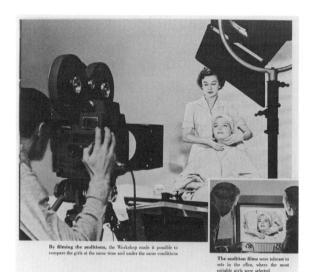

By filming the auditions, the Workshop made it possible to compare the girls at the same time and under the same conditions

The audition films were telecast to sets in the office, where the most suitable girls were selected

Casting for television commercials for beauty products like Pond's cold cream rivaled the audition process for a Hollywood film. (John W. Hartman Center, Duke University)

Which girl would do justice to the product?

● Products of the Pond's Company have always been associated with women of exquisite taste. Thus, it was extremely important to find exactly the right model for each Pond's television commercial.

More than twenty girls were tested on film by the Workshop. Thompson executives then compared the girls under actual telecast conditions. In this way, they were sure —*before* going into production—that the girls selected would do justice to Pond's.

As an advertiser, you naturally expect your commercials to convey the quality you associate with your product. The Television Workshop gives you the opportunity of achieving this goal.

Members of the staff check the staging of the Kraft Caramel commercial on a set in the J. Walter Thompson Company office

Because "children are unpredictable," agencies like J. Walter Thompson carefully choreographed each step of commercials that employed kids before live airing. (John W. Hartman Center, Duke University)

Was it asking too much of a child?

● Creative imagination called for children to demonstrate the use of Kraft caramels in making different kinds of candy.

But children are unpredictable, and in a television commercial there can be no deviations. Timing must be perfect . . . cue lines must be remembered.

Using the children who would do the commercial, the Workshop explored the best way to stage the demonstration. The solution proved convincing—yet every step was easy for the children to do.

This kind of service is invaluable. The Workshop gives Thompson the opportunity to study *all* the important details of a commercial under actual telecast conditions.

nine original plays for television, without sponsors or advertising agencies looking over his shoulder. As in radio, advertisers still held virtually complete control over program content in television, as those who paid the bills demanded to call the creative shots.[16]

The constraints that ad agencies and their sponsors placed on television writers had much to do with the clichéd and repetitive nature of programs in the early 1950s. Men seemed to be frequently carrying guns, the writer Shellaby Jackson noted at the time, and couples often engaged in some form of domestic discord. Actors almost always remained indoors (to avoid the branded car issue), usually in a one-room apartment with nondescript decor (to avoid showing any branded items other than those of the sponsor). Conflict between characters would then ensue, perhaps revolving around some missing jewels. Passionate speeches by the protagonist (clad in a trench coat) to a blonde woman against a bare wall would then form the dramatic thrust for the remainder of many shows. Because many television shows even during this, the golden age, were so tepid and familiar, it was often the commercials that stood out to viewers, for better and worse. Jackson saw television advertising as "a kind of frenzy. Sell, sell, sell—dozens of men with white teeth, pushing packages of cigarettes at you, dozens of well-groomed women batting their eyes and pushing packages of soap at you." Juxtaposed against the blandness of many television dramas, the aggressiveness of commercials became even more conspicuous, instrumental in making shopping, as Lipsitz put it, "the cornerstone of social life . . . in the postwar era."[17]

This "aggression" was, however, also proving to be a major problem for television advertising. By spring 1953, the distrust of television advertising appeared to be reaching epidemic proportions, with many viewers and critics alike finding commercials too long, routinely offensive, and often fraudulent. As television viewers themselves, business executives could not help but reach the same conclusion. "Television commercials have almost reached the point where I don't believe a doggone thing I hear on the air," a General Electric district representative said, subsequently admitting that a current commercial of his own company was also fraudulent.[18] Paul Price, a television critic for the Los Angeles *Daily News,* called on the NARTB to abandon the "Seal of Good Practice" it had adopted in March 1952 because it was not being complied with. Price wrote:

It [the Seal] doesn't mean a thing. . . . The very stations that have been permitting dishonest pitchmen to peddle the mastic paints, carpets, and freezer food plants—all completely discredited now—are the same ones that make much of their Seal of Good Practice. Seal of Malpractice would be more fitting.[19]

Price suggested that legitimate marketers might have been avoiding all advertising on television because they did not want to be associated with the medium, and that viewers may have reached the point where they were suspicious of all commercials. He called on station owners to refuse to air misleading or offensive commercials, and to follow the lead of KTLA-TV in Los Angeles, which had offered $350,000 worth of time for free public service advertising. Local stations in Los Angeles were consistent innovators in television advertising, a function of their proximity to Hollywood and commercial production firms. On KTLA in 1954, for example, Cliff Saber and announcer John Wingate of the locally produced *Pass the Line* appealed on air to advertisers to support the struggling show, a rare occurrence. Another Los Angeles station, KABC-TV, came up with the brilliant idea of arming their seven salespeople with portable GE television sets to sell media time. With sets in tow, the salespeople visited Southern Californian ad agency media buyers on the day and at the time desired to be sold. The salesperson and media buyer would then proceed to watch the show for sale on the portable set, as close to a product demonstration someone in television sales could hope for. "Nearby secretaries delight in the innovation," boasted the station in a press release about the gimmick, the first of such a kind in the country (radio had been used this way before). KABC-TV claimed that the scheme was an immediate success, creating "a sales boom for men in gray flannel suits."[20]

Many others besides Paul Price found television advertising to be insufferable and tasteless. Universally hated were hard-sell spokesmen who abrasively assaulted viewers with pitches for products such as vacuum cleaners or dog food. Marya Mannes of *The Reporter* considered them to

have faces that belong in a psychology textbook or a police line-up; their voices, gravelly or fruity, would, if requesting admittance at your back door, warrant the unleashing of Rover. . . . Since their continued presence on TV indicates some measure of success in selling, I can only shudder at the type that is persuaded by them.[21]

Because of such characters, Mannes wrote in March 1954, "There is no question that the rebellion against commercials is rising daily." Mannes thought advertisers as a whole were "still back in the early days of the circus barkers, attempting, with coyness, noise, and hyperbole, to lure the crowd inside." This was not the first Barnumesque accusation of television advertising, as the medium came to be seen by its harshest critics as a high-tech version of medicine show–type salesmanship. Mannes's and others' criticism of the lowest form of commercial life carried on a long tradition by the trade press to chastise those responsible for bad advertising. Marchand noted that between the world wars, industry journalists had attacked that era's new wave of "super-advertising," that is, ads that were clearly in bad taste, stretched the truth, or overused superlatives.[22]

One clever entrepreneur decided to create a business opportunity out of television advertising's "seal of malpractice." Blab-Off, an actual device allowing viewers to remotely turn off the sound of commercials deemed objectionable, was invented by an anonymous advertising executive of a nationally known corporation. Knowing firsthand of the big opportunity to be had, the renegade executive priced his product at $2.98 and, rather ironically, tried to advertise it on television and radio. After a slew of advertising agencies refused to handle the Blab-Off account, Leonard M. Sive & Associates came to the product's rescue, although many stations would not sell the agency media time. A modest campaign generated sales of 15,000 in just a few weeks, an impressive figure given the product's limited media access. With great word of mouth, sales of Blab-Off soon hit 2,000 per day, six of which were to ex-President Herbert Hoover, who planned to use them as Christmas gifts. Five thousand letters of thanks flooded into the manufacturer's mailbox, including one from a Brooklyn woman who wrote, "Tonight we really enjoyed TV for the first time in five years!" In these days before the remote control mute button, channel surfing, VCR zapping, and TiVo skipping, the ability to turn down the sound of annoying television commercials was considered by many as a godsend.[23]

The People Speak

An esteemed public relations consultant, Edward L. Bernays, had a different idea regarding how to improve the state of television advertising. Bernays was and is considered by many to be the "father of public relations" in the U.S., having almost single-handedly created the field in the 1920s. Firing what he called the "opening gun in a movement to improve [their] quality and effectiveness," Bernays mailed a questionnaire to 575 influential people, asking them how they felt about commercials. One hundred eleven people replied, considered by Bernays to be "a cross-section of businessmen, educators, sociologists, officials of associations of all types, and representatives of other phases of American culture." Out of these respondents (who, all being listed in "Who's Who" or the *World Almanac,* hardly constituted a balanced sample), only twelve believed that television commercials fulfilled broadcasting's mission of serving the "public interest, convenience, and necessity." Opinions were diverse but nearly unanimously vitriolic, with only the seemingly invincible Betty Furness earning kudos. Grayson Kirk, president of Columbia University, called commercials "insufferably repetitious and far too obtrusive . . . [having] cast a withering blight over the early development of an important communications medium." Dr. Pitirim A. Sorokin, professor of sociology at Harvard University, replied that "intellectually, the commercials, as well as the programs, are on the level of semimoron." Dr. Reinhold Niebuhr of the Union Theological Society was "amazed that . . . actors and performers are drawn in to be the 'hucksters' to sell the goods." [24]

In general, Bernays's group of elite viewers wanted shorter commercials, fewer and less violent interruptions, less exaggeration, and more intelligence. There appeared to be a consensus that "in the long run people may come to associate quality of product with quality of presentation," and that advertisers who offered commercials in bad taste were ultimately hurting themselves. With the publishing of his findings, Bernays was both applauded and criticized. The results were certainly interesting, but the "eggheads" that Bernays had hand-picked were hardly representative of the population as a whole. Acknowledging this, Bernays released the results of a second survey two months after the first, reporting opinions from bartenders, barbers, beauticians, and butchers. Interestingly, the findings were essentially the same, with almost all of the 115 "non-Who's Who" conveying equivalent dislike of commercials, if expressed in less erudite terms. Alfred J. Beasley, a bartender from Cincinnati, suggested that "they [commercials] break up the program too frequently and do not blend in, which gives the programs the air of limburger." Bernard Stern, a New York City barber, was of the opinion that "a great majority of them are fakers, liars, and nerve-racking to listen to . . . There ought to be a law." The similar findings from the two samples suggested that class was not a major factor in the way that Americans felt about commercials, contradicting previous research and suggesting that by 1953 television had reached a level playing field. [25]

If Bernays's two nonscientific studies were bad news for the advertising industry, worse news came via some hard numbers. At a November 1953 Radio and Television Executives Society meeting, the advertising research firm Daniel Starch & Staff presented some rather startling findings based on a six-month survey of 5,000 television viewers. The study showed that only 41 percent of television viewers actually saw an average commercial on a network show, a much lower percentage from the "practically 100 per cent" that many advertising salespeople claimed. One-third of viewers said they missed all commercials, and as much as 85 percent of the sample could not remember having seen some of the spots on shows they said they watched. The Starch report created a small furor in the television industry, but most advertisers continued to have unflagging faith in the medium's ability to reach viewers and sell product. Ien Ang has written extensively of the measurement problems associated with television ratings, and the gap between what the industry has historically imagined its audience to be and reality. Whether measured by Arbitron's viewer diary or Nielsen's electronic setmeter, "watching television" typically does not take into account factors like viewers temporarily leaving the room, not paying attention, or not understanding the show or commercials. These issues were revealed in the Starch research, although no one in the industry wanted to believe this was really the way that Americans watched television.[26]

Another study published about a year later added to the growing amount of research challenging the effectiveness of television advertising. At an October 1954 American Association of Advertising Agencies (AAAA) convention, Horace Schwerin announced that "of over $400 million which will be spent on TV advertising this year, well over $100 million is going down the drain." Advertisers (especially department store tycoon John Wanamaker) had long understood and accepted the fact that a certain percentage of their dollars were inevitably "wasted," that is, would never translate into sales, but this research suggested that advertisers were at fault. Since 1946, Schwerin Research Corporation had tested more than 3,500 commercials among more than 1 million viewers, finding that many standard advertising techniques were simply ineffective in both retention and persuasion. Companies such as General Mills, Borden, and Colgate-Palmolive used Schwerin as an independent source to measure the effectiveness of the commercials their ad agencies created. Schwerin believed that many commercials failed because agency people were "college men . . . not in rapport with the people they are communicating to." Although this prompted snickers within the advertising community, Madison Avenue couldn't argue with Schwerin's advice that "agencies . . . can no longer . . . play this medium by the seat of their pants." Before the end of the decade, marketers and their ad agencies would heed

Schwerin's advice by investing more money in statistically reliable, nationally representative commercial pre- and post-testing to find out if they were getting their media money's worth.[27]

As Schwerin was suggesting, the demographic gap between advertising executives and viewers was related to both class and geography. The physical universe of television advertising actually had two very different capitals, but each could hardly be said to be representative of life between the coasts. The more glamorous side of the business was in Hollywood, where many programs now originated, while the more crass, commercial side was in New York because of the concentration of agencies and networks. Hal Humphrey described Madison Avenue as consisting of "intense young men wearing unpadded Brooks [Brothers] suits and short haircuts." Intense or not, agency executives of the early 1950s often made important decisions without sophisticated research, creating an occupational climate of high risk and high rewards. Viewer mail was thus welcomed as a valuable means of literally reading public opinion about a particular show. A small number of positive letters were known to have saved shows from cancellation, while an equal number of complaints could lead to a show's total overhaul. The public thus had a direct voice in determining what shows they would see, a real example of democracy in action in the otherwise tightly controlled universe of television.[28]

Agency executives and marketers were not the only ones interested in the popularity of sponsored shows and the effectiveness of television advertising. In 1953 NBC commissioned the research firm W. R. Simmons to do a "before-and-after" study of 7,500 television households in Fort Wayne, Indiana (recognized as a demographically "average" American city to this day). The first survey was completed in fall 1953, before television broadcasting came to the city, the second in spring 1954, after two stations had been on the air for some time. The study focused on the impact of television on brand preference and purchase, that is, whether viewership had an effect on the products consumers decided to buy. One of the key findings revolved around the purchase activity of Camay soap. Those "exposed" to Camay commercials increased their purchase of the soap by 48 percent, while the "non-exposed" decreased their purchase of the brand. With this sort of evidence in hand, networks had hard data showing that television advertising did in fact work, an issue being called into question by other quantitative research and Bernays's anecdotal evidence.[29]

Left Brain vs. Right Brain

After making the leap that television advertising did indeed work and was thus worth the investment, advertisers had to determine what kind of commercials worked best for their brands. Most professional critics and laypeople considered the most effective television commercials to be those that provided information in some way. Documentary-style commercials, such as those that aired on *March of Medicine* on NBC, *See It Now* on CBS, and *The U.S. Steel Hour* on ABC, were considered by many viewers to be extremely interesting and informative. The mini-documentary was obviously well suited for political commercials, conveying a sense of truthfulness about candidates and their values. For the 1956 presidential campaign, the Democratic party adopted the documentary style to promote its ticket to the American people. In one spot, presidential candidate Adlai Stevenson (D-Illinois) and vice presidential candidate Estes Kefauver (D-Tennessee) were joined by Senator John F. Kennedy (D-Massachusetts) in a discussion about the party's youth and vigor. "Young people have to participate in government," said Stevenson, although it would be another four years before American politics truly embraced the idea of youth. In addition to the documentary commercial, product demonstrations were generally viewed as among the best of the "rational" school of television advertising. Young & Rubicam ultimately earned a place in the Clio Hall of Fame, for example, with its 1954 demonstration spot for Remington, "Peach of a Shave." Viewers were not only told but shown that Remington's 60 Deluxe Electric Shaver was so powerful that it could shave a hair brush, but gentle enough to shave a peach. The old adage that seeing is believing took on new resonance for advertisers who could now show their products in action.[30]

As opposed to the documentary or product demonstration, animated commercials were used to stretch the boundaries and limitations of reality by appealing to viewers' imaginations. Animated commercials accompanied by jingles were thought by most viewers to be harmless and often amusing entertainment, yet persuasive in their own way. Young & Rubicam used animation for a popular 1953 spot for Jell-O, "Busy Day," which was also ultimately nominated to the Clio Hall of Fame. In the commercial, a housewife tries to simultaneously quiet her crying baby, talk to a door-to-door salesperson, and answer the telephone, a not too farfetched slice of postwar domestic life for many women. "Wait," the announcer tells viewers, "it's not too late to make dessert, because . . . Jell-O Instant Pudding . . . needs no cooking," a classic case of product-to-the-rescue. Marketers like General Foods presented their products as modern-day messiahs, opportunities for homemakers to ease the very real pressures of family life and turn food preparation into a domestic science. In another memorable spot, "Smoking Penguin," Kool cigarettes combined animation and film, a common visual technique of the day. Created by Ted Bates and Company, the 1954 commercial starred "Willie the Penguin" walking on a bed of hot coals, while the announcer suggested that viewers switch "from hots to Kools." Filmed footage of a stream flowing through a winter landscape was placed between the animated segments, reinforcing the idea that the product was indeed "snow fresh Kool." Packard automobiles also combined animation with film for a commercial for its Clipper. The 1955 spot sandwiched an animation sequence of the car's "unique suspension system" between segments of a live-action scene of the Clipper on a rough country road, and added a jingle for full audiovisual effect. Combining animation with film was viewed by ad executives as a best-of-both-worlds blend of entertainment and information, and served as another way that popular culture and consumer culture were brought closer together through television advertising.[31]

Although animation was considered entertaining and artistic, most industry experts believed that the most effective commercials were those employing the aggressive, "hard-sell" approach. Many commercials of the 1950s were unapologetically didactic, reflective of the postwar era's core values of competitive spirit, rational argument, and scientific expertise. In the wild west of mid-century American television advertising, many if not most advertisers and stations had few if any scruples regarding what they would put on the air. In a classic case, American television networks were offered free use of the BBC's films of Queen Elizabeth's 1953 coronation, with the "gentleman's agreement" that it would be shown with a minimum amount of commercialization. At least one of the networks broke the agreement, interrupting the coronation at inappropriate moments with obnoxious sales messages. Deodorant ads ran during the event, as did one spot starring the popular monkey J. Fred Muggs (Dave Garroway's simian sidekick on *The Today Show*). Perhaps worst of all, however, was that just as the Queen was enthroned, the broadcast was interrupted by a commercial declaring, "Here's a car that's a real queen too!" after which the network returned to the solemn religious ceremony. Many Brits, hearing of how the coronation was turned into American-style commercial fodder, were not surprisingly angry and shocked, and given a valuable lesson in the potential hazards of advertising-funded television.[32]

Across the Pond

This lesson would prove valuable indeed as Britain prepared for its own interpretation of commercial television, emerging out of a radically different broadcasting history and culture. Television and radio broadcasting in Britain was controlled exclusively by the British Broadcast Corporation (BBC), which was chartered by Parliament in 1927 with the purpose of disseminating "information, education, and entertainment." The BBC had actually pioneered mass television in the 1930s, well before American networks, but it remained conservative and lethargic as a governmental, noncommercial monopoly. The BBC was, as Charles W. Morton described it, "a somewhat flustered despotism which [the British] have come to regard with a kind of affectionate despair." A popular saying was that the bishops of England expected the Second Coming to be announced on the BBC with understated dignity. The organization retained total control over what went out over the air, assuming the roles of "engineer, impresario, censor, producer." The BBC earned its income ($46 million in 1953) by charging citizens a one-pound annual licensing fee per radio, two pounds a year per television. Advertising was completely forbidden, with many British government officials viewing commercial television in the same league as the anti-Christ. Like a few American critics, the Archbishop of York claimed television to be at least as powerful as the atom bomb, adding that he certainly wouldn't hand the bomb over to commercial sponsors. One House of Lords member preferred a different analogy, likening American television to the bubonic plague.[33]

After more than four years of debate, however, the Television Act of 1954 was passed by Parliament, which would expand programming in the country. Although Britain's Socialist party favored commercial television, the Conservative and Labor parties (as well as the *London Times*) vigorously opposed it. Because of sponsorship involvement, opponents correctly pointed out, the American public was considered a market rather than an audience, tainting the beneficial role television could play in society. The British viewed television as a positive social force, capable of uplifting the country's intellectual and moral standards, while Americans looked at it as a way to sell cars and soap, despite its legal charter to serve the public's interest. Historical class differences in set ownership between the two countries played a key role in the different perspectives. While ownership of a set in the United States initially skewed toward upper income groups, most of Britain's 2.5 million sets in 1953 were owned by low-income families. Business in British pubs and movie theaters, in fact, fell significantly as television ownership grew in the early 1950s, as more working-class Brits stayed home to watch the telly.[34]

As Britain debated whether its own system should be commercial or remain advertising free, America's interpretation of television was viewed as the worst case scenario. Opponents of commercial television in Britain, not too surprisingly, pointed to American advertising as the bottom of the cultural barrel. The opposition noted the American advertisers' penchant for turning the sacred into the vulgar, citing one marketer's television jingle for its Beecham's pills:

Hark the Herald Angels sing,
Beecham's pills are just the thing.
Peace on earth and mercy mild,
Two for man and one for child.[35]

Even those in support of some form of British commercial television characterized American advertising as unacceptably overbearing, something ordinary citizens simply would not put up with. The "coronation incident" was considered by many to be vivid proof that consumer capitalism and public service did not happily mix, at least in the U.K. All agreed that advertisers should have no involvement with the production of programs, the heart and soul of American sponsorship up to that point. Unlike American agencies, the British advertising industry had no desire to be in the entertainment business, although American-owned agencies in the United Kingdom (including J. Walter Thompson and Young & Rubicam) not surprisingly actively promoted a commercial-type system. One of the primary fears among opponents regarding commercial television in Britain was that American marketers with a presence in the United Kingdom (such as Procter and Gamble, Lever, Ford, and Kellogg) would recycle their taped shows originally broadcast in the States, putting British writers and actors out of work. Commercial television proponents themselves suggested that actors appearing in programs should not be permitted to appear in spots on the same channel in order to maintain a distance between advertising and entertainment, realms that American advertisers brought together at every possible opportunity.[36]

The commercial system that began to develop in Britain in 1954 thus looked very unlike that of American television. Firm rules were established regarding the development and dissemination of programming to keep British television from copying the American model. Commercial shows were to be created by four specially licensed "program contractors" who, after buying time from the governmental Independent Television Authority (ITA), would sell it to advertisers. Commercials would be permitted to appear only at the beginning and end of shows or at "natural breaks." Religious, political, or strike-related advertising would not be allowed. Commercials could not be so long as to detract from the aesthetic value of the programs. The ITA was forbidden from buying sole broadcast rights of "public ceremonies, public spectacles, and important sporting events," another key difference from that in the States, where advertisers actively sought to link their brands to the civic arena. Needless to say, no advertising in proximity to an appearance by royalty would be allowed. Perhaps most different from American advertising, sponsors would not be allowed to give the impression that they were responsible for bringing the show to viewers, nor did they have any say as to the program content which surrounded the commercials. In sum, consumer and popular culture—intimate partners in American television—were viewed in the U.K. as strange bedfellows that should keep separate televisual quarters.[37]

As the debut of British commercial television neared, *The American Daily*, a London newspaper for Americans overseas, imported a number of television shows from the United States, complete with commercials, and showed them to five hundred British journalists and business executives as a sort of public service. The reactions were mixed. Philip Phillips of *The Daily Herald* objected to a scene in one commercial in which an actor playing King Henry VIII gulped down beer. William Hickey of *The Daily Express* was also put off by the king swilling pints of beer, but found a Philip Morris spot "interesting." Mr. Hickey was particularly fond of the Johnson Wax commercials, "marvel[ing] at the brilliance of the presentation." "It was fun," Mr. Hickey thought, "to see the children leaving the dirty marks on the kitchen equipment [and] fun to see 'Momma' coming along—with a smile—and wiping them off with the NEW polish." Peter Black of *The Daily Mail* found the advertisements to be "vivid and amusing" and that "the menace of the commercial spot has been greatly exaggerated." Sir Kenneth Clark, chair of Britain's Independent Television Authority, however, had a rather different view of American television advertising. After a fact-finding mission to the United States, Mr. Clark stated that "what I saw there was pretty hair-raising." "People do say they have very good things in the U.S.," Mr. Clark continued. "Perhaps I struck it unlucky."[38]

With time running out, opponents of commercial television in Britain desperately positioned advertising as the cause for everything bad about American culture. Robert Harling, a reporter for the *Times*, had perhaps the harshest view of American television advertising and of the threat commercial television posed to English viewers. Harling warned fellow Brits of the horrors of that resided overseas:

The terrifying impact of TV on that vague but durable old institution The American Way of Life has to be seen to be believed. It has been reliably estimated that each American TV household spends five hours every day at its set or sets. Children become willing salesmen on behalf of exigent sponsors urging parents to buy named brands of cereals and drinks. Even the dining table has been rearranged so that the whole family can watch whilst eating. Neighbors are invited in not for their conversation, but just to look and listen . . .

Almost all the intrusions made by the advertiser into the programmes are evolved by the advertising agencies. These "commercials," as they are known in the States (and "spots" as they will be known here), are written and designed with demoniacal skill and ingenuity. . . . The "live" salesman and saleswoman, whose counterpart we shall see all too soon in this country, are persuaders of nauseating persistence . . .

They annoy and disgust: for frequently, yet not altruistically, they are seeking to rectify the more distressful failings of our bodies. One hates their unctuous injunctions, their hypnotic hucksterring.[39]

Despite Mr. Harling's call to save the British empire from banning commercial television, broadcast advertising finally arrived in September 1955. With the ITA in control, the restrictions were considerably greater than those in the United States. The six minutes of commercial time per hour of broadcasting was a firm rule rather than just an oft-ignored code guideline. Commercial television was broadcast only 52 ½ hours per week, less than half of the 130 hours shown in the States. British screens were blank on Sunday morning to avoid competing with church activities. No commercials could be accepted from a long list of marketers considered too shady for mass public display. These included moneylenders, matrimonial agencies, fortune-tellers, undertakers, and bookmakers, as well as manufacturers of slimming, bust development, contraceptive, smoking cure, and alcoholic treatment products. Guarding the public trust for the ITA was Dr. Charles Hill, Great Britain's Postmaster General. "Hamlet," he promised, "will not interrupt his soliloquy to relate the sort of toothpaste being used at Elsinore."[40]

With all the restrictions and scrutiny, the first commercials to hit British television not surprisingly looked quite different from American-style advertising. *Time* magazine was of the opinion that British commercials "sounded about as American as tea and crumpets." Harry McMahan, vice president in charge of television commercials at the New York office of McCann-Erickson, said that "in all the [British] commercials I've seen, there is a wonderful simplicity, no gimmicks, and an earnest desire to give information." After just two weeks of commercial television, the *London Times* even softened its stance, editorializing that "offensive would be too strong a word by far for these comic little interruptions of entertainment." "But one did feel, nonetheless," the newspaper continued, "that a thick skin of resistance to them will be needed before long." One British viewer agreed, saying that "they'll wear a bit thin after a while," an accurate forecast of things to come.[41]

Pushing the Envelope

Much of the ITA's concerns revolved around the potential threat of commercial television toward children, a concept lost on American advertisers, who viewed the targeting of kids as an extension of their capitalistic freedoms (the trump card in an era that worshipped free enterprise). On British television, Sunday afternoon shows could not be directed at children, the fear being that the shows would conflict with Sunday school. As on Sunday mornings, screens went dead every evening between six and seven o'clock (as they did on BBC radio, a period popularly called the "toddler's truce") so that parents could put their children to bed without televisual interference. The ITA's code also stated that advertising should in no way exploit children's natural credulity and sense of loyalty, which was of course perfectly fair game in America. "Advertising must not result in mental, physical, or moral harm" to children, the code prescribed, nor should advertising encourage children to talk to strangers or "to be a nuisance."[42]

The British system's guards against exposing children to too much or to potentially harmful commercials obviously differed greatly from standard practice in the United States. Children, as an important consumer segment, had been considered a primary, legitimate target audience for many advertisers since the very beginnings of the medium, a legacy of what had been established a generation earlier in radio. By 1955, the American baby boom was in full swing, with 18 million children under the age of five and 16 million between the ages of five and nine. With two-thirds of American households owning at least one television set, commercials were indeed reaching most children, a fact backed up by research showing that children exposed to commercials often had amazing recall and retention abilities. Findings from the Youth Research Institute, for example, showed that "youngsters eagerly repeat television and radio commercials which strike their fancy. Even five-year-olds sing beer commercials over and over again with gusto." This finding, interestingly, was remarkably similar to those reported by British television scholar David Buckingham almost forty years later. In his research, Buckingham found that kids under ten years old became highly engaged when exposed to television advertising, finding it difficult to stay in their seats when viewing a musical commercial. Although children today are unquestionably more sophisticated when it comes to media viewing than their parents were in the 1950s, the effects of a good jingle on kids are apparently timeless.[43]

American advertisers' vision of children as junior consumers was made most apparent through the offering of premiums in commercials. As they did on radio, a number of companies used premiums to entice children to purchase or have their parents purchase products, but television promotions in the postwar years were a much larger, more coordinated affair than those of Depression-era radio. "Nationwide merchandising schemes and their implementation began to hit high gear by 1954," noted Michael Kammen, as marketers went all out to use television advertising to promote their products to a national audience of children. General Electric, for example, advertised a sixty-piece circus, a magic ray gun, and a space helmet to children who brought their parents into stores to see a demonstration of new GE refrigerators. GE's competitor, Sylvania, offered a Space Ranger kit, complete with space helmet, disintegrater, flying saucer, and space telephone to children able to persuade their parents to inspect a new line of television sets. Nash automobiles advertised a toy service station to children who convinced their parents to visit a dealer showroom. Quaker Oats sent a pouch of Alaskan dirt to every child who mailed in 25 cents and a box top. Sunkist Growers offered four circus masks for a quarter and a wrapper from a three-can package of juice. General Mills stuffed millions of Lone Ranger masks in boxes of Wheaties and millions of Lone Ranger comic books in boxes of Cheerios. Standard Brands put free Howdy Doody coloring cards into boxes of Royal pudding, while Armour gave away baseball buttons with the purchase of its hotdogs. Tagging commercials with such premium offers undoubtedly achieved advertisers' objective of using children to influence adults' brand selection, and traded upon icons of popular culture to move consumer goods.[44]

The willingness, even eagerness, among marketers to aggressively target children was reflective of the gold rush orientation of postwar consumer culture. As marketers scrambled for sales and profits, advertisers in many consumer product categories chose television as the primary battleground to wage their wars. Cigarette advertising was among the most competitive of these years, filled with supposedly scientific claims and statistics to "prove" the superiority of brands. Goodman Ace, a television writer and acute observer of the American television scene for the *Saturday Review,* humorously suggested in February 1953 that "the promises of the cigarette campaign now being waged on TV have become such a major proportion of the clamor and ballyhoo which emanate from our screens these nights that required dress for an evening of viewing has become a smoking jacket." To lend an air of legitimacy to its "thirty-day Camel test" campaign, the makers of the brand hired well-known newsman John Cameron Swayze. Leveraging his popularity as a reporter and anchor, Camel featured Swayze in a commercial in which he interviewed three corporate executives at the company's brand new research facility in Winston–Salem. With this new building, the executives claimed, the company would be able to develop the best cigarettes possible by identifying the best tobacco. Through "objective" spokespeople such as Swayze, marketers like Camel achieved a greater level of credibility among an increasingly skeptical viewing audience. Corporate America's employment of real journalists for commercial purposes had the larger effect of turning voices considered to be in the public domain into those of private interests, in effect "branding" reality as an especially potent marketing strategy.[45]

Although cigarette advertising had yet to be seriously challenged on health or moral grounds, selling alcohol on television was a more controversial issue. Legislators in states such as Michigan tried to ban the advertising of beer and wine in the state to no avail. Beer advertising on television was and is, of course, a staple of sports broadcasting in local markets across the country, strongly associated with a particular team's identity. Millions of New Yorkers, for example, became familiar with the various beer slogans of baseball's salad days, brought to them by radio and television advertisers. Mel Allen, the not yet legendary announcer of Yankee games, was a spokesperson for Ballantine, excitedly exclaiming that "it's the beer that chill can't kill!" "No matter what the temperature is outdoors," Mr. Allen informed armchair Yankee fans between innings, "it's always winter in your refrigerator." Across town at Ebbets Field, Connie Desmond, announcer of the Brooklyn Dodgers games, reminded viewers that the makers of Schaefer's Beer had not lost their skill. Russ Hodges, now an announcer for the New York Giants, stuck to promoting Chesterfield cigarettes on baseball broadcasts, although he did pitch Pabst Blue Ribbon Beer when he called boxing matches. (Mr. Allen and Mr. Desmond also represented tobacco products, White Owl Cigars and Lucky Strikes, respectively.) As Goodman Ace observed, "Drinking and smoking seem to be the stuff athletic broadcasts are made of." Television advertising was an integral part of the sports experience for many Americans, as the same announcers who called the games urged viewers to patronize sponsors' brands.[46]

Still, some politicians viewed alcoholic beverage advertising on television the way temperance advocates viewed alcohol a half century earlier. Although brewers' expenditures on television and radio accounted for just 3 percent of all advertising spending (and only .31 percent of total time), Rep. Eugene Silver (R-Kentucky) was on a mission to stop "booze broadcasting" in its tracks. Not only did Silver introduce a bill to the House Interstate and Foreign Commerce Committee, but he followed it up with a tirade to the House on the evils of alcohol. Silver compared John Barleycorn to "the rattlesnake, the brothel, the stalking murderer, and the insidious thief," and claimed that unrestrained advertising of it "may cost more than the damage and loss of life of both the Chicago fire and Johnstown flood combined and multiplied by two." Silver's bill failed to get very far, as banning the advertising of beer was too reminiscent of the failure of Prohibition, and ran directly counter to the classical American tenets of free speech, free trade, and laissez-faire consumerism.[47]

Network, agency, and corporate executives wisely tapped into these themes when television advertising was attacked, a smart business strategy. In May of 1955 at the U.S. Brewers Foundation convention in Los Angeles, for example, Robert C. Kintner, president of ABC, confirmed that his network welcomed brewers' business. Alongside brewing dignitaries such as Anheuser Busch, president of the eponymous brewer, Mr. Kintner told the group that

I would not have accepted your invitation if A.B.C. was not a willing servant of the beer industry. . . . I say that advisedly because . . . I have heard people criticize the broadcasting business, as a public franchise, for taking beer advertising. As far as A.B.C. is concerned, we not only actively solicit it; we definitely want it; we believe it is a basic part of the American scene just like our radio and television business is. . . . And may I compliment, very sincerely, the United States Brewers Foundation and its advertising agency, the J. Walter Thompson Company, for the building up by advertising and public relations of the concept that "beer belongs" as the family drink of a freedom-loving people.[48]

Framing the advertising and consumption of beer as an inalienable right was brilliant posturing, effectively accusing those holding oppositional views as being "un-American." With the Red Scare still very much alive and well, criticizing anything smacking of "freedom" was dangerous ground to tread.

Although liquor marketers voluntarily abstained from airing commercials, there was no objection to television advertising for products intended to mix with liquor. One such product, Schweppes tonic water, was a visible televisual presence in the mid-1950s due to its memorable commercials. In a 1955 spot for the brand, "Was It Paris?" Ogilvy, Benson & Mather commissioned Commander Whitehead, a fictional sea captain who had appeared in Schweppes print ads. With an over-the-top British accent, Whitehead asked a beautiful woman where they had previously met. "Was it Hong Kong? Beirut? Cairo, perhaps?" The woman remembers that the Commander had a gin and tonic, the latter having told the waiter "to make jolly well sure" that the drink was made with Schweppes. Whitehead responds by saying it could have been anywhere because Schweppes is famous the world over. Although ridiculous by today's standards, "Was It Paris?" captured postwar viewers' imaginations, leveraging Americans' high-brow values of formality, elegance, and international sophistication.[49]

Big Business

Supported by an ideological backbone equating consumer capitalism with America's basic freedoms, television advertising continued to soar. A generally healthy economy, an unprecedented demand for consumer goods, and effective commercials like "Was It Paris?" were all major factors contributing to a ninefold increase in television advertising billings from 1949 ($68.4 million) to 1953 ($688.7 million). Notably, television was beginning to steal more revenues from other national media, forcing radio networks to abandon their once bread-and-butter profit source of prime time entertainment. According to figures from the Publishers Information Bureau (PIB), many advertisers were continuing to cut purchases of both radio time and magazine space and investing the money in television instead. *Tide*, an advertising trade magazine, confirmed the PIB findings, noting that more than a third of the nation's top one hundred advertisers had cut radio and print budgets and increased television budgets in the past year. Procter and Gamble, for example, increased its television budget by $3.5 million in 1954 by appropriating $3.3 million in "new" money and taking $200,000 from other media. The introduction of Swanson's frozen TV dinner in 1954 seemed an apt symbol of the impact television had made on the nation's cultural landscape.[50]

By April 1955, there was no doubt that television advertising was seriously threatening the "selling power" of other national media. As in the early 1930s, when the exploding medium of radio triggered a decline in national magazine advertising, a new gunslinger was taking over the town. As network television brought in a record $320 million in 1954 (a 40 percent gain over the 1953 level), magazine spending remained flat while radio spending dropped 14 percent. A closer look at the numbers reveals that while magazine spending was indeed flat, rate increases were making up for a drop in actual advertising pages. Increased spending in the food, toiletries, and home furnishings categories was most responsible for television's large gains. Although magazines remained the number one medium in total revenues, big advertisers were now determining what they wanted to spend on television before setting their print or radio budgets. This was due to the undeniable prestige of television as a more "modern" medium than print or radio, and the ability for marketers to tell their stories through both sound and images.[51]

As network television rose to the top of the media heap in the mid-1950s, its impact within the retail arena became more evident. Retailers were very aware of which companies were running commercials, and they stocked more brands which were advertised on television, gave them better shelf space, and promoted them more through in-store displays. Equally important, more advertising by national manufacturers lessened the need for local retailers to create awareness of what goods were available. Victor M. Ratner, a vice president at McCann-Erickson, concluded that the role of selling was passing from the local merchant to the national manufacturer, observing that "advertising is becoming more a primary partner in marketing than it once was . . . [as] the selling job has shifted to the manufacturer." Arno Johnson, a vice president at J. Walter Thompson, believed that network television advertising was contributing to nothing less than the decline of the urban department store as local retailers cut back on their own spending. Whether national advertising was good or bad for local retailers, there was no doubt that television advertising was redefining the way America did business by becoming the medium of choice for large marketers.[52]

Shower of Cars

Helping to drive national advertisers' spending in 1954 and 1955 was the introduction of expensive and extravagant shows called "spectaculars." Spectaculars were one of NBC president (and former ad exec) Sylvester "Pat" Weaver's innovations, a means of challenging habitual viewing by turning an ordinary broadcast into a national event, thereby justifying higher rates. Often ninety minutes or longer and costing $200,000 to $500,000 to produce, spectaculars represented the longest and most expensive television shows created to date. CBS spectaculars included *The Best of Broadway,* a once-a-month revue of thirty years of musical comedy and dramatic hits sponsored by Westinghouse, and *Shower of Stars,* a once-a-month extravaganza featuring Betty Grable and sponsored by Chrysler. In addition to their frequent sponsorship of spectaculars, automobile manufacturers parked themselves all over the dial. Ford offered the *Ford Star Jubilee* on CBS, while General Motors spread money across a number of shows on its favorite network, NBC. Chevrolet sponsored *The Dinah Shore Show,* Buick *The Milton Berle Show,* Pontiac the *Red Buttons* and *Jack Carson* shows, Cadillac the *Today* and *Tonight* shows, and Oldsmobile a series of specials such as *Max Liebman Presents.*[53]

With annual style changes modeled after the fashion industry (what Karal Ann Marling called "Sloanism," after Alfred P. Sloan, the GM president of the late 1920s credited for the idea), automobile companies were seizing the televisual day. Driven by their goal to sell each American household a new car every year, car manufacturers (along with profit-driven networks and local stations) pushed commercial time to twelve or more minutes per hour, twice that "allowed" by the NARTB. Goodman Ace joked that with the number of Chrysler spots it aired, the *Shower of Stars* should be called *Shower of Cars.* Increased horsepower was often the focus of automobile advertising, as Buick increased its horsepower on its basic model from 220 to 236, Cadillac from 230 to 250, and the clunky DeSoto from 170 to 185. Television advertising in the automobile category dovetailed perfectly with the economic, social, and geographic dynamics of the 1950s, promoting America's love affair with the road and helping make the automobile an even more ubiquitous and necessary possession. With the creation of the interstate highway system in 1956 and the parallel rise of road culture (e.g., drive-ins, motels, fast food), most Americans couldn't wait to get behind the wheel. Automobile marketers were seizing this confluence of cultural forces with a vengeance, creating record-level advertising budgets to position cars not as a mere consumer product but as a cornerstone of postwar life. At the nexus of commuting, shopping, and vacationing, the automobile was the American Dream on wheels, the ideal mode of transportation for the modern suburban family.[54]

For car manufacturers like Chevrolet, television also offered an unprecedented opportunity to visually demonstrate new technologies. In one 1955 spot, for example, viewers were told that Polynesian navigators have known for centuries that an outrigger provides greater stability to a canoe, and explained that Chevrolet engineers adopted the idea in the rear-end design on its 1955 models. Handling and cornering were further inspired by "glide ride," technotalk for an innovative front-end suspension system. We see the car riding over a rough road with a pitcher of water placed on its hood with not a drop spilling, proving that the automobile is, as Chevrolet claimed, "Motorific." By turning technological innovation into visual demonstration, advertisers like Chevrolet were taking full advantage of the seeing-is-believing power of television advertising. General Motor's top-of-the-line division, Cadillac, relied on more emotional appeals to sell its automobiles. In one of its 1954 commercials, a sophisticated couple is shown getting ready to go out for the evening. The announcer tells viewers that for occasions such as this one, there is only one car—Cadillac. Drawing upon classic 1950s peer pressure and desire for upward mobility, the announcer suggests that viewers imagine "how proud they will be when they arrive and find themselves the subject of admiring glances." As an icon of the American Dream, Cadillac had a large carrot to wave in front of those wanting to tell others (and themselves) that they had indeed "arrived." [55]

Marketers of more practical automobiles such as Mercury conceded luxury in favor of safety. In the fall of 1955, Mercury called on spokesperson Ed Sullivan to personally point out the many safety features of its Custom model. On his show, Sullivan told viewers about the car's safety brakes, safety beam headlights, padded steering wheel, and high-powered engine. Sullivan, whom David Halberstam considered the "Minister of Culture" of the 1950s, was the ideal person to deliver Mercury's message of prudence and common sense. Ford's answer to its sister company Mercury was its "life-guard" design, developed at the company's "proving ground" in Dearborn, Michigan. Ford's commercials in 1955 featured "safe-guard" door latches designed to keep passengers from being thrown from the vehicle in a collision. In these pre–seat belt days, such safety devices were about the best car companies could do to reduce the staggering number of injuries and fatalities resulting from crashes. Studebaker took a novel approach to entice consumers with feelings of greater security when driving. Rather than focusing on technology, not one of Studebaker's strongest suits, the company had spokesperson Gene Raymond make a special offer for a $20,000 insurance policy to purchasers of its automobile. Executives at Studebaker's agency, Benton & Bowles, apparently believed that the idea of leaving a legacy for one's loved ones was a more compelling selling proposition than featuring another "me-too" safety device, an interesting strategy designed to capitalize on parents' fear of the worst case scenario.[56]

Mixed Messages

With or without a strong selling proposition, marketers continued to rely heavily on what they believed were the two most effective techniques of the golden age of television advertising, celebrity testimonials and integrated advertising. The level to which commercials were integrated into the story lines of television shows actually rose in the early 1950s as sponsors recognized the value of a seamless presentation of program material. Story lines often referenced not just products but brands, as on a *Milton Berle* episode when guest star Gertrude Berg (in character as *Mama*'s Molly Goldberg) asked the star to donate a Buick to a raffle her ladies' auxiliary was holding. Integrating a product into programming was not only a way to weave a brand into a televisual slice of life but also a clever way of getting around the limits of commercial time recommended by the NARTB. According to the code, mentioning a sponsor's product during a program was not considered a commercial as long as the product was considered "new." The names of new car models thus found their way into the scripts of many variety shows, purely to gain more advertising impressions "off the clock." This loophole in the NARTB code led Goodman Ace to wonder what would prevent a sponsor from introducing a square aspirin, a circular refrigerator, a rectangular cigarette, or a laxative that actually tasted like a laxative instead of chocolate.[57]

Even if it was considered advertising by the voluntary code and thus subject to time constraints, getting a brand on stage as a plot device or celebrity foil was a marketing coup. As Arthur Godfrey was proving every week, plugs for food products could easily be turned into televisual spectacle. Hosts of other shows went to school on Godfrey's success by using food as show business prop. On *You Asked for It*, a popular audience participation show, for example, host Hugh Conover demonstrated three different methods of removing Skippy "Old Style" peanut butter from the roof of one's mouth to roars from the live crowd. Such blending of entertainment and commercialism made it difficult for viewers to discern between the two, elevating the status of brands like Skippy by making them virtually synonymous with their respective product categories.[58]

Although Godfrey and a handful of other stars and announcers were certainly adept at branding their shows, Jack Benny remained the undisputed champion of integrated advertising. Lucky Strike renewed its sponsorship of *The Jack Benny Program* through 1953 and 1954, consistently reaping advertising time during the entertainment portion of the show in addition to regular commercial breaks. In a January 1953 episode, for example, Don Wilson performed the Lucky Strike commercial as a ballet dancer wrapped in a tobacco leaf costume. In a September show themed around a trip to Honolulu, the spot was presented with hula music and dancing. Three weeks later, the Sportmen Quartet sang the lyrics of the Lucky jingle to the tune of "By the Light of the Silvery Moon," while in November the show's scriptwriters somehow created the possibility for Rochester to sing the jingle to Don. In May 1954, within a sketch set in an English drawing room, the Sportmen Quartet sang the Lucky commercial to the tune of "Mad Dogs and Englishmen Go Out in the Noonday Sun." A few weeks later, as part of a show titled "On the Road to Nairobi," the group reappeared in African dress, singing the commercial to the tune of "Digga Digga Doo." Rochester reprised his presentation of the Lucky jingle in October, singing and dancing alongside guest stars the Four Sports.[59]

Many other show hosts closely aligned themselves with sponsors' brands in a variety of ways. Some hosts had been major movie stars who now found themselves, in the world of commercial television, advertising spokespeople. Douglas Fairbanks Jr. and Adolphe Menjou rejoiced over Rheingold and Schaefer beer, respectively, while James Mason, host of *Lux Video Theatre*, pitched Lux soap. Loretta Young kept a box of Tide detergent on her grand piano, while Groucho Marx spoke of the glories of owning a DeSoto. Steve Allen personally presented commercials throughout much of his tenure as host of *The Tonight Show*. A few stars — most notably Sid Caesar — refused to mix entertaining with selling, maintaining the purity of their creative genius. With both film and big band music in decline and television on the rise, however, most stars of the day took advantage of the opportunities within the sponsor system. Eddie Fisher, Coca-Cola's major television spokesperson in the early 1950s, was one such entertainer-turned-show host. The singer hosted a 1953 series on NBC, *Coke Time*, in which Fisher was often shown relaxing at home drinking a Coke. On their show *I Love Lucy*, Lucy and Desi plugged their sponsor's product, puffing on Philip Morris cigarettes on episodes such as "The Diet," which originally aired in February 1953. Near the end of a live pitch for Nescafé instant coffee on *The Jackie Gleason Show* in May 1953, Art Carney made a seemingly impromptu appearance, turning the commercial into a comedy skit. Jack Benny's predisposition to promoting anything in sight, which was of course consistent with his character's obsession with money, worked to the advantage of stars who appeared on his show. On an October 1953 show, Benny thanked guest star Humphrey Bogart for appearing, sneaking in a plug for Bogie's new film, *Beat the Devil*.[60]

With commercial television the biggest and best means of gaining instant exposure and making fast money, the most popular stars from movies and music were, like it or not, prominent advertising spokespeople. Frank Sinatra not only happily plugged Timex watches but occasionally lent his magic voice to sponsors' jingles, as when he crooned the "Halo [shampoo] Song" on a November 1953 episode of *The Colgate Comedy Hour*. Even an actor of such stature as Henry Fonda decided that he was not above doing an occasional commercial. As host of *Henry Fonda Presents,* a CBS show that premiered in June 1954, Mr. Fonda's duties included endorsing a brand of beer. When asked why he would agree to pitching a product on television after his distinguished movie career, Fonda said simply, "Money. I will make as much doing these as I would from a movie." For the thirty-nine weeks, over the course of which Fonda simply introduced the play and made a short sales pitch, the actor made $150,000 (which he promptly sent to the IRS as payment for back taxes). Seduced by the big money, popular culture's finest talent were becoming television advertising's principal players, their careers imprinted with the role of product pitchmen. Through the massive power of commercial television, film stars and singers were increasingly complementing their artistic personas with that of the voice of consumption.[61]

Recognizing the great power of celebrities to move product, some advertisers sponsored shows principally because they would then have access to stars' time outside of television. In addition to their on-camera role, television spokespeople had valuable merchandising value, extendable to tie-in newspaper, magazine, and outdoor advertising and point-of-sale promotion. Actors' selling responsibilities thus frequently went well beyond the television show he or she starred in. Most spokespeople had to be available for such duties as signing autographs in supermarkets, attending groundbreaking ceremonies for new plants, or acting as toastmaster at dinners for sponsors' friends. As depicted in the *Milton Berle* "raffle" episode, famous actors were even expected at times to help sponsors' wives raise money for their favorite charities, while others were asked to perform private shows for boards of directors. After Jimmy Durante finished his television show in Los Angeles in December 1954, for example, he flew to New York to do a command

performance for Texaco's board. Durante even paid his own way to enter-
tain his sponsor, although he was hoping to land a performance on an NBC
"spectacular" to cover his expenses. That same month Art Linkletter flew to
New York to emcee the annual Grand National Bake-Off Awards luncheon at
the Waldorf-Astoria hotel as a perk for his sponsor, Pillsbury. Ed Sullivan's
trips for Lincoln-Mercury had a more specific agenda, to persuade dealers
to continue to contribute promotional money to keep *Toast of the Town* on
the air. General Electric used its television personalities to boost morale of
plant employees, having Ronald Reagan, host of *General Electric Theater*,
tour the company's factories, a duty which was formally outlined in his contract. Reagan perhaps ultimately got the better of this deal, capitalizing on
his popularity with working-class Americans in his future career as public
servant.[62]

Other big stars, such as Danny Thomas, also made themselves available
for speeches to employees of their sponsor, as did the indefatigable Betty Furness, who made coast-to-coast public appearances for Westinghouse. Sponsors believed that personal visits were not only good public relations but that
they actually drove up show ratings. Some television personalities, however,
would not honor requests to be a corporate goodwill ambassador. Jack Webb,
for example, made one trip to a Liggett & Meyers factory, but did not plan to
make any other visits. "They are very nice about that sort of thing and realize
how busy I am," explained Webb. Groucho Marx also opted out of sponsors'
requests for off-camera appearances, which, given his penchant for off-the-
cuff insults, was probably just as well. After Ronald Colman was asked by his
sponsor, International Harvester, to make a commercial film for distributors
of the company's products, Colman balked at first but soon recognized that
he had best give in if he was to keep his cushy job. Hal Humphrey agreed
with Colman's decision, believing that most actors who wanted to stay on
television "were going to have to hit the road more often for these special clam-
bakes." Sponsors considered that such services should be gratis, covered by
the huge costs they were paying to produce the shows. Even Lassie had to
participate in corporate events, purportedly having ten puppies in November 1954 so that the show's sponsor could award pups as prizes in a contest.
The promotion was, in fact, not an imposition at all to that season's Lassie,
who was a male in real life.[63]

If Jack Benny was the king of integrated advertising in the 1950s, Ed Sullivan was the best all-around product spokesperson. Host of *Toast of the Town*
and later *The Ed Sullivan Show,* Sullivan's dryness was more than made up

by his enthusiasm for promoting Lincoln and Mercury automobiles both on the show and offscreen. He appeared at both regional dealer meetings and at events sponsored by Lincoln or Mercury, such as the Portland, Oregon, Rose Festival and the crowning of the Cotton Queen in Memphis. Sullivan truly went beyond the call of spokesperson duty, giving blood in San Francisco, landing in a helicopter in Boston Common, and submerging in a Navy diver's suit, all to generate publicity for the car manufacturer. Although Sullivan's stunts varied, a shiny motorcade of Lincolns and Mercurys was an essential part of one of his personal appearances. When on air, Sullivan was keenly aware that the Lincoln, rather than himself, needed to be the real star. Each time a particularly renowned guest appeared on *Toast of the Town,* such as Sam Goldwyn, Oscar Hammerstein, or Walt Disney, in fact, Sullivan made sure the guest's wife received a new Lincoln as a gift. "That gets a lot of caste-conscious people buying Lincolns," Sullivan correctly believed. Sullivan's efforts, along with those of his colleagues in show biz, helped forge the symbiotic, synergistic relationship between entertainment and consumerism of these years. Television advertising was ground zero for this relationship, packaging consumption within the cult of celebrity.[64]

Some celebrities, such as Alfred Hitchcock, chose an alternative path by which to promote a sponsor and its products. On his CBS television show, *Alfred Hitchcock Presents,* the host took refreshing potshots at sponsor Bristol-Myers, treating the company's commercials with what *Time* magazine called "the equivalent of a fastidious man brushing a particularly repellent caterpillar off his lapel." Hitchcock routinely offered snide, ironic comments immediately after the airing of Bristol-Myers commercials, such as when he said sarcastically, "Over so soon? My, time certainly passes quickly when you're being entertained." After a particularly long spot, Hitchcock said, "You know, I believe commercials are improving every day. Next week we hope to have another one—equally fascinating. And, if time permits, we shall bring you another story." On occasion, the camera would find Hitchcock counting when the commercial was over, murmuring to himself, "five hundred and eleven, five hundred and twelve, five hundred and thirteen! Thank you, sir." Rather than be miffed at this abuse, Bristol-Myers executives, like advertising manager Richard Van Nostrand, were elated with Hitchcock's mocking, as the show was earning a 29.5 Nielsen rating, four points more than its rival on NBC, *The Alcoa Hour.* Hitchcock's digs at his sponsor also endeared the famous director to many viewers. Research showed that not only did many viewers remember the products advertised on the show, they could recite the order in which the spots appeared, a rare accomplishment. What viewers did not know was that Hitchcock's barbs were not impromptu ad libs, but actually carefully scripted lines submitted to Bristol-Myers for review prior to filming. Hitchcock himself did not even come up with the pithy comments, composed instead by a copywriter named James Allardice, who confessed that he found the opportunity to poke gentle fun at his client a very rewarding experience, a means of venting some of his own job-related frustrations.[65]

Whether through Sullivanesque sincerity or Hitchcockian sarcasm, celebrity appeals were a powerful way that business was using commercial television to turn postwar America into the promised land that many dreamed it could and would be. Through its "shower of stars," programs-as-commercials, and sheer volume, television advertising was acting as a cheerleader of prosperity, rooting for Americans to realize their personal American Dream. Now a fixture in most Americans' living rooms, television had strengthened the domestic orientation of the American Dream, making home, more than ever before, sweet home. The role of television advertising in American life would only grow in the latter half of the 1950s, as the pressure to turn myth into reality intensified.

PART TWO

Keeping Up with the Joneses

*

Chapter Three

The Spark Plug of Prosperity, 1956–1958

The exciting car for years to come.

John Cameron Swayze, speaking of Ford's new automobile, the Edsel, in 1958

As executives from the television and advertising industries planned for the 1956–1957 season, they could each look back at what had been achieved to date with some deserved glee. The year 1955 had been a key moment in advertising history as television passed all other national media for the leading position. Television accounted for 15 percent of total national advertising expenditures, but network executives envisioned the day when the medium would account for a full half of all promotion spending. Especially exciting to industry executives was that advertising as a percentage of total national income was approaching pre–World War II levels. In the consumer-driven economy of the 1920s, advertising as a percentage of national income was about 4 percent. In the Depression years of the mid-1930s, the ratio was about 3 percent, while during the war years the percentage was virtually nil because there were hardly any consumer products to sell. In the postwar years, however, the ratio gradually crept upward, from 1.6 percent in 1946, to 2.5 percent in 1952, to 2.6 percent in 1953, and to 2.7 percent in 1954. It certainly appeared that television was playing a major role in the recovery of the advertising industry and in stirring Americans' desire to be consumers.[1]

In addition to growing as a percent of total income, advertising as a whole was taking a decided shift toward national media and away from local or regional media. This also had much to do with the record levels of television viewership, as well as advertisers' use of the medium to reach a nationwide audience in one fell swoop. In the mid-1930s, before commercial television, the split between total national and total local advertising was around 50–50. By 1949, however, the ratio was 57 percent to 43 percent in favor of national advertising, and in 1954 about 60–40. As national television's "share of voice" increased, so did its rates, as networks took advantage of increased demand of a medium of limited supply. Throughout the first half of the 1950s marketers had complained about how expensive television advertising was, but networks continued to sell out their schedules. As Frank Stanton, president of CBS, succinctly put it, "Advertisers wouldn't pay these [high] prices if it didn't [sell goods]."[2]

More than just creating demand for individual products or services, however, television advertising appeared to be lighting a fire under the entire American economy. When an expected recession after the end of the Korean War in 1953 and 1954 turned out to be relatively mild, some theorized that the selling power of television advertising persuaded Americans to keep consuming when they might have otherwise slowed down on spending. CBS's Stanton and NBC's Pat Weaver went even further in assessing the economic and cultural impact of television advertising. Stanton observed that the nation's production and sales volume had each doubled since the end of World War II, a fact he correlated with "television's explosive entry on the American scene." Weaver saw television as "the spark plug of a never-ending prosperity," creating "such an itch to buy, have, see, and do all the things shown on TV that everybody will work better to make more money to spend." Stanton and Weaver had located the postwar American Dream somewhere between the entertainment television offered and the commercials that brought them to viewers, making abundance for all a self-fulfilling prophecy.[3]

David Halberstam has summarily captured the paradigmatic shift in national identity that occurred during the 1950s as consumerism became our dominant ethos. This was, he writes,

not simple old prewar capitalism, this was something new — capitalism that was driven by a ferocious consumerism, where the impulse was not so much about what people *needed* in their lives but what they needed to consume in order to keep up with their neighbors and, of course, to drive the GNP endlessly upward.[4]

As commercial television urged, cajoled, and enticed viewers to keep up with the Joneses and improve their standard of living, American citizens were well on the way to becoming, first and foremost, consumers.

The Tower of Babel

Prosperity and abundance for all, however, did not come cheap, as some television advertisers continued to abuse their power. Some sponsors, like Minute Maid orange juice, were turning television into a televisual tower of Babel, earning legitimate candidacy for the Seal of Malpractice. On New

Year's Day of 1956, for example, NBC telecast the annual Rose Bowl Parade, brought to viewers by Minute Maid. The hosts, Betty White and Bill Goodwin, interrupted the ninety-minute broadcast every five or six minutes to promote the sponsor's brand, drawing quite a number of letters from viewers upset about the number and frequency of Minute Maid orange juice commercials. One particularly irate viewer went so far as to create Orange Juice Anonymous, an organization whose members swore to forego the citrus beverage for life. The invasion of commercial interests into a domain historically considered within the public realm alienated many viewers, especially because of the excess involved. Sponsors were literally commercializing icons of popular culture such as the Rose Bowl Parade, integrating pitches for products like orange juice into nearly every sphere of everyday life in America. As advertisers appropriated any event likely to reap high ratings, watching television as a form of leisure relied increasingly on subscribing to or at least tolerating the endless urging to consume more products.[5]

Writing for *Holiday* magazine in the 1950s, Alfred Bester captured the incestuous, symbiotic relationship between leisure and consumption as expressed by television advertising. Bester was deeply disturbed by the seemingly endless cycle of viewing and buying, believing that

the noble aim of the TV commercial is to provide America with more leisure which . . . America needs like a hole in the head. . . . Millions of families will trudge out, hypnotized by the words "new" and "different," to buy the gadget which will provide more leisure to watch TV and discover new timesavers which will provide more leisure to watch more TV and discover more timesavers which will provide more leisure to . . .[6]

Other observers of the contemporary scene criticized television advertising in their own way. Armed with an insider perspective, the best television comics of the day found ample opportunity to satirize the inescapable presence of commercials in postwar America. In May 1956, for example, Ernie Kovacs performed a commercial for witch doctor kits as a sketch, perhaps poking fun at the often phony claims made by advertisers of real over-the-counter health remedies. In January 1957, Carl Reiner and Sid Caesar did a mock television commercial for the "Fiasco" automobile, a gentle slap at the "shower of cars" on the air. It was no coincidence that it was these comedians who demanded as much independence as possible from sponsor control.[7]

Critics' concerns and comics' ridicule, however, only confirmed that television advertising was now at the forefront of the national consciousness, as American as mom, apple pie, and, of course, Chevrolet. Expectedly, those involved in the television commercial business reaped the financial rewards associated with the dominant medium of the day. Unlike in radio, where commercial announcers were among the poorest paid people in the business, television announcers and actors were compensated extremely well, reflecting the higher stakes and budgets (not to mention the need to look reasonably physically attractive). In 1956, the scale talent fee for television commercials was $70 for the first performance plus an additional $50 each time the spot was shown. That may not sound like very much by today's standards, but consider that some commercials were shown eight times a day for three months, some even longer. For a few hours of work, then, some actors would eventually collect $36,000, a lot of money by any standards and particularly so in 1956. Stars, of course, got paid significantly more than scale. Big-name talent were put under contract and paid yearly retainers starting at about $1,000 per week, with the top twenty commercial announcers or actors grossing around $70,000 a year. With these sorts of fees, some considered a role in a television commercial even more prestigious than one on Broadway. "The blonde who pestered daddy for a walk-on in the Follies," wrote Alfred Bester, "now yearns for a bit in a commercial." [8]

Higher talent fees were matched by an equivalent rise in the overall production values of television advertising. The production of filmed television commercials in the mid-1950s, which were increasing in number over live spots, was often as complex and expensive as staging a Broadway play. After approval of the script and storyboard, commercials typically were assigned to one of the many production studios based in New York or Los Angeles. It took about a day to shoot a sixty-second spot, with cost averaging $4,000 (but ranging anywhere from $1,500 to $15,000). It was not unusual for a studio to shoot 5,000 feet of film to produce an air-worthy thirty-second spot. Often complicating matters were "commercial mothers," who made stage mothers seem benevolent. Clients were frequently as difficult as they were popularly believed to be, particularly when it came to how to refer to their products. A leading executive of a company that made electric ranges reportedly had a fit if anyone said "stove" in his presence, while a refrigerator marketing executive reacted similarly at the word "icebox." Clients were also known for their desire to ensure that their commercials would appeal to middle class tastes in order to hit the fat bull's-eye of the mass market. Anything that could be considered either high-brow or low-brow was thus not likely to make it on the air. One agency turned this idea into a compliment for copy it considered air-worthy. "This is so good it's almost mediocre," went its stamp of approval.[9]

Mediocre or not, companies continued to invest heavily in television advertising and looked for different ways it could contribute to their total marketing efforts. In the mid-1950s, companies began to aggressively use television advertising as a key part of their test marketing programs. With spot television, marketers had a means of advertising a new product on a mass scale in a limited part of the country. Television advertising was superior to both radio and magazines in this respect, as both of these media had more "spill," that is, reached more readers and viewers outside of the test market. While some marketers chose local markets which were representative of the country as a whole, others chose markets based on the likelihood of achieving favorable results. For example, because Green Bay, Wisconsin indexed very high on candy consumption, new candies were often tested there. Because soaps and shampoos did well in cities with hard water, Chicago and New York City were often selected as test markets for brands in these product categories. Anything to do with the home was, not surprisingly, tested in Southern California, the leading edge of domestic lifestyle trends throughout the postwar years. The unique geographic "containability" of television advertising thus became an important resource for national marketers, a tool by which to influence consumption habits in a specific area of the country before a national rollout.[10]

The $64,000 Question

Commercial television was steaming ahead not only in the States but, somewhat surprisingly, in Britain. By February 1956, just six months after it was introduced, commercial television was already outdrawing the BBC in homes that had access to the extra channels. Sixty percent of viewers, in fact, preferred watching a commercial station to the BBC during prime time evening hours. The only thing preventing even more Brits from switching their dials was that not enough people had television sets that could pick up commercial stations. Either the station did not broadcast in their area, or viewers had not yet invested in the converter that was required for older sets. Advertisers were thus reluctant to buy time on commercial stations, being too expensive for their limited reach. By its one-year anniversary, commercial television was pulling in 70–80 percent of the total audience that had a choice, but it was still not making money. About $28 million of advertising time had been sold,

$8 million short of the break-even point. The inability of British commercial television to turn a profit in its first year was hardly surprising given the complete lack of any form of commercial broadcasting tradition in the country. American television had the benefit of some twenty years of commercial radio, borrowing heavily (perhaps too heavily) on the development and production of advertising from one medium to the other. Although print advertising was, of course, a mature art form in Britain in the mid-1950s, agencies had little knowledge of how to plan a television campaign and put it on the air. Again, agencies in the States built on their familiarity with radio campaigns when television advertising took off after World War II, while British agencies had to essentially start from scratch when it came to commercial broadcasting.[11]

As British entrepreneurs in commercial television increasingly looked to the American system for inspiration (i.e., to make money), British spots began to more closely resemble their cousins across the pond. Despite all the restrictions, British advertisers quickly adopted much of the American hard-sell approach and techniques to get their commercials seen and heard. "At first, we were spending forty-five seconds entertaining and only fifteen seconds selling," one British agency executive said, "[but] we decided that was silly and I don't think we've made the mistake since." Some American marketers selling their products in Britain, such as Kellogg's cereals, even used the same film shown in the United States dubbed with a different soundtrack. The harder sell tactics, in addition to the greater number of sets able to pick up commercial stations, were largely responsible for a much more successful second year of commercial television in Britain. Gross revenues rose from $33 million in 1956 to $84 million in 1957, with commercial television producers making ten times the amount in profit. One year later, no BBC television program would even be a serious contender for the top ten rating spots. The American model of commercial television was becoming the global industry standard and, in the process, helping to turn citizens of other countries into consumers.[12]

Despite the undeniable cultural impact of television in the States and soon the world, all parties concerned—networks, advertising agencies, and marketers—continued to look for firm proof that the medium did indeed sell goods. Inside advertising agencies, an "unpublicized but virulent" war was raging between younger "TV men" and older "print men." Halberstam has referred to the print versus television advertising war of the 1950s as "a generational thing," with the battle lines drawn between the printed word and the televisual image. Who would win this war had huge implications for the long-term success of the magazine and television industries, as it was these "men" who told Corporate America where to put its advertising money. To help resolve this internal war and make the best use of clients' budgets, more research was commissioned by agencies and networks to more accurately determine the effectiveness of television advertising. Two new studies revealed that the younger generation were likely to keep their jobs. The first, a follow-up study of the NBC-Simmons test in Fort Wayne, showed that sales of products advertised on television rose a full 33 percent among set owners. The second, another by A. C. Nielsen, tested the impact of a single commercial in three markets, one without a television station (where the commercial could obviously not be seen), one with a single station, and one with several stations. The study revealed that sales of the advertised product, a specialty food item, remained flat in the market without television, rose 22 percent in the market with multiple stations, and jumped 29 percent in the market with a single station (where viewers were more likely to see the commercial).[13]

With the number of television sets now exceeding that of bathtubs in the United States, statistical research only confirmed the obvious ability of the medium to move product. Television fever was raging in 1956, fueled in part by success stories which both networks and ad agencies no doubt helped circulate. After a year on television, for example, sales of Dow Chemical's Saran Wrap had gone from 120,000 to 3.8 million rolls a month. The biggest, most lauded case history was, however, that of Revlon, sponsor of *The $64,000 Question.* In the year that Revlon sponsored "64," as it was known in the trade, the company's sales rose 54 percent, its earnings rose 200 percent, and its stock went from $12 to $30 a share. The company was swamped by retailers demanding product to sell. Daniel Seligman, writing in *Fortune,* observed that by sponsoring *The $64,000 Question,* Revlon could sell just about anything. "It is no reflection on the quality of Revlon's merchandise," Seligman wrote in April 1956, "to suggest that one could, apparently, sell an outright facial corrosive in quantity if the program were hawking it."[14]

Because brand loyalty was relatively low in cosmetics, marketers like Revlon had to spend a high proportion of their sales on advertising and promotion to win over consumers. Revlon budgeted a whopping 25 percent of its retail sales on advertising and promotion, spending $7.5 million to persuade women to buy its lipstick, nail enamel, powders, and hair spray—a rate that exceeded even that of companies in traditionally high-spending product categories. (Just as e-commerce advertising today favors greater spending for standardized products like books and CDs, so television advertising of the postwar era favored certain product categories, specifically beer, cigarettes, cars, and health and beauty aids.) Revlon's confidence in the medium rested on its ability to successfully translate its "consciously arty and 'expensive looking'" print advertising into television commercials. Consistent with the feminine ideal of the 1950s, the "Revlon look" was a complex blend of sex and wholesomeness. One agency executive described the Revlon woman as one who "only goes out at night and looks at first like a high-class tramp, but you know, somehow, that she's really a nice girl."[15]

The high percentage of sales Revlon was investing in advertising and promotion was a reflection of its prestigious position as sponsor of *The $64,000 Question*. The show was an unparalleled hit in the history of television, pulling in some 55 million viewers each week. From July 1955 to April 1956, the show finished first in the ratings nearly every week. Viewership was so high that it did not matter so much that a good portion of the audience of *The $64,000 Question* was "wasted." At the time, Revlon made no products for men or children, but the company was quickly developing deodorants and cologne for the former, trying to exploit its advantage of reaching so many men on the most popular show on television. In addition to introducing new products, Revlon was seizing the televisual day by spinning off multicultural versions of *The $64,000 Question* for viewers in foreign countries. England had *The 64,000 Shilling* and Mexico *The 64,000 Peso*, each sponsored by Revlon and each seeding American-style consumer capitalism. The show's success in the States was even more remarkable given the internal controversy that surrounded it during its heyday. In 1956, NBC tried, and almost succeeded, to steal *The $64,000 Question* from CBS, while Revlon replaced its agency (and conceiver of the show) Norman, Craig & Kummel with BBDO.[16]

The next television season, however, another quiz show, *Twenty-One*, topped *The $64,000 Question* in the Trendex television rating index. As contestant Charles Van Doren increased his winnings to $143,000 in March 1957, NBC's *Twenty-One* passed both *The $64,000 Question* and CBS's top-rated show, *I Love Lucy*, something the network had been aggressively trying to do since 1951. The sponsor of *Twenty-One*, Pharmaceuticals, Inc., was as delighted with the coup as Revlon had been with its *The $64,000 Question* a year previously. Pharmaceuticals, Inc. was an unknown corporate entity to most Americans, but the company's products were not. As the nation's eighteenth largest buyer of network television, Pharmaceuticals spent $10 million advertising brands like Geritol, Geritol Jr., Serutan (a laxative), Zarumin (a pain killer), Sominex (a sleeping agent), RDX (for losing weight), and Nyron (for adding weight). In two years, Pharmaceuticals and its hit show *Twenty-One* would be at the epicenter of the biggest scandal in television history.[17]

The Boy/Girl Next Door

Of course, no single agency, show, or individual could remain at the top of the only-as-good-as-your-last-campaign world of television advertising for too long. In 1956, queen of commercials Betty Furness was finally dethroned, as Julia Meade emerged as the new It Girl of television advertising. Ms. Meade, a twenty-eight-year-old actress, had already matched Furness's salary of $100,000 a year by plugging Lincolns on CBS's *The Ed Sullivan Show,* Hudnut hair products on NBC's *Your Hit Parade,* and *Life* magazine on ABC's evening news show, anchored by John Daly. Although there was some initial concern among Lincoln executives regarding a woman's ability to convincingly talk about torque, transmissions, and ball-joint suspensions, research showed that both men and women found her very believable. Researcher Horace Schwerin, in fact, found that "no one in our experience has had a higher acceptance with women . . . [with] 90 percent of the women questioned [giving] her very high scores." By January 1957, Ms. Meade was getting two hundred fan letters a week, and achieved celebrity status when sighted motoring in her "flamingo pink" Lincoln Premier convertible. Meade attributed much of her on-camera success to her "well-groomed invisibility," and more specifically, to her necklines, which did not reveal "even a shadow of cleavage." Another female automobile spokesperson, Mary Costa, considered her own ability to gracefully get in and out of Chryslers on the shows *Climax* and *Shower of Stars* to be largely responsible for her success. When viewers asked why her skirts never rode up, Ms. Costa said that "it's a simple matter of placing more weight on the calves than on the thighs, as women usually do."[18]

Careful, perhaps fanatical, consideration was given to the selection of female spokespeople, with "the-girl-next-door" type the overwhelming preference among advertisers. In 1957, Dinah Shore was considered the universal ideal of postwar womanhood—articulate, wholesomely attractive, but not too sexy. Clients and agency people—virtually all male through the 1950s—were known to audition fifty women before selecting one for a part in a commercial. Ruth Burch, a leading commercial casting director in Hollywood, wondered whether all this time and effort was genuine or "just a case of liking to look at lots of girls." Generally forgotten from the annals of advertising and entertainment history is Marilyn Monroe's brief career in television commercials. In 1950, Burch cast Monroe in a motor oil spot as a "dumb blonde" who had to have her car pushed to a service station. When the attendant told her the oil was low, she replied, "Oh! I didn't know cars had to have oil, too!" Monroe, not surprisingly, wore a tight sweater in the commercial.[19]

Just as the popularity of female spokespeople relied upon a certain kind of innocuousness, their male counterparts also had to make sure they did not outshine the sponsor's product. One of the biggest male stars of television commercials between 1955 and 1957 was William Lundigan, the announcer on *Climax* and *Shower of Stars,* both sponsored by Chrysler. The car company sold a half-million fewer Chryslers, DeSotos, Dodges, Plymouths, and Imperials in 1954 than it did in 1953, a loss in sales of a billion dollars. For the 1955 model year, Chrysler's designers completely restyled their lineup of cars, while the company's ad agency, McCann-Erickson, created a new campaign based around the theme "The Forward Look." Wanting to project an image of vigor and strength, Chrysler approached Cornell Wilde, Clark Gable, and James Stewart to be its new product spokesperson, each of whom promptly declined. The company settled for Mr. Lundigan, a relatively unknown actor with "just enough foundation but not too much superstructure." Lundigan proved to be an overnight success and an extremely credible pitchman, evidenced by his receiving many letters from Chrysler owners requesting advice on clutch and transmission problems.[20]

Taking no chances, however, McCann-Erickson initiated in February 1956 a new research methodology to test Lundigan's long-term appeal. Using its "Electronic Program Analyzer," the agency measured his performance along a number of dimensions including awareness, likability, convincingness, and effectiveness. (Lundigan passed with flying colors.) In addition to survey data, however, the study included research techniques quite new to business applications such as attitude testing, role playing, and projective methods. McCann-Erickson's advanced research was emblematic of a new era in advertising that borrowed from theory and practice in the social sciences. The evolution of advertising research in the 1950s was directly tied to the impact of television as a new, more powerful medium. Because television involved both sight and sound and the financial stakes were so much higher, advertisers looked to a variety of "experts" to maximize efficiency and reduce waste. The Advertising Research Foundation, an industry trade group, itself looked to the social sciences for guidance, publishing "The Language of Dynamic Psychology as Related to Motivational Research" as a guide for its constituents.[21] Even Ernest Dichter, a prominent neo-Freudian and head of the Institute of

Motivational Research, took note of and supported Madison Avenue's new interest in psychology, observing that

The successful advertising agency has manipulated human motivations and desires and developed a need for goods with which the public had at one time been unfamiliar—perhaps even undesirous of purchasing. . . . It is going to take study of scientific publications outside of the advertising field to keep one step ahead of your competitor and in step with the constant reorientation of the buyer's mind.[22]

Dichter was retained as a consultant by some companies and agencies, in hopes he could reveal hidden "human motivations and desires," long considered the skeleton key to advertising success. His theories, founded in the conflict between pleasure and guilt, directly addressed marketers' desire to displace traditional puritanism and Calvinism with the self-indulgence and hedonism that were integral to the new postwar consumerism.[23] Whether legitimate "science" or theoretical snake oil, motivational research struck a chord with industry executives because it offered answers to the biggest questions of advertising—how and why it worked.

Star Search

Sponsors and agencies would have no doubt combed through the most obscure psychological or scientific journal if the formula to a hit show or popular personality resided somewhere within its pages. Over the course of the 1956–1957 season, many sponsors suffered from "rating-itis," the compulsion to quickly drop a show if a large audience did not develop. Walter Winchell and Herb Shriner lost sponsors for their respective programs after thirteen weeks, as advertisers decided they were not realizing an adequate return on their investment. By the end of the season, no fewer than fifty-six network shows had been canceled by their sponsors. As Elvis Presley burst onto the scene in 1956, one trade journal wondered if he could be the answer to a sponsor's dreams, asking, "Can Elvis Sell Soap?" Upon hearing that Ed Sullivan had booked Presley for three appearances, one NBC executive had doubts about The King's selling abilities. "What the h—— does Sullivan want with him? The audience Elvis appeals to doesn't buy Lincolns—they steal the hubcaps!" Hal Humphrey remained adamant that no actors should endorse products on television, bothered at the likes of Bing Crosby promoting gas appliances in his kitchen. "Crosby in a kitchen would be like Zsa Zsa Gabor working in a hand laundry," Humphrey bemoaned.[24]

Eager to appeal to postwar norms, clients were, in fact, notoriously choosy about talent in their commercials, more interested in cultural stereotypes than in social reality. Ruth Burch's search for a "Mexican calypso" [sic] guitarist and a rumba dancer, for example, was more problematic than anticipated as each pair she found was considered by her client to not look like what a Mexican calypso guitarist and rumba dancer *should* look like. Complicating the situation was the popularity of dancing in commercials, as dancers were often considered too exotic looking for sponsors' (and their wives') liking. Sports scenes also presented a problem, as it was difficult to find actresses or models who, in Hal Humphrey's words, "look trim and neat in swimsuits and shorts but who are not endowed with extensive or voluptuous curves." "Around Hollywood," Humphrey observed, "this is not easy." Consistent with the molded, hourglass aesthetic of Christian Dior's "New Look," the ideal feminine body type of the 1950s—busty, full-figured, zaftig—was just a little too sexy for more conservative television advertisers.[25]

The safest bet in terms of using talent in television commercials remained the celebrity testimonial or endorsement, already a "venerable advertising technique" when radio took off in the 1920s, as Roland Marchand has noted. Marchand reasoned that testimonials were so popular because public figures assume an aristocratic role in a democracy, and thus endow a brand with high status when endorsing it. Testimonials flourished in print and radio advertising between the wars, with some famous figures loaning their names to multiple products. The literal and figurative queen of testimonials in the 1920s and 1930s was Queen Marie of Romania, who rented her image to so many advertisers that at some point just bringing up her name in a room full of executives would produce loud guffaws. One generation and revolutionary medium later, whether or not a star "cheapened" himself or herself by appearing in commercials continued to be a hotly debated issue within the trade. *Printer's Ink* went so far as to solicit the opinions on the matter among fifty authorities, asking a variety of executives, performers, and critics what they thought. Some of the responses were surprising. Robert F. Lewine, vice president of network programs at NBC, was opposed to stars in commercials, thinking they destroyed the illusion of character and detracted from the reality of shows. Lewine saw some leading television personalities, such as Ed Sullivan, not as stars but as salesmen, directly referencing the blur between entertainment and consumerism which the medium was responsible for. Sullivan too admittedly saw himself as much more of a salesman or perhaps impresario than as a true entertainer. Surprisingly, however, Sullivan believed that stars should not perform commercials, thinking that viewers did not find them credible as spokespeople and that doing so could be career threatening. He was true to his word on this point, never allowing esteemed guests such as Clark Gable, Helen Hayes, or Tallulah Bankhead to deliver a commercial on his show.[26]

Garry Moore, host of his own CBS daytime show for eight years, agreed with Sullivan that commercials were "below" star entertainers. Also like Sullivan, however, Moore himself was a shameless pitchman, personally delivering or supervising as many as twelve commercials in a one-hour show. After beginning to think that he and his cast were spending more time rehearsing commercials than on the routines in the show, Moore boldly decided to step down as host. "It got so I couldn't remember which was crunchy and which was crispy," Moore said in December 1957. John Crosby, syndicated television critic for the *New York Herald Tribune* (and occasional performer), felt that leading stars like Jack Benny and Frank Sinatra made it impossible for lesser entertainers to refuse to do commercials, thus setting up an entry barrier for less-than-famous entertainers. Jack Gould of *The New York Times* agreed, on record as being "100 per cent against stars being used as candy butchers." Gould considered Sinatra's singing commercials as "wretched ... doggerel," Gertrude Berg's spots for Maxwell House "shattering," and Basil Rathbone's performance for Tums "worthy of giv[ing] any viewer indigestion." [27]

Janet Kern of the *Chicago American,* however, believed that stars did not lose any stature by doing commercials. "Stature, smature," she sneered, reflecting the laissez-faire orientation of her Hearst-owned newspaper. "If the performer is big enough to have stature he won't be hurt by delivering commercials," Kern continued. "It isn't degrading." Most sponsors, understandably, saw no problem with stars performing commercials on television. Carnation was pleased as punch with George Burns and Gracie Allen's spots on their show, which resulted in increased sales of its products. From the kitchen set used in *The Burns and Allen Show,* Allen offered Carnation recipes in her dizzy persona and unique vocal style. The show's announcer, Harry Von Zell, was responsible for the harder sell, often saying, "It's so easy, even Gracie can do it." Burns had the freedom to both approve commercial material and help with the writing, but still had to abide by a contract binding himself and Allen to do commercials if requested. Lever Brothers' relationship with stars went back decades, solidified by "Aunt Jenny's" long-running radio show, during which sales of Spry shortening climbed considerably. The company subscribed to what it called "personal salesmanship," considering entertainers such as Arthur Godfrey, Art Linkletter, Garry Moore, and

Bill Cullen extended salespeople for the company. Lever carefully matched brands to its roster of spokespeople, choosing stars other than Richard Boone of *Have Gun Will Travel*, for example, to pitch less-than-macho products like Lifebuoy soap or Good Luck margarine on the show. Rather than lease their image to companies for money, many stars chose to use their fame to promote causes that they supported in public service announcements (PSAs). In 1958, for example, Janet Leigh volunteered her time for a public service announcement for the American Heritage Foundation. Leigh told viewers of their civic responsibility to vote in the following year's presidential election, and that it was an opportunity to shape the future. Many other stars took part in PSAs, using the power of television advertising to help those in need or, perhaps, to improve their own public persona.[28]

Although advertising executives disagreed on the relative value of using stars in commercials, most agreed that credibility remained the key issue. Credibility was defined as whether a star's personality would enhance the appeal of the advertised product. Ronald Reagan was viewed as an excellent spokesperson for General Electric's defense equipment, for example, as the star's screen persona complemented the company's image as a powerful, competitive force. Roger Pryor, vice president of radio and television at Foote, Cone & Belding, believed that when it came to star credibility, psychological forces were somehow at work. Echoing advertising theory of a generation earlier, when Freudian psychology was infiltrating the industry and culture at large, Pryor postulated that "the viewer's subconscious mind must play a large part in causing his hand to reach for the products which . . . people of . . . importance are recommending." Norman King, president of Celebrity Consultants, Ltd., a star–advertiser matchmaking firm, agreed that psychology played a large role in the success of celebrity testimonials. The "halo effect" of star worship, King believed, was responsible for raising the prestige of the advertiser's product, a reprise of Marchand's theory of populist aristocracy and Dichter's theory of audience involvement. King also had a more nuts-and-bolts rationale for the effectiveness of celebrity endorsements. "Viewers reason that stars wouldn't perjure themselves for money because they have plenty," he reckoned.[29]

Most agency executives, including Mitchell Johnson, television director for William Esty, strongly supported the use of stars. For its client Camel cigarettes, the agency used Phil Silvers on his self-titled show and Ida Lupino and Howard Duff on *Mr. Adams and Eve*. The agency also encouraged integrated advertising, with Silvers and the rest of the cast apt to light up Camels at any point of his program. Many other stars continued to oblige their sponsors by providing live testimonials from within their stage personae. On *The Steve Allen Show,* the host often personally delivered sponsors' messages, carrying on the tradition of *The Tonight Show,* where he frequently performed on-stage commercials with announcer Gene Raymond. On *The Steve Allen Show,* co-sponsored by Polaroid, Steve Allen often took snapshots of guests using Polaroid Land Cameras, as when he took a Polaroid photograph of singer Abbe Lane during a November 1957 show. For Fresh deodorant, Allen routinely ignored the scripted commercials, even making snide comments about the product in Hitchcockian style.[30]

Some hosts, like Dave Garroway and especially Jack Paar, enjoyed doing commercials. Paar found creative ways to deliver commercials from the stage of his live show, such as in November 1958 when he played a tune on a Hi-Fi-Lophone, a toy xylophone made by advertiser Louis Marx and Company. On another 1958 show, however, Paar's freewheeling style caught up with him. Merely as conversation, Paar mentioned a number of times that he had a headache, finally saying, "I think I should have taken an aspirin." Paar seemed to have forgotten that Bristol-Myers and its Bufferin brand were the show's sponsor, making any promotion of regular aspirin a televisual faux pas (Bufferin was and is, of course, buffered aspirin). Paar, however, saw the opportunity to turn the aside into an opportunity, saying, "Now, now, that was just a slip. I take Bufferin all the time, and I'm going to take one right now to show you." Paar took the cap off a bottle of Bufferin, but was unable to get the tablets past the cotton wadding. With the studio audience now laughing, Paar decided to turn the embarrassing situation into a comedy act. He poured some water into the bottle, raised it in a toast to the audience, said "Skoal," pretended to drink, and resealed the bottle. Paar appeared to have cleverly bailed himself out. About twenty minutes later, however, in the middle of a talk with guest Abe Burrows, the bottle of Bufferin exploded, its cap hitting the ceiling. White blobs of wet Bufferin splattered onto the suits of both Paar and Burrows. Mass hysteria reigned for the remainder of the show.[31]

Seeing an opportunity to get even more mileage out of the snafu, Lee Bristol Jr., a top-ranking executive of Bristol-Myers, asked Paar to keep the joke running. On the next evening's show, Bristol himself presented Paar with a giant bottle of "non-explosive" Bufferin and awarded the host with a citation for achieving the "greatest booboo in the whole history of Bristol-Myers sponsorship of radio and television programs." For more than a week, guests appearing on Paar's show referred to the incident, while newspapers across the country ran stories about it. New York's *World Telegram,* in fact, devoted a four-column spread to the story on page 1 under the headline, "Paar Pops Off, So Does Product." Bristol-Myers executives were, of course, delighted with its unexpected public relations bonanza, gaining tremendously more brand name exposure than if Paar had performed the commercial as planned.[32]

State of the Art

Like Paar, Jack Benny was pleased to shill products for corporate sponsors, losing no "stature" in the process. Benny's partnership with Lucky Strike was amiable from 1956 to 1958, with the brand's jingle popping up on his show in every situation and format imaginable. In an April 1956 episode, Harlow, Don Wilson's teenage son, attempted to sing the jingle but couldn't quite manage it, a classic case of the character's ineptitude. In a December show of that year, Rochester once again joined the Sportmen Quartet to sing the jingle, this time as part of a sketch set in Trinidad. Occasionally audience members would take part in the Lucky Strike commercial, as in a January 1957 show when *The Burns and Allen Show* announcer and guest audience member Harry Von Zell read the spot. He performed it so well, in fact, that Benny subsequently pretended to consider firing Don and hiring Von Zell. In a September show of that year, Don read the Lucky Strike commercial in calypso style, but Benny kept interrupting him. Don's wife then made Benny call the sponsor to explain that the botched spot was the host's fault, not her husband's. In two December 1957 shows, the commercial was directly integrated within the story lines of each week's sketch. In one show set in a department store, the Sportmen Quartet sang the Lucky Strike jingle in an elevator, while two weeks later they sang it from a Rose Bowl Parade float (the parade would be held later that week).[33]

Rather than trying to hide the sponsor's role, afraid perhaps that overt plugs would hurt ratings, Benny looked for every opportunity to bring the idea of commercial sponsorship out into the open. In a February 1958 episode, for example, Benny met his "sponsor" at a racetrack, where they tried to persuade each other to bet on a particular horse. In a March show of that year, Jack was off to New York City to meet with his sponsor. (At the hotel, Don unpacked the suitcases to check if they had taken the Luckies. They had.) During Benny's opening monologue of a show in October 1958, someone from the "Announcers' Guild" appeared to read the Lucky Strike spot in place of Don. He claimed not to smoke but, after trying a Lucky Strike offered by Benny, became otherwise persuaded. By presenting the concept of sponsorship in entertainment terms, Benny offered a product that satisfied both viewers and the backer of the show. This form of advertising was, as research would prove in a few years, more effective than any other because of viewers' level of trust in their favorite stars.[34]

Sponsors also looked to integrated advertising as a means of preempting viewers' predisposition to leave rooms en masse during commercial breaks. Water department officials in many cities noted that water consumption did indeed rise on the hour and half-hour, the time when most commercials ran. This nightmarish finding was a factor in agencies' shift away from hard-sell tactics typical of the early 1950s to a more entertaining, creative approach in the later 1950s. To keep viewers in the room, many advertisers invested more money in the production of commercials, foregoing heavy-handed demonstrations for more glamorous and stylistic presentations. Bernard J. Carr, president of Cascade Pictures, a leading commercial production firm, reported that advertisers were spending 25 percent more in 1956 to produce an average one-minute spot than they had in 1954. Advertisers were also finally beginning to realize something that viewers had known at the inception of the medium, that certain products did not have to be shown in use. Women did indeed know how to wash their hair, for example, a fact which had apparently been lost on many shampoo marketers over the course of the first decade of commercial television.[35]

Less reliance on heavy-handed television commercials opened the window for advertisers to experiment more with modern animation technique. Considered perhaps the most entertaining genre of commercials, animation continued to evolve as an advertising art form in the latter half of the 1950s. Young & Rubicam used animation for its well-loved spots for Piel's beer, featuring the voices of comedians Bob Elliot and Ray Goulding. In a 1957 spot, "Bull's-eye," the Piel Brothers' "high concept" voice-over complemented the intentionally rough, almost primitive animation style. Young & Rubicam used animation much differently for another 1957 commercial, "Chinese Baby," for Jell-O. In a faux Chinese accent, the announcer introduced the spot as "an ancient Chinese pantomime." The visual portion depicted a mother serving her baby Jell-O, "a famous Western delicacy." The baby is seen having difficulty eating the gelatin using chopsticks, causing his mom to hand him a spoon, "invented for sole purpose of eating Jell-O." As a coup de grace, the announcer asked viewers, "Is pretty good commercial, no?" Despite being politically appalling by today's standards, the commercial was elected to the Clio Hall of Fame.[36]

For marketers of children's products, animation was naturally viewed as a means to instantly capture kids' attention. For the Uhlmann Company, Fletcher, Richards, Calkins & Holden created "I Want My Maypo," a 1956 spot which lives on in the memory of many baby boomers. In the commercial, a child wearing a cowboy hat refuses to eat breakfast. After persuading the child to sit down and remove his hat, the boy's father suggests he try Maypo cereal, as "cowboys love Maypo." As incentive, the dad samples the cereal himself and, liking it, is reluctant to give it to the boy. "I want my Maypo!" the boy screams, a slogan which undoubtedly echoed in kitchens across America. The Maypo story was a classic case of the power of television advertising. Before going into television advertising in 1956, the company believed that Maypo's sales had peaked. The company's agency at the time, Bryan Houston, however, recommended television to reach children, and the rest was history. The brand's animated spots, featuring the mischievous brat "Marky," consistently ranked among the ten "best-liked" commercials as measured by the Advertising Research Bureau. The commercials were inspired by the real-life experiences of the campaign's cartoonist, John Hubley, whose tape-recorded conversations with his son were translated into copy selling points. John Van Horson, the agency's account supervisor, considered the campaign's success a result of what he termed its "subtle sell," claiming that "the viewer isn't aware of where the sell begins or ends." By intentionally disguising Maypo commercials as regular cartoons, the company was exploiting children's less than fully developed ability to distinguish between entertainment and selling. (Another standard technique in advertising to children was to present food in settings in which it appeared that the child was eating voluntarily, rather than submitting to parental authority.) Heublein, which bought the brand from Uhlmann, further leveraged the popularity of Marky by setting up displays in supermarkets featuring the character, a device that attracted an unusual amount of attention among kids. Sales boomed as Heublein rolled out Maypo across the country, backed up by its aggressive television and promotion strategy.[37]

In addition to raising the entertainment value of commercials, advertisers were finding innovative ways to make their products appear superior to the competition's. In April 1957, Westinghouse led in a new era in competitive advertising in the most controversial commercial and campaign of the year. Westinghouse broadcast a commercial live from a private home—the first time such a feat had been attempted—as part of a campaign running on *Studio One,* a CBS drama on Monday nights. The campaign featured a demonstration of a towel-filled Westinghouse automatic washing machine in which sand had been poured. The first installment of the campaign, which first aired live on September 24, 1956, from CBS studios, involved New York City "club women" washing towels in competitive machines, with only the Westinghouse getting them clean after the sand pouring. On November 12, the company had a group of skeptical viewers repeat the live demonstration, in which only the Westinghouse again got the towels clean. Westinghouse found two neighbors, Mrs. Asay and Mrs. Spangler, in Columbus, Ohio who repeated the head-to-head demonstration on live television from their homes.[38]

The idea of Westinghouse's remote broadcast was based on Edward R. Murrow's popular show on CBS, *Person to Person,* in which he interviewed notable people in their homes. It cost the company $23,000—twice as much as an ordinary commercial—to produce the spot, which required remote equipment, a special power transformer, and two temporary parabolic antennas to handle the extra load of electricity. Along for the ride were a crew of fifteen and the queen of appliances, Betty Furness, who had emceed all the sand test spots. The extra effort was well worth it. Gallup & Robinson tests rated the commercial as one of the top five in television advertising history in terms of audience recall, and the best ever for home appliances. Jack D. Lee, the Westinghouse laundry equipment manager who spearheaded the campaign, claimed that "the sand test has meant more to Westinghouse in direct sales than any other laundry equipment commercial." Indeed, the company realized a 20 percent rise in sales each time a sand test spot ran, with dealers even picking up on the idea by doing sand tests in their showrooms via a promotional kit provided by Westinghouse. Their hackles naturally raised, competitors accused the company of both rigging the test and instigating negative advertising that would ultimately hurt the entire industry and retailers. Knocking the competition would, however, serve as the rule rather than the exception in the years ahead as advertisers fought for market share over the airwaves. In a classic competitive spot of 1958, for example, Josephine the Plumber demonstrated via a comparative test how Comet was superior to its chief (but never mentioned) rival, Ajax. Compton's commercial for Procter and Gamble's brand showed viewers how Comet "gets out stains better than any other leading cleanser" in a head-to-head scrubfest. The doors to competitive advertising had been swung wide open, drawing upon the good-guy-versus-bad-guy creative genre and political model that was so pervasive in 1950s culture.[39]

Biggest Bang for the Buck

As advertisers tried to keep up with the Joneses, total media costs for the 1957–1958 television season rose to an all-time high of $1.5 billion. Higher time, production, and talent costs were making it significantly more expensive to be a television advertiser. Talent fees in particular had skyrocketed, a result of networks entering into bidding wars with Hollywood and Broadway in the search for new television faces. As the top television stars of the day—Lucille Ball, Jackie Gleason, and Bob Hope—battled for the biggest fee per show, production costs continued to rise beyond the budgets of single sponsors. For a half-hour weekly show under exclusive sponsorship, an advertiser would have to spend a minimum of $5 million. "Maintaining effective continuity at today's TV prices presents a real problem to many advertisers," admitted Sigurd Larmon, president of Young & Rubicam. Because of the higher costs, decisions about expenditures on television were being increasingly made by corporate top management, whereas previously they had been made by middle management or by agencies. If there was any good news to advertisers, it was that household penetration of television sets continued to rise as well; 20,000 television sets *a day* were sold in 1956.[40]

Because of rising costs, the number of television advertisers was falling, although total billings continued to rise because of higher media rates. The industry was consolidating, with just nine agencies accounting for over half of network television billings in 1956. The trend toward formula buying based purely on audience share and cost per thousand was squeezing out advertisers on the air mainly to gain consumer goodwill. Still, some of these latter companies found different ways to cut costs while maintaining a presence on television. Alcoa and Goodyear Tire and Rubber dropped their one-hour shows and instead bought half-hour shows. Lever Brothers dropped its long-running *Lux Video Theatre* (a descendant of the old "Lux Radio Theatre" show), also in favor of a half-hour show. Notably, Lincoln dropped out of its shared sponsorship of *The Ed Sullivan Show*. The eight-year partnership between Lincoln and Sullivan had been one of the longest and happiest on television, but became a victim of high costs. "The minute TV networks started spreading out and costs per thousand began zooming up, the one-sponsor show was doomed," Sullivan said sadly. Eastman Kodak, however, quickly picked up the $5 million shared-sponsorship tab for the show. Other sponsors went to the alternate week plan, which evolved into two or more sponsors advertising one week and a different team the following week. With alternate sponsorship, advertisers were keeping their names in front of viewers at a lower cost, and reducing their risk in case a show flopped.[41]

Total sponsorship of a show, however, remained the best opportunity to execute a full advertising blitz. NBC's *The Kraft Music Hall* was, of course, chock-filled with commercials for Kraft Foods. On one November 1958 show, viewers licked their lips to spots for Parkay margarine, miniature marshmallows, jelly and preserves, and Philadelphia cream cheese. The next week, the menu was all-purpose oil, Velveeta cheese spread, salad dressings, and American cheese. Another full-sponsorship program, *The DuPont Show of the Month* on CBS, featured much less appetizing fare, serving up commercials for chemical research, color conditioning for paints, and DuPont consumer products. The Timex-sponsored *All-Star Jazz Special* on CBS featured the all-time great demonstration commercials for the watch and John Cameron Swayze's equally memorable line, "It takes a licking but keeps on ticking."[42]

Because of television's spiraling costs, it was taking longer for the networks to sell all of their time to advertisers for the 1957–1958 season. Not helping matters was another recession and a growing sense of anxiety, discontent, and fear among many Americans. Cold War tensions had escalated with the Soviet launch of *Sputniks I* and *II*, and racial unrest in Little Rock reminded Americans that broad prosperity had not solved the nation's social problems. Popular books like Russell Lynes's 1954 *The Tastemakers,* William Whyte's 1956 *The Organization Man,* C. Wright Mills's 1956 *The Power Elite,* and John Kenneth Galbraith's 1958 *The Affluent Society,* in addition to a number of follow-up books by David Riesman to his 1950 *The Lonely Crowd,* offered persuasive evidence that postwar America was not turning out to be the twentieth-century Eden many had expected. Vance Packard's *The Status Seekers* too would soon suggest that the American Dream may be just that, a dream. With the country in a sour mood and television advertising costing more than ever, an unusual amount of unsold time remained late in the summer selling period. Clients' and agencies' reluctance to commit to a show was largely a function of their admitted search for another *Gunsmoke, I Love Lucy,* or *The $64,000 Question.* It was difficult for sponsors to concede that television viewership had leveled off and that the days of achieving a 40 percent or more audience share were over. Seeing the writing on the wall, however, advertising agencies were no longer sticking their necks out to sell clients a particular show. NBC vice president Robert Lewine admitted that the networks were experiencing "a softer market than in previous years." His boss, the legendary "General" of NBC, Robert W. Sarnoff, added that "no responsible television executive can look you in the eye and say this has not been a 'hard sell' season." Although this hardly meant serious trouble for the networks, one executive believed that the days when shows could be sold over the phone were over. Sarnoff observed that "network salesmen have worn out more shoe leather this selling season than at any time in my memory." [43]

Complicating matters was that sponsors and programs were shifting from one network to another more than ever before, as advertisers jockeyed to get the biggest bang for the television buck. Part of this shifting around was due to the emergence of ABC as a serious network contender. In February 1953, ABC had only seven principal affiliates, reaching just 38 percent of television homes; by the fall of 1957 its presence had grown to 85 percent. Advertisers thus had three rather than two legitimate networks to choose from when it came to making sponsorship decisions. (The Du Mont network had folded in 1955.) To try to hang onto sponsors in a more competitive environment, networks continued to develop elaborate and costly specials or "spectaculars" likely to attract high viewership. Pepsi-Cola sponsored the 1957 NBC spectacular "Annie Get Your Gun," using Harpo Marx to deliver a silent but manic sales pitch from the stage. [44]

Although such specials almost always generated many viewers, sponsors disagreed on how "spectacular" television shows should be as commercial vehicles. John Bricker, vice president of marketing of Whirlpool Corporation, looked for shows that did not overshadow his company's commercials. Consistent with one popular theory at the time, Bricker believed that viewers' emotional involvement in a show left them unable to absorb commercial messages. Westerns in particular, according to Bricker, had "too much excitement in them," leaving viewers "emotionally exhausted." He also refused to sponsor *I Love Lucy* during its run, thinking it too drained viewers' energy. Instead, Bricker chose *The George Gobel* show for the even-keeled star's ability to generate a sense of empathy with its viewers (the show largely had to do with the trials and tribulations of married life). Gobel was also "very co-operative when it comes to touring the various Whirlpool plants and putting on little impromptu shows for the employees." Employees reading in the company newsletter that Whirlpool was spending $21 million a year on advertising and promotion felt better after meeting the star, Bricker noted, not mentioning that Gobel's visits also helped ensure his own job. [45]

The deployment of contracted stars—analogous in some ways to the studio system of film's yesteryear—thus jumped across corporate departments, from marketing and sales into human resources or personnel. On the basis of experience, companies justified the larger amounts of money being spent on television advertising by including relationship-building with employees or franchisees as part of the total package. In January 1958, for example, Plymouth orchestrated a closed-circuit telecast from Hollywood to thousands of its dealerships in forty-one cities across the country. According to Jack W. Minor, Plymouth's vice president of sales, telecasts such as these were "industry's greatest sales aid for getting a story over to salesmen quickly and dramatically." The hour-long show from ABC's Hollywood studios included stars from the television shows Plymouth was sponsoring. Bob Hope, Lawrence Welk and his orchestra, Betty White, Bill Lundigan, and other stars under contract joined Plymouth executives in announcing its new "sales-stimulating program." Through this program and the company's new "all star salesmen's club," Plymouth was confident it would get consumers who owned paid-off 1955 models to buy new 1958s. Plymouth was banking on its dealers getting extra motivated to move cars off of lots, knowing they were on the same corporate team as Bob Hope and other big names.[46]

Getting the most mileage from stars with advertising contracts was also a way to reduce sponsors' high degree of occupational exposure. Sponsors were typically blamed for television show flops, as everyone knew that entertainment was not their primary business. Although this was true, it was the sponsor who assumed the lion's share of the financial risk involved in producing a show. Advertisers at the time were obligated to pay the agreed-to rate regardless of the realized cost per thousand viewers, and not reimbursed in any way for shows which generated low ratings. Surprisingly, little thought was given to competition when networks set the cost of shows; that is, no discount was assigned if a show was up against a top-rated program. Sponsors' great power was thus countered by the great financial risk that came with the territory, a fundamental difference between print and broadcast media. Although advertisers were not given control over editorial content of magazines and newspapers, as critics of the sponsor system eagerly pointed out, it was publishers, not advertisers, who carried the risk in print media. Because of this risk, sponsors' ultimate control in television was thus believed to be warranted by most in the television and advertising industries.[47]

Sponsors' great power and exposure to risk were directly connected to the censorship that pervaded the television industry through the postwar years. Rod Serling, a writer for CBS's *Playhouse 90* in the 1950s, saw sponsor pressures as responsible for limiting television's singular ability to create controversy. Because of its immediacy and reach, television had the potential, Serling believed, to force American society to face up to its social and economic problems (particularly those involving race). With show content essentially just a vehicle to deliver advertising, however, this potential was not being realized. "I've always felt that the only way that you could get controversy to be accepted is to have a line of delineation between what is the commercial product and what is the entertainment involved," said Serling in 1958. In his series *The Twilight Zone,* Serling recast social commentary in the guise of science fiction in order to get controversial issues past nervous sponsors and network censors. Serling, of course, had personal experience with sponsor interference, with scripts such as "Noon on Doomsday" having been significantly altered by the time they reached the air. (For his masterpiece "Requiem for a Heavyweight," Serling was asked to delete the phrase, "Got a match?" because one of the sponsors was a manufacturer of lighters.) By containing controversy, the sponsor system both reflected and helped to shape an intolerance for divergent views of American postwar society, and reinforced consensus values concerning gender, race, and class.[48]

No amount of script doctoring by sponsors could help alleviate the recession in 1958, lift the nation's generally sour mood, or, for that matter, boost ratings for many shows during the 1957–1958 season. If the market was shrinking and seasoned viewers were more likely to turn off mediocre television shows, sponsors thought, advertising simply had to become more persuasive. Although sponsors spent only about 10 percent of total show cost on commercials, this percentage was rising as more emphasis was put on advertising. More campaigns were developed around the same theme rather than running a single commercial over and over. Additionally, production values continued to become more elaborate and original. For its client Chemstrand, a maker of nylon stockings, Doyle Dane Bernbach used a twenty-piece orchestra as background music for a commercial which appeared to be a series of high-fashion print ads. Compton looked to the popular Broadway musical comedy for inspiration, casting a group of teenagers in a song-and-dance routine for a spot for Procter and Gamble's Royal Drene Shampoo. In addition, creative demonstration of a product's special feature was considered state-of-the-art advertising in 1958; for example, Ogilvy, Benson & Mather showed a Pepperidge Farm pastry actually puff up in an oven.[49]

To keep down costs of more elaborate commercials, producers were finally beginning to use more scale talent than big-name stars. More and better preproduction planning also helped to keep costs in check, and shooting a few commercials all at once rather than one at a time afforded additional savings. Clients could then rotate spots over the course of a year, avoiding excessive repetition and having to go back to the studio. Advertising executives, however, had to continually remind themselves that they tired of commercials much faster than viewers did. Marketers of disinfectants such as Lestoil and Lysol apparently took this message to heart, notoriously known by the trade and viewers alike for running a single commercial for years. "Repetition in itself is the basis of advertising and not necessary an evil," defended Dick Seelow, product manager of Lysol. Copy research and pretesting were also being increasingly used by advertisers to maximize the return on their investment. Agencies often did not charge clients for these services, believing that research was, in effect, a form of quality control (and a way to keep the account!). Although many different kinds of research methodologies were used, motivational guidance copy research was the choice of the day. This Dichterian technique purportedly identified the emotions commercials appealed to, in hopes that the "right" emotions were being tapped. Such methods, rooted in the behavioral sciences, reflected the greater degree to which business was looking to psychology to sell consumer products and services. More broadly, the psychology trend in popular culture and democratization of psychoanalytic therapy had brought the field out of America's postwar closet, and advertisers were determined to figure out how to use it to their advantage.[50]

Some even suspected that psychology might be being used for nefarious purposes, with the concept of subliminal advertising getting widespread media coverage in 1957. Popular reports claimed that there were increased sales of popcorn and Coke after the words "eat popcorn" and "Coca-Cola" flashed during a movie at $1/3,000$ of a second every five seconds. Worry quickly spread that the technique could be used to sell liquor and sleeping pills on television in order to get people addicted. Similar fears about the use of subliminal advertising in political commercials brought to mind George Orwell's *1984*. Most advertising people scoffed at the whole idea of subliminal persuasion, claiming it was simply a hoax. Not taking any chances, however, the NARTB Television Code Review Board recommended to subscribers that any proposed use of "subliminal perception" be referred to the board for review and consideration. Whether subliminal advertising worked or not, the board made clear that television should not be used as an experimental medium for such efforts, knowing that the last thing the industry needed was even a passing acquaintance with the idea of mind control. The brief (and sensationalized, due in large part to Vance Packard's *The Hidden Persuaders*) subliminal perception affair was television advertising's interpretation of the postwar theme of mind control by an outside force, popularized in film, television, and literature (with all kinds of subtexts ranging from Russian totalitarianism to alien invasion). Although subliminal advertising made good press, advertisers have always prioritized making their messages work at the conscious level, as consumers are rarely unconscious when they go shopping or make purchase decisions.[51]

Jingle Bells

If Americans' secret desires couldn't be shaped by subliminal messages, advertisers had to work harder at the more pedestrian process of creating good commercials. The new competitiveness of television advertising and overall maturing of the medium trickled down into all aspects of creative development and production. High-powered talent, such as Piel Brothers Ray Goulding and Bob Elliott, formed their own production companies to capitalize on the demand for more effective commercials. More agencies were commissioning original music for television commercials, a trend that had started in 1955 in radio advertising. Jingle writing in particular became more professional, with composers from Broadway applying their talents to the commercial field. In April 1957, Frank Loesser, composer of *Guys and Dolls,* created his own jingle-producing firm, boasting a stable of superstar talent borrowed from other creative arts. On the staff of Frank Productions, Inc. were Hoagy Carmichael (composer of such hits as "Stardust"), Vernon Duke (composer of "April in Paris"), and Harold Rome (composer of "Fanny"). For good measure, Loesser hired Ogden Nash to write lyrics. Not to lose out on any business, Raymond Scott, composer of the popular Lucky Strike jingle, "Be Happy, Go Lucky," immediately formed his own firm, The Jingle Workshop. Scott perceptively assessed the importance of jingles in the consumer-oriented postwar years, stating that "to me, they've become as much a part of the American scene as any native art form." *Time* magazine went even further, claiming that "the singing commercial has become as entrenched in U.S. culture as the madrigal in the Italian Renaissance." Leading composers and lyricists were going to where the action and money were, applying their trade to the hottest show in town.[52]

Advertisers had a wide range of options when it came to commercial music. Some, like Rheingold beer, a regional brand distributed in the Northeast, chose songs such as its "Banana Boat Song" from the public domain because they were free. Just because songs were free did not mean advertisers skimped on the production end. On *The Nat King Cole Show* in October 1956, the great singer performed Rheingold's jingle from New York's Philharmonic Hall, definitely one of the highlights in jingle history. (Cole's talent, unfortunately, could not save his show from cancellation in 1958, a casualty of sponsor fear of being identified with an African American artist.) Many other leading singers of the day performed in television commercials, including the McGuire Sisters for Coca-Cola, Patti Page for Oldsmobile, Eddie Fisher for Chesterfield, Vaughn Monroe for RCA, and Burl Ives for Eveready batteries. Sponsors occasionally purchased commercial rights to hit songs, such as DeSoto's use of Cole Porter's "It's De-Lovely," which cost the car company thousands of dollars. Large agencies typically retained a staff of jingle writers (Young & Rubicam had twelve in 1957), while J. Walter Thompson went even further to secure the best songs for its clients. In an exception to J. Walter Thompson's stodgy reputation (its nickname was J. Walter Tombstone), the agency presciently hired people with particular skill in spotting songs likely to be hits so that they could be placed in commercials before peaking in popularity.[53]

Initially, songwriters were reluctant to "lease" their songs to television advertisers, afraid that commercial use would taint both the song and their own reputation. By 1957, however, most composers welcomed the interest among advertisers to use their songs in commercials. The rationale was, of course, money. Composers not only got fees from publishers of commercially used songs but also ASCAP or BMI royalties each time the commercial ran. Additionally, songwriters came to the opinion that commercial use of their tunes could help sell records or tickets to shows in which they appeared. Loesser, for example, offered White Owl cigars the title song of his Broadway show *Most Happy Fella*, even having the six principal actors in the show record it for the commercial. Loesser believed that commercial exposure would make people want to see the show, an early example of the cross-promotions that are so much a part of entertainment marketing today.[54]

The question of whether a commercial jingle could cross over into popular music was answered rather resoundingly between 1956 and 1958. Almost immediately after running a spot for Duquesne beer, the brewery and television stations across six states began receiving hundreds of requests for the jingle's words and music. The jingle, "Have a Duke," was even adopted by Elder High School of Cincinnati as a school rouser (with different words, thankfully). With sales boosted by the popular jingle, Duquesne recorded the song in six versions (Dixieland, polka, swing, calypso, march, and instrumental), rotating the versions to avoid listener saturation. Around Christmas, Duquesne successfully skirted the sensitivity of advertising alcoholic beverages by running a version of the commercial with melody alone, played on a celeste. "Since practically everybody hearing the wordless commercial already knew the words by heart, it got its message across appropriately and delightfully," glowed Vic Maitland, president of the advertising agency that created the campaign. Although new jingles such as "Have a Duke" gained greater legitimacy by entering the orbit of popular culture, using existing songs in commercials was generally considered "slumming." Some songwriters, in fact, went to court to demand compensation for work that ended up in commercials. Ray Gilbert, writer of the lyrics to the song "Muskrat Ramble," for example, won a judgment of $10,000 from Hills Brothers coffee and its agency, N. W. Ayer & Son, in August 1958. The company had used the melody of "Muskrat Ramble" in a commercial which, according to Gilbert, "cheapened the value of the words he had written for the tune." Edward (Kid) Ory, who wrote the music, had given the agency permission to use the song for commercial purposes but apparently didn't let his writing partner in on the decision. The judge agreed with Gilbert that the song was a "jazz classic" whose lasting value would be jeopardized through commercial use.[55]

In addition to the commercial jingle, the star's personal plug became a greater presence on late 1950s television. It became increasingly common for entertainers appearing on shows to mention their most recent book, magazine article, film, record, or public appearance, something we now take for granted. Without today's formula, personal plugs sometimes reached epic proportions. On a single show in 1958, in fact, Bob Hope plugged his current movie no fewer than thirty-three times. Edward R. Murrow's *Person to Person* was custom-fit for the plugging of personal projects, a practice that was a predecessor to today's talk show circuit. A wide range of guests appeared on Murrow's show to promote their projects, including the Duchess of Windsor, who pushed her book of memoirs. It was rumored that producers of one top show did not even pay scale fees to guests, knowing the value of a plug on national television. The plugging of songs on television shows left one particularly unpleasant imprint on our entertainment landscape—the phenomenon of "lip synching"—as singers opted to move their lips to their record rather than perform it live.[56]

To keep things in perspective, however, it should be noted that prod-

Former Vice President Richard Nixon plugs his book on The Jack Paar Show.
(Library of Congress)

uct plugs on American television were relatively invisible compared to their presence on Japanese television. As in the States, most bars, restaurants, and coffeehouses owned sets to attract customers, with quiz shows, baseball games, and American programs being especially popular (Emperor Hirohito's favorite show was *Superman*). Although there were nineteen government-run stations, most Japanese viewers preferred commercial stations, which increased in number from seven in 1958 to thirty-nine in 1959. Although it is difficult to fathom, commercials were routinely integrated into program plots and settings to an even greater degree than on American television. For example, in a scene from *A Comic Housemaid,* a Japanese soap opera, the heroine complained of a headache, proceeded to swallow a remedy from the Arakawa Drug Company, and then announced, "Now I'm ready for anything." On a dramatic show, a private investigator used a drugstore — whose shelves were clearly filled with the sponsor's products — as a rendez-vous. In a samurai episode, the hero felt a mysterious breeze coming from a shrine, only to reveal its source as an air conditioner. "It's Nippon Electric's latest model," the samurai exclaimed.[57]

Car Wars

If some advertisers both East and West occasionally went to extreme mea-sures to get their products seen, others went to equal extremes when it came to keeping new products a secret. Ford was furtive if not downright para-noid as it developed the first commercial for its new medium-priced car, the 1958 Edsel. To produce the campaign, Ford's agency, Foote, Cone & Beld-ing, hired Cascade Pictures, a firm familiar with top-secret projects, having produced films for the Atomic Energy Commission and the guided-missile program. Five Edsels were shipped to a Hollywood studio from New Jersey, unloaded at night, and kept under around-the-clock security. Actors were auditioned with no mention of the product. Enclosed vans carried the auto-mobiles to outdoor locations, which were then sealed off by police. The cars even had a stand-in for rehearsals to minimize exposure. All usable film was kept in a safe overnight, with unusable footage burned, and the finished spots were hand-carried back East by a courier and personally delivered to the networks. The top-secret campaign ultimately achieved its objective — to get people into Ford showrooms — but confirmed the maxim that good advertis-ing will always hurt sales of a bad new product more than bad advertising. Three million Americans rushed to see the Edsel only to learn that it was big, ugly, and overpriced.[58]

For the 1959 model year, Ford decided to give the Edsel another shot by restyling and repositioning the car, hiring a new ad manager and changing ad agencies. Two versions of the 1958 Edsel, the Citation and Pacer, were dropped, leaving only the Corsair and Ranger for 1959. Prices also were dropped, and some "extras" offered as standard equipment. Edsel also changed sponsorships, dropping *Wagon Train* for the higher profile *The Ed Sullivan Show*. Eldon Fox, Edsel's new ad manager, considered Kenyon & Eckhardt's campaign "hard-hitting and competitive," but the 1959 Edsel tried to be too many things. Perhaps trying to repeat the success of Timex's com-mercials, Ford had John Cameron Swayze tell viewers that the Edsel was designed as a mid-priced car but could be had for the same cost as a Plymouth or Chevrolet. Although the car promised "more of everything—size, comfort, and power," the Edsel proved to be a classic case that more may be, in the consumer's view, less. Another automobile, the Studebaker, was on the way toward extinction because its advertising confused viewers and promised too much. Trying to make a televisual splash, Studebaker plunked its 1957 Golden Hawk smack dab in front of NBC Studios at New York's Rockefeller Center. Leveraging the car's name and the glamour of air travel (the commercial jet had just debuted), Studebaker told viewers that the car's "slipstream styling gives you the feeling of flight, even at a standstill." Studebaker's message didn't get too far off the ground, however, with the Golden Hawk labeled as "America's only family sports car with supercharged power," a convoluted mish-mash of adtalk. The car company further confused consumers by adding its slogan, "Craftsmanship Makes the Difference," to the commercial. By trying to be all things to all people, the Golden Hawk soon went the way of the dodo bird.[59]

Chevrolet, on the other hand, had a clearly defined brand identity based on wholesome, quasi-patriotic values. The company's major spokespersons—Dinah Shore and Pat Boone—were cut out of the same American quilt, despite being used in different ways. Ms. Shore was used for symbolic purposes, representing Chevrolet through her singing and personality but never making an actual sales pitch. Boone, on the other hand, was considered the "nuts and bolts" spokesperson, urging viewers to visit showrooms and talking at length about technological features. Additionally, with a full line of cars, Chevrolet was able to position its models away from each other and effectively segment the market. For its 1957 station wagon, obviously targeted to families, Chevy created a spot filled with characters seemingly out of a Norman Rockwell painting. For its basic 1957 model, however, Chevrolet focused on technology, specifically its new "positraction" feature. The spot showed other cars getting stuck in mud and then the Chevrolet driving up a ramp covered with axle grease. "Positraction is just one of the many reasons you get more to be proud of in a Chevrolet," viewers were convincingly told. Mercury also found success through a single-minded selling proposition supported by a compelling demonstration. For the 1958 Mercury, Kenyon & Eckhardt tapped into one of the primary entertainment genres of the day, westerns. Halberstam has theorized that Westerns resonated so much in the 1950s because they embodied the myth of American individualism, particularly powerful stuff in an era when conformity ruled. In the Mercury spot, a saddle was placed on top of a pole attached to the hood and connected to the front wheels of the Mercury. A cowboy then sat in the saddle to "show how the 'Big M' rides over a rough road." While the cowboy bounced up and down, the announcer in the front seat remained still, showing living room buckaroos that Mercury was indeed "the new performance champion for 1958."[60]

While other car companies had found their niche, General Motors' Buick division was struggling to find a winning formula in its television strategy. After taking a year off from network television, Buick paid NBC $250,000 to sponsor the Floyd Patterson versus Hurricane Jackson boxing match in August 1957. During the broadcast, one after another "dull, lumpy" announcers, as *Time* magazine referred to them, were paraded out to sell cars between rounds, each one more annoying than the last. Worse, just as referee Ruby Goldstein signaled a technical knockout for Patterson, another Buick commercial came on in place of the frenzied activity in the ring. Four hundred letters of protest flooded into the company's offices, to which Buick general manager Ed Ragsdale responded in a public statement. "As a fight man myself," Ragsdale said, "I was incensed at the inept handling and bad timing . . . and assure those interested that this will not happen again on any public-service telecast by Buick."[61]

Unfortunately, Buick faced another public relations flub in the fall of 1958, after it approached doctors in the New York City area to appear in commercials. McCann-Erickson, Buick's ad agency, developed an idea for a spot in which a real doctor would be shown woken up in the middle of the night to make an emergency house call. The doctor would then express his relief that he owned a Buick because of the car's outstanding dependability. It was critical that the protagonist be an actual doctor in order to comply with the FCC's ruling that actors could no longer portray medical practitioners in television commercials after January 1, 1959. As enticement to appear in the commercial, Buick offered numerous doctors $750 in cash, the chance to buy a new Buick at "factory prices," and an excellent trade-in value on their present car. News of the offer spread to *New York Medicine,* the official publication of the New York County Medical Society. The society urged doctors to resist Buick's attractive offer by not "capitalizing on [an] M.D. degree as a subterfuge for an actor who had previously done the job." Buick not surprisingly abandoned the idea for the commercial, making the excuse that it wouldn't fit in with the mood of *The Bob Hope Show,* on which it was scheduled to run.[62]

The End of the Golden Age

Despite the occasional blunder, large marketers like General Motors knew that they were in the driver's seat when it came to television advertising. Just fifteen companies spent almost half of all network television advertising dollars in 1958, with these same companies also responsible for almost a third of all spot television. Under pressure as commercial television became more expensive in the late 1950s, marketers decided to flex their financial muscles by demanding more flexibility through shorter contract commitments and program escape clauses. Networks justified higher time, talent, and production costs by relying on their ace-in-a-whole, cost-per-thousand efficiency. Hugh M. Beville, NBC vice president of research and planning, claimed that cost per thousand for all networks had actually dropped some 11 percent since 1955, a result of higher television set ownership. Indeed, according to the Advertising Research Foundation, 42 million households owned sets in 1958, 10 million more than in 1955. Television advertising costs were going up, but not as fast as the audience was growing. Despite the valid efficiency argument, it was becoming clear that network television had simply become too expensive for most advertisers, an option only to marketers with very large promotion budgets. The number of network advertisers had peaked in 1956 at 321, dropping to 293 in 1957. The economic recession of 1957–1958 also pushed sponsors to look for more ways to cut television outlays. Chrysler decided to kill its long-running show *Climax,* while General Electric looked for more product identification by bowing out of *Cheyenne* and picking up the new drama *Man with a Camera* (whose title character conveniently used G.E. flashbulbs). Other advertisers committed to 26 or 13 week schedules rather than the standard 39. The 52-week contract, once the norm, was becoming all but extinct.[63]

The economic pressures placed on television advertisers were leading to nothing less than the breakup of the sponsorship system that had been the foundation of the industry over the course of its first dozen or so years. By 1958, the alternate sponsorship plan of cutting costs was evolving into even more affordable "participations," whereby three or four companies bought commercials in a single program. Historian William Boddy has argued that participation sponsorships were also a mechanism for the networks to "recession-proof" their shows by attracting advertisers from different kinds of industries. In a larger sense, as both Christopher Anderson and Michele Hilmes have suggested, participation sponsorship had the net effect of shifting the balance of power away from sponsors and their agencies to the networks by appealing to a wider range of advertisers. Joint sponsorships were thus a key factor for making the "magazine format" a reality, ultimately changing the entire nature and power structure of commercial television. Originally created by radio host and cooking expert Ida Bailey Allen in the 1920s, as Susan Smulyan has pointed out, the magazine format was gradually becoming the television industry standard. NBC President Pat Weaver had introduced the format to television in the mid-1950s, allowing advertisers to purchase time on programs as they purchased space in print advertising, that is, with no authority over editorial. Starting with the *Today* and *Tonight* shows and newscasts, Weaver recognized that broad application of the magazine format represented the means by which networks could regain control over programming, something not held by broadcasters since the early days of radio.[64]

Increasingly enamored of the magazine format because of its affordability, many advertisers wanted yet more flexibility by buying one-minute time slots in prime time, but only ABC offered to sell such units on selected shows. ABC's willingness to sell one-minute spots on prime time was not only financially driven, however. The network was rapidly earning a reputation as the guerrilla of the industry through its looser "must buy" policy and its unexpected plunge into daytime television in 1958. Via a unique partnership with Young & Rubicam, ABC added three hours a day to its weekday network schedule, selling two of these three hours directly to the agency for exclusive use by their clients, General Foods, Johnson & Johnson, and Bristol-Myers. Executives at CBS and NBC criticized ABC's strategy by suggesting that the network was selling time too cheaply and that the deal gave an agency too much programming control. In one fell swoop, however, ABC had become a serious contender for the business of the 138 advertisers who were using daytime television to reach the prized female audience.[65]

In the absence of innovative solutions to advertisers' money crunch, there was always the tried-and-true strategy of watering down the product. The three networks' simplest solution to make advertising more affordable was to develop shows which cost less to produce, leading to the dumbing down of television and the end of its golden age. Filmed Westerns became especially popular because even reruns earned solid ratings (*Gunsmoke* was the #1 show in 1957, 1958, and 1959). Live game shows flourished primarily because of their low production cost, but for a number of other reasons as well. Kinks in the shows were easy to fix, they were sold in thirteen-week blocks rather than a full year, and they ranked very high in sponsor identification. Advertisers loved game shows for their ability to accommodate their company or brand name in virtually every scene.[66]

This more formulaic, cookie-cutter model of commercial television was not, however, a panacea for the problems which faced the industry. Because of its own unprecedented success and impact as a promotional vehicle, television advertising had taken on many of the qualities of a pressure cooker. Pressure for better ratings, bigger audiences, and more efficient costs per thousand were continuing to mount, pushing advertisers and their agencies to take shortcuts and bend if not break the rules. The single-sponsor system was now in rapid decline, a casualty of rising costs and the networks' commitment to gain preeminent control over the medium. Moreover, TV commercials were taking on a more competitive, somewhat nastier tone, reflecting the pressure being put on sponsors to turn their advertising into sales and ultimately profits. Still, investment in the medium continued to grow, and advertisers looked to any and all ways to get their brands in the hands of consumers. Would the bubble ever burst?

Chapter Four

A Mist Settling on Our Pond, 1959–1960

You can believe the following words.

The first words of a proposed Dictaphone commercial, as jokingly suggested by A. Donald Brice, vice president of advertising for the company

As America rocketed toward the 1960s, television advertising was pushing its own envelope, heading out to new, unexplored frontiers. Despite the upheaval in the shift in power in the sponsor-agency-network relationship, television advertising was proving to be highly resilient, in part because its host medium was still growing. Household penetration of television sets had hit 85 percent in 1958, bringing television ownership closer and closer to that of radio, which had flattened out at 96 percent household penetration earlier in the decade. Audience levels were thus higher than ever, even if viewers were more selective about particular shows. Most encouraging, many people in the advertising business believed television commercials had begun to improve, and surveys showed that viewers too thought some progress had been made in terms of commercial "likability." Interestingly, television shows and commercials were considered to be moving in opposite directions in the first half of 1959. A survey taken by *Printer's Ink* among a panel of advertising executives revealed that 65 percent believed that the quality of programming was declining, while 75 percent of them felt that commercials were becoming more imaginative, creative, and exciting. The 70 percent failure rate of new shows during the 1958–1959 season was evidence that television had become too derivative and too reliant on formulaic Westerns, thrillers, and detective series, and that sponsors and network executives were becoming increasingly impatient with poor ratings.[1]

But it was criticism by publications such as *Printer's Ink* that drew the wrath of at least one leading advertising executive. In May 1959, Douglas L. Smith, advertising and merchandising director of S. C. Johnson & Company, delivered a stirring speech to the Association of National Advertisers in Chicago. Before a closed (member only) session, Smith attacked critics of commercial television, saying it was

one of the greatest assets which we the advertisers, possess. We must respect it, use it, maintain it, even cherish it. Never again shall we see such a phenomenal media impact on our business.[2]

With close to 80 percent of Johnson's $9 million advertising budget directed to television, Smith had a personal stake in defending the medium. He was particularly angry at representatives from the print media who bad-mouthed television for what Smith believed were self-serving purposes. "I have yet to see a tv network or a station use its *air time* to attack another medium," he declared. As rebuttal, Smith hinted that because television was a driving force of the nation's economy, critics of the medium could be considered "un-American." Drawing further upon McCarthyesque "un-Americanism," Smith linked the medium to patriotic values, exclaiming that

television has had the most important single effect upon our daily lives of anything that has happened in this century. . . . I believe that much of our prosperity during these wonderful 1950's must be truly attributed to the force of television in moving merchandise, and thereby keeping our great productive processes flourishing.[3]

Smith's speech located commercial television not just as a tool of business, but as an essential element of the postwar American Dream, a virtually foolproof ideological stance.

Waste Not, Want Not

Considering how important television had become to the national economy and specifically Corporate America, industry executives had good cause to defend it. Total advertising spending passed $10 billion in 1959, a 49 percent rise over 1951's spending of $6.7 billion. Television advertising was responsible for a significant part of that growth, as spending doubled between 1951 and 1959 to reach about $1.5 billion. "The fifties was a decade that revolutionized Madison Avenue," David Halberstam has mused, adding that "with television, the sizzle was becoming as important as the steak." Forty-four million of the nation's 51 million households now owned one or more television sets, completing what Miller and Nowak considered "the most sudden and huge communication change in history." Total consumer sales in the United States had almost kept up with the pace of ad spending over the eight-year period, rising about 41 percent, suggesting a clear link between television advertising and the booming postwar economy. The importance of television advertising to a national marketer of consumer goods was not open to debate; how to stand out in the televisual crowd and get a fair return on one's investment, however, was the source of much consternation as the end of the 1950s approached.[4]

Some marketers looked to compelling visual icons as a way to set themselves off from the competition. Jack Dreyfus, president of the Dreyfus Investment Fund, instructed his agency, Doyle Dane Bernbach, to use the visual device of a real lion to symbolize the strength of the fund. In the classic 1959 "Lion in the Street," an announcer told viewers that Wall Street had been Dreyfus's territory for twenty years, symbolized by a lion roaming the financial district. The lion comes up the stairs of a subway station (actually a mock station filmed in a Hollywood studio) and appears to walk through the streets of New York (the film of the lion was overlaid on the street scene). The effect was so startlingly real, however, that some viewers called and wrote to Dreyfus, asking if the lion endangered any lower Manhattanites. The slogan, "With Dreyfus, you get the lion's share," completed the king of the financial jungle analogy. In a 1959 spot for Kleenex napkins, Foote, Cone & Belding created Manners, a diminutive butler, to symbolically elevate the brand over the competition. After a housewife who is portrayed in various roles (e.g., homemaker, maid, and chauffeur) concedes she could use some help, Manners comes to the rescue with a box of Kleenex napkins. Manners tells the housewife (and viewers) that the product is soft enough to use as facial napkins but tough enough to soak up spills (and would not slide off laps!), situating the brand as a hero of domestic life. Maxwell House coffee also used visual iconography to set its brand apart from competitors. In Ogilvy, Benson & Mather's 1960 "Perking Pot," a percolating coffee pot was shown as the announcer explained that Maxwell House tasted as good as it smelled. The brand's slogan, "Always good to the last drop," perfectly complemented the visual mnemonic, and remained in the popular lexicon for decades.[5]

Networks also responded to sponsors' desire to set themselves off from their competition by offering more than four hundred spectaculars over the 1959–1960 season. Advertisers linked their names to these specials in order to garner maximum brand identification, seduced by what historian Christopher Anderson termed "monuments to corporate stature." Programs such as the Westinghouse-sponsored *Lucille Ball-Desi Arnaz Show* in April 1960 (in which the wacky duo was teamed up with voice of reason Betty Furness) united the appliance company with television stars. *The Kraft Music*

Hall kept churning with its sponsor's commercials for oil, margarine, and cheeses, as did the *Hallmark Hall of Fame* and its sponsor's spots for greeting cards and gift wrap. Car manufacturers also looked to one-time specials as a means of gaining greater brand exposure. The *Pontiac Star Parade* featured music and dance by such artists as Victor Borge and Gene Kelly, while Ford countered with Leonard Bernstein in its *Ford Christmas Startime.* Chevrolet offered *The Chevy Mystery Show,* and Plymouth the *Steve Allen Plymouth Show* (co-starring a young Don Knotts). *The Frank Sinatra Timex Show* on ABC featured Swayze's "keeps on ticking" spots, with one show teaming up one generation's singing icon with another, Elvis Presley, who had just returned from his stint in the Army.[6]

As clients looked for any way to make their advertising work harder, the concept of "efficiency" emerged as a near obsession within the industry. Since the early part of the century, of course, business had continually pursued the idea of efficiency, mostly in the manufacturing area. America's machine age of the 1920s and 1930s and militarization in the 1940s had led to amazing strides in efficiencies in production, but equivalent efficiencies in the distribution end of business were considered not yet realized. One executive even had numbers to back up this theoretical disparity. Halsey V. Barrett, manager of television sales development for the Katz Agency, somehow arrived at the claim that "production efficiency since 1940 has increased by 64 percent while distribution efficiency has increased by 22 percent." Although a statistical mystery, Barrett's attempt to measure the gap between production and distribution efficiencies illustrated how much postwar advertisers wanted consumption to equal production—capitalism in its purest form (and Marx's worst nightmare). Many wondered how the same sort of scientific principles that were used to make things could be applied to advertising, and to television advertising in particular. Even in the abundant 1950s, any form of waste was considered un-American, a vestige of the nation's puritan ethic and a legacy of the scarcities of the Depression and war years. The inability to accurately correlate advertising and sales was maddening in an era where everything was supposed to be able to be quantitatively measured and scientifically proven. "It may even be a disservice to even try" [to correlate advertising and sales], Dr. Morgan Neu of Daniel Starch reluctantly admitted. Attempts to measure the effectiveness of commercials, noted *Television Magazine* in July 1959, "have yielded only a few buried trinkets in the depths of human motivation, rational and irrational."[7]

The failure to identify a reliable method of measuring commercial effectiveness was not for lack of trying. There were a number of methodologies in use to do just that, although none could be considered particularly accurate. Research firms such as Gallup & Robinson, Pulse, Daniel Starch, and Trendex focused on commercial recognition and recall, Schwerin on commercial impact, and various others (including Dichter's Institute of Motivation Research, the Institute for Social Research, and the Psychological Corporation) on commercial impression. More emotionally based methods, such as the Thurstone psychological test, were used to measure commercial persuasion and liking. Although even researchers themselves considered their work simply one set of factors to consider, clients often used research results to dictate decision making. Reliance on such "truth" was an efficient means of moving the creative process through the typically many levels of client management (Lever Brothers, for example, had nine layers of bureaucracy in 1959). Agency executives, however, knew that advertising was as much art as science, and tried to steer their clients away from using test findings as gospel. Executives such as Charles Feldman, vice president of copy at Young & Rubicam, pointed to highly successful campaigns which tested poorly, such as the General Foods "Busy Day" spots and the Piel's beer "Bert and Harry" commercials. "Only small and sophisticated groups recognize creativity in the beginning," astutely explained Harry Wayne McMahan, who had been an executive with McCann-Erickson and Leo Burnett. Arthur Bellaire, vice president of television and radio copy at BBDO, had even less confidence in pretesting commercials. He believed that the only reliable method of pretesting was via posttesting, that is, applying lessons from past commercials to the development of new ones.[8]

Still, pretesting commercials was becoming standard procedure for large agencies with large clients (and large budgets), a result of the higher financial stakes involved and the trend toward image-based advertising. The undisputed leader in pretesting was Schwerin Research, which was founded in 1946 and claimed to have 70 percent of the market in 1960. Other firms, including the Institute for Advertising Research (IAR), Television Audience Research, and Communication & Media Research Services, also offered independent commercial pretesting services, as did most large advertising agencies. IAR had split off from its parent company, Social Research, specifically to compete in the growing field of commercial pretesting. In addition to statistical analysis, IAR had professionals with backgrounds in psychology, sociology, and anthropology on staff to interpret findings from personal interviews. For example, IAR behavioral science experts found deep meanings embedded in competitive detergent commercials for Lestoil, Mr. Clean, and Handy Andy. While "women believe[d] Lestoil will 'float the dirt away'" and thought of Mr. Clean "as a personalized helper, even in a romantic way," IAR research also showed that "Handy Andy and his four arms disturb[ed] many of the viewers," specifically that "his frantic qualities reinforce[d] the distasteful aspects of his four arms." Although odd in virtually any other context, such insights were exactly what advertisers were paying research firms big bucks for.[9]

The rising interest in commercial pretesting was only one of various attempts to reduce the high degree of risk of television advertising, due to its generally ephemeral nature. Advertisers were pouring money into the medium despite the many unknowns when it came to what they were in fact getting. Unlike newspapers and magazines, which could accurately estimate circulation based on the number of copies printed and sold, broadcasters had to rely on market research rating services. In 1960, there were 50 million television sets in 45 million homes, each one tuned in an average 35 to 40 hours per week. The Nielsen TV Index, largest of the media ratings services, however, used a sample of only about a thousand homes to electronically estimate the size of national television audiences by show. The American Research Bureau, with its Arbitron diary system, sampled 2,200 homes, while Trendex, through its unique overnight telephone survey technique, monitored between 600 and 1,500 homes, depending on time period. Sample sizes were thus microscopically small, with a very wide range of potential error. A 1954 study commissioned by the television industry, in fact, had found that none of the ratings services could accurately measure viewership but, as rough indicators, were better than no data at all. Combined with the inevitability of some inaccurate reporting by sample participants and no way to measure attention, it could be expected that numbers-oriented sponsors looked in any and all places for some firm quantitative grounding. As Ien Ang has written, industry executives were "turn[ing] television consumption into a presumably well-organized, disciplined practice, consisting of expandable viewing habits and routines."[10]

Just as research was being used in the attempt to maximize the reach and effectiveness of commercials, clients were putting more money into their production for similar purposes. Higher professional standards were being applied across all aspects of commercial production, reflected by rising costs. Talent costs for television as a whole, for example, rose more than 300 percent between 1954 and 1959, with production costs rising 50 percent over this same period. The industry leader, MPO Television Films, consistently added Hollywood talent to its staff, including cameramen who had won Oscars and the writer of the film *Hell's Angels*. "Someone had to sponsor Michelangelo, too," said MPO head producer Marvin Rothenberg, defending television commercials as an art form. The innovation of videotape also had much to do with advancing television advertising production at the turn of the decade. Tape greatly reduced the amount of time necessary to produce a commercial, and unlike film, allowed for immediate playback. Retakes could thus be shot in the same day should they be necessary. Tape was also cheaper than film, and was an easier material with which to create special effects. Hardware to play videotape still remained scarce, however, and the cost of making tape duplicates or dubs was extremely high. Modeling agencies too had evolved considerably, now keeping detailed files organized by body part (voice, face, hands, hair, teeth, feet, and breasts). For one tissue commercial, no fewer than forty actresses were invited to a sneezing audition to determine who could explode nasally with perfect conviction and pitch. For Alka-Seltzer, hundreds of people were auditioned in a nationwide talent search for the voice of Speedy, the brand's diminutive, animated spokescritter. A little person got the part.[11]

Quiz Show

Despite the progress commercial television had made as a business tool and art form, sponsor "rating-itis" would threaten to bring the medium down like a house of cards. In the fall of 1959, contestant Charles Van Doren shockingly confessed that his $129,000 winnings on *Twenty-One* were a result of the show's being fixed. Handsome and popular with the television audience, Van Doren was fed the questions he would be asked on the show to keep him winning and earning big ratings. Higher show ratings, of course, meant more Americans would be exposed to Pharmaceuticals, Inc.'s advertising, driving up sales of Geritol and other of the company's brands. As the details of the scandal unfolded, a number of instances of collusion were determined to have existed between contestants and producers on the television quiz shows *Twenty-One*, *Tic Tac Dough*, and *The $64,000 Question*. In the competitive battle for ratings, it was clear that the industry had violated its commitment to serving the public's "interest, convenience and necessity," which the Communications Act of 1934 stipulated. As federal and New York State investigations searched for who exactly was to blame, sponsors and advertising agencies were implicated along with producers and contestants. In a House subcommittee hearing, testimony indicated that executives of Rev-

Master of Ceremonies Jack Barry with Charles Van Doren and Vivienne Nearing after Van Doren lost to Nearing on Twenty-One *in March 1957. Nearing, a New York City attorney, had tied Van Doren a number of times before her victory. (Library of Congress)*

lon, sponsor of *The $64,000 Question,* were "fully aware" that its show too was fixed, allegations which head executives Charles and Martin Revson each denied.[12]

Subsequent testimony revealed, however, that Revlon was undeniably obsessive about the ratings of *The $64,000 Question,* and that the fixing was directly connected to advertising. Revlon, like all major competitors in the cosmetics and toiletries category, was highly dependent on television's ability to reach a mass audience. In terms of television media spending, the category was now second only to food; 19 cents of every dollar spent on television advertising was for food, while cosmetics and toiletries accounted for 14 cents of every dollar. During the height of Revlon's sponsorship of *The $64,000 Question,* Revlon executives were so interested in the show's audience levels that they considered the weekly turnaround provided by the regular ratings services to be "too little, too late" information. Revlon not only purchased Trendex overnight telephone survey information to determine audience share of the show, but correlated them with the names of the contestants who were appearing on the show. Any dip in ratings led to Revlon's providing contestants with the questions to be asked and, in effect, the answers to the questions. "The tacit assumption of all concerned in this process," said Attorney General William P. Rogers, "was the direct connection between a highly rated program and increased product sales."[13]

With the quiz show scandal forcing an examination of every aspect of the television industry, much more scrutiny was given to the role of sponsors and Madison Avenue in the entertainment business. The key question was whether or not either party could ever present entertainment in a responsible manner, given that each had a commercial mission. Some critics, such as Philip Cortney, president of Coty, another maker of cosmetics, suggested that advertisers should get out of programming completely. In newspaper ads and speeches, Cortney asked the $64,000 question: why advertisers had the power to influence television programming when they did not have equivalent control over editorial and entertainment sections of print media. He urged the FCC to amend the Communications Act of 1934 by making it illegal for any

Jack Barry with contestants James Snodgrass (left) and Hank Bloomgarden (right) in sound-proof insulation booths on the May 22, 1957, broadcast of Twenty-One. *The show was soon canceled and producer Albert Freedman arrested on a two-count indictment charging he committed perjury in denying he supplied questions and answers to contestants. (Library of Congress)*

Dr. Fred R. Bollen, second from left, a dentist from Little Rock, Arkansas, came within two cents of guessing the correct amount of the $16,356.44 seen here on the "Big Names Game" part of the April 15, 1958, broadcast of The $64,000 Question. *The game, in which the closest guesser won the money, was a new audience participation feature of the show, drawing more than one-and-a-half million letters from home viewers. The show's master of ceremonies, Hal March (left), is watching Dr. Bollen help load the money into a canvas bag as bank guards prepare to transfer it to an armored car outside the studio. Five runners-up each won $500 in U.S. Savings Bonds. (Library of Congress)*

advertiser to exercise control over programs. Cortney believed that networks were not capable of serving the public interest through quality programming either, as doing so would create a "conflict with their economic interests which require mass audiences for the advertisers." Cortney agreed with noted syndicated columnist Walter Lippman, who wrote that television had become the servant or prostitute of merchandising, and that "as long as advertising remains the only source of income of the television stations, we cannot leave it to them to interpret the meaning of the words 'public interest.'"[14]

Cortney went further by urging sponsors involved in the scandal to donate profits made off the quiz shows to charity. Cortney was attacked by a number of agency executives, who correctly observed that at this point, independent producers and the networks had more control over programming than did sponsors. Executives from Revlon, Coty's arch rival and one of the key players in the scandal, not surprisingly took Cortney's criticism somewhat personally. "We sincerely regret that a competing cosmetic manufacturer has undertaken to set himself up as accuser, judge, and jury," a statement from Revlon read. Mr. Cortney did, however, have his supporters. Responding to calls that the FCC and FTC should more firmly regulate television programs and commercials, critic John Crosby wrote that, "We must remind ourselves that already there is censorship of the airwaves so complete, so blinding, so choking, so single-mindedly devoted to selling Flama Grande [a Revlon product] that no government body can make it much worse."[15]

John Crosby emerged as perhaps television's most vocal critic, announcing that the state of the medium had gotten so bad that it no longer deserved a daily column; instead, Crosby told his readers, he would write about it only sporadically. Crosby was nostalgic for the golden era of the early 1950s, when live drama filled the airwaves and sponsors were willing to take some risks. "Their [advertisers'] aim is not to amuse or instruct or inform you," Crosby wrote. "It is to sell soap and that aim gets in the way of everything else." It was Crosby's opinion that viewers were more annoyed at the aesthetics of commercials than concerned about their fraudulence. Crosby sided with Walter Lippman, who believed that the entire television industry was to blame for the quiz show scandal. "There has been an enormous conspiracy to deceive the public in order to sell profitable advertising to the sponsors," Lippmann wrote. Writer Gore Vidal, whose television scripts had been consistently censored by sponsors, also saw advertising as the root cause of the industry's problems. "It is my dream," Vidal emotionally wrote, "that one day advertisers will buy only time on the air as they buy space in magazines; that they will exercise no more control over the programming of a network than at present they do over a magazine's editorial policy."[16]

Other critics attributed occasional deception and fraud simply to television being, above all, a commercial medium. "Television is owned, body and soul, by the seller of products," *The New Republic* wrote, and "lives not to produce good programs but large audiences for the spiel of the salesmen." *Common-*

weal agreed, saying that "sponsors are, with rare exceptions, uninterested in public culture, information or even entertainment; all they want is maximum advertising exposure." Robert Horton of *The Reporter* wrote that although television was "obligated by law to place public service over private profit, . . . the economics of broadcasting, as presently organized, run directly counter to the basic law that governs the industry." The pursuit of the mass audience and the tyranny of ratings were viewed as responsible for the sorry state of television at the close of the 1950s, with the quiz show scandals the networks' coup de grace for assuming control over programming. In early 1960, the networks gained favor with the FCC by arguing persuasively that it was advertising agencies that held the smoking gun in the quiz show crimes against the public.[17]

As the investigations surrounding the quiz show scandal continued in late 1959, the FTC and the NARTB review board each took a much closer look at potential violations in television advertising. Although a number of surveys (by television trade magazines) indicated that most viewers were not terribly bothered by the fraud the quiz shows had committed on the American people, many in the industry believed that public trust in television—and therefore television advertising—had been seriously damaged. The quiz show scandals had opened up a huge can of worms for television advertising, exposing for the first time the degree to which the industry tweaked reality to sell more product. A. Donald Brice, vice president of advertising for Dictaphone, jokingly suggested that his next commercial would begin, "You can believe the following words." Other advertisers and agency executives claimed that scandal or no scandal, it was their right to use everything at their disposal to present products in the best possible light. Wilbur Jones of the Hoover Company rejected any changes in commercial production techniques or giving up product plugs. "Sure we throw liquid on the floor when we're doing a shot for our polisher," Jones said, "it makes the floor glisten more."[18]

Indeed, in the rush to create commercials that were "more real than reality," the strange but true maxim of advertising (and Disneyland), virtually any trick of the trade was considered fair game. Automobiles were routinely photographed with wide-angle lenses to make them appear longer and wider. Beer foam was typically augmented by salt and other chemicals to create a headier head. One production company found an even easier solution. After discovering that another brand foamed up perfectly, producers simply poured out the client's product and refilled the bottles with the competitive beer for the shoot. No one doubted that such practices misled viewers, but most television advertising techniques that were being viewed as potentially deceptive by the FTC and NARTB were in fact standard practice in print media and, for good measure, the movies. In print ads, women photographed in bubble baths always had on bras and tights under the suds, and bubbles in the bath were created by a hose connected to an air compressor, not soap. Visual tricks in fashion photography for print advertising were also standard. Back halves of gowns often did not exist, and extraordinary measures sometimes had to be taken to keep them on. "If you could [only] see the rear side of some of these girls in the photos," said a well-known fashion photographer, who used clothespins to pull gowns tight. "The girls look like pincushions from behind." Producers of commercials had also learned well from their Hollywood film brethren, where snowflakes were often cornflakes, smoke or fog was dry ice in water, wind was created by a blade-whirling machine, and thunder was simply a sound effect. Most filmgoers even recognized that mountains and seascapes behind actors were often just a color slide, and the scene was being shot not on location but in a comfy Hollywood studio. If print advertisers, fashion photographers, and Hollywood filmmakers could present an artificial interpretation of reality for commercial purposes, why couldn't television advertising, one could ask.[19]

Largely as another outgrowth of the quiz show investigations, the FCC decided to focus its efforts on product plugs on television. Like the FTC, the FCC's resources were being strained by the pressures required to properly regulate the huge broadcasting industry. John Crosby viewed the commission as "an overburdened, largely passive body of lawyers and rate experts who have no experience with, liking for or knowledge of programs." As a result of the February 1960 hearings in Congress investigating bribes made to radio disk jockeys, however, the FCC was making some progress in cracking down on payola in the music industry. In this more critical climate, the FCC began to view product plugs as another form of payola. Plugola had by the end of the 1950s become rampant on television. On his appearances on the *Jack Paar* and *Person to Person* shows, for example, George Jessel unfailingly steered the conversation toward Bulova watches. Bob Hope joked that "The NBC peacock is really a plucked pigeon with a Clairol rinse," while Jerry Lewis finished off a gag with the punch line, "Look, Mom, no cavities!" a Crest toothpaste slogan. Steve Allen performed an entire skit around Gardol, an ingredient in Colgate toothpaste, while the Three Stooges used Polaroid cameras as a story line device. Dean Martin once asked guest Frank

Sinatra if he was wearing the cologne My Sin (he was), while another show starring Sinatra and Bing Crosby featured a filling station set clearly labeled Union Oil. Anyone who was anyone in the advertising business in the late 1950s was aware of what was called "The List," the names of marketers interested in getting a product plug into a television script for a payment in cash or goods. A legendary plugola story concerned Bud Abbott and Lou Costello, who were performing a sketch about Thanksgiving on a television show when Southern Comfort whiskey and Dr. Scholl's foot pads were on "The List." "Boy! That's good stuffing in that turkey," said Abbott. "Tell me, what did you put in it?" "Dr. Scholl's Footpads and Southern Comfort!" shouted back Costello.[20]

Interestingly, stars themselves rarely accepted payment for product plugs, instead typically giving the free merchandise they received to their writers. Stars competed with each other to get the best writers, and pampering them with free products was one way to keep them loyal and motivated. Hollywood legend had it that Jack Benny once fired off five plugs to furnish the home of a writer about to get married. There was no disputing the fact that after mentioning Schwinn bicycles on television, Benny did once look directly into the camera and flatly state, "Send three." It was also known that another top comic received a case of whiskey each time he mentioned "bowling" on his show, and that he was somehow able to mention the word thirty times in as many minutes. Sometimes plugging a product was a bit more challenging. One writer was having trouble finding a way to work the name of a drug product into a skit about horse racing, for example, until he hit upon the brilliant idea of naming a horse Anahist. Cultural and legal forces were starting to turn against plugola, however. The FCC was taking a harder look at the practice, and TV critics too were becoming more critical. Commerce was tainting the purity of entertainment on television, legal and popular thought now went, fouling the natural creative process of the stars. The actor Walter Slezack quipped, "Everybody has become so suspicious that if you say 'Oh, my God!' on television, people think you're being paid off by the Holy Father."[21]

The floodgates now open, however, critics high and low vented their disapproval of the worst of television advertising. *The New Yorker* considered obnoxious commercials that aired during election night in 1960 to be a "degrading form of hazing." "Our method [commercial television] puts the watcher in the position of a mission bum who must listen to a sermon before he receives his sandwich," the magazine complained. Even pro-industry *TV Guide* felt that viewers deserved better, given that they were effectively paying to see commercials. The magazine estimated that the average viewer spent $81.14 a year to operate a television set on electricity, repairs, and depreciation. Dividing this figure by 1,853, the average annual number of viewing hours, each family spent 4.3 cents per hour or $1.53 a week to watch television. Given that about one-sixth of every hour on television consisted of advertising, the average viewer paid roughly 25 cents per week to watch commercials. *TV Guide* urged advertisers to give viewers their money's worth by avoiding commercials which "annoy, bore, or disgust." [22]

Some of the creative elite joined the railing against television advertising. The poet Carl Sandburg believed that "More than half the commercials are . . . filled with inanity, asininity, silliness and cheap trickery." [23] The author E. B. White also felt compelled to offer his opinion on television advertising, which, he observed, "has given liver bile and perspiration a permanent place in the living room." Like Gore Vidal and an increasing number of authors, White found the sponsorship element of television to be a structural flaw particular to the medium. If the world of journalism were like television, where Chevrolet partnered with Dinah Shore, Kraft Cheese with Perry Como, and General Electric with Ronald Reagan, White concluded, "you'd have Walter Kerr reviewing the theater for Hart, Schaffner & Marx, and you'd have Walter Lippman cleaning up the political scene for Fab." When it came to advertising, White believed television should be similar to newspapers and magazines, where

they don't buy a writer or an artist, they don't create material, and their products are dissociated from the work and the personalities of the men and women who do create the editorial content.[24]

White was most disturbed that television had seduced almost all performers into becoming spokespeople. He saw actors, singers, and athletes living double lives on television, interrupting their performances to pitch a product. Although in fact celebrity testimonials in some form dated back to the nineteenth century in the United States, White asserted that "this is a relatively new cloud in the American sky, this practice of commandeering people in the arts for advertising and promotion." White was less bothered by payola, which he believed to be an evil but inevitable part of any business in which money could purchase promotion. Much more troublesome was performers compromising their talent in order to sell products on television, that is, the merging worlds of popular and consumer culture. "The steady drift of people from the lively arts into the ranks of advertising," White concluded,

> . . . is a mist settling on our pond. The old clarity simply isn't there any more. In its place we have the new, big, two-headed man, one mouth speaking his own words, smiling his own smile, the other mouth speaking the words that have been planted, smiling the smile that has been paid for in advance. This is nationally demoralizing . . . Any person who, as a sideline, engages in promoting the sale of a product subjects his real line of work to certain strains, and fogs the picture of himself in the minds of all.[25]

As an artist himself (and with no one knocking at his door to ask him to endorse products), White believed that the realms of entertainment and advertisement should be kept as separate as church and state. Other critics subscribed to White's vision of televisual purity and believed that the medium had to be reinvented, with proposals ranging from a commercial-free network like the BBC to calls for pay television.[26]

Some more elitist critics, however, believed that commercials in bad taste should not only be tolerated but be expected. At an Advertising Federation of America (AFA) meeting, Dr. Lawrence C. Lockley, a professor at Columbia University Graduate School of Business, conceded that television advertising was "blatant, lacking in refinement, [and] materialistic." Rather than running counter to the national standards, however, Dr. Lockley believed that "the general tone of advertising is in tune with the general tone of the American people." The professor went so far as to recommend to the advertising professionals present that it would be a mistake to try to raise the sophistication level of television commercials. "If we attempt to add refinement, delicacy, and moderation to advertising," Dr. Lockley concluded, "we shall have put it out of phase with the consumer, whose wishes and moods it now meets." The professor may have been the minority voice in seeing nothing wrong with the state of television advertising, but viewership and the marketplace bore him out. Americans were in fact not turning off their televisions because of bad commercials and, further, were rewarding those marketers who advertised by buying their products. Almost all research showed that television advertising usually worked, regardless or perhaps because of its typically unidimensional, repetitive nature.[27]

Indeed, at least for those of the old school, there was clearly no substitute for the pure massive power and efficiency of television. Leading advertising theory for packaged goods in particular held that constant reinforcement of a singular commercial message was a virtually no-fail strategy to move product. This idea was the heart and soul of Ted Bates's Unique Selling Proposition, or U.S.P., a leading advertising approach of the postwar era. For "low-interest" products such as hair tonics, headache remedies, cigarettes, or soap, television offered the intrusiveness that print or even radio simply could not. Supporters of television admitted that the medium might not be particularly pretty, but it was able to get a message across to the greatest number of people at the lowest cost.[28]

Do's and Don'ts

Now under pressure from all sides and in the public spotlight, sponsors and their agencies not surprisingly became even more conservative regarding program content. Even outside the single-sponsor system, advertisers retained censorship power when it came to the shows they were paying to produce and, because of the escalated fear of drawing criticism and alienating viewers, became downright paranoid regarding show content. Upon seeing a preview of a documentary on the Hungarian revolt, for example, one agency executive representing a cigarette client suggested that the show should not "have too many Russian officers smoking cigarettes," afraid of any association whatsoever with communism at the peak of the Cold War. Another agency representing a manufacturer of filter cigarettes demanded that villains be shown smoking only non-filters. One sponsor based in the South insisted that a drama that included a lynching be moved from Mississippi to New England, and that all references to Coca-Cola (a "Southern drink") be removed. When Associated Gas & Electric sponsored a show about the Nuremberg trials, an agency executive sitting at the control panels turned off the sound when he saw the words "gas chambers" coming up in the script. Perhaps most extreme was the case of the Ford executive who ordered a shot of the New York skyline to be deleted from a show because the Chrysler Building could be clearly made out.[29]

The FCC's television investigation on the West Coast revealed more programming taboos enforced by Corporate America. The vice president of programming of Screen Gems, a major producer of shows, admitted under cross-examination that sponsors, via their ad agencies, had the ultimate say on "taste and policy." General Mills and its agency, Dancer-Fitzgerald, Sample, had a full-fledged manual, "Television Program Policies," consisting of twenty-two program do's and don'ts. Steeped in postwar consensus values dictating what did and what did not constitute morality, the company's television guidelines made clear that the "moral code of the characters in our dramas will be more or less synonymous with the moral code of the bulk of the American middle-class." Ministers, priests, and "other representatives of positive social forces," including "men in uniform" were not allowed to commit a crime or be placed in an unsympathetic role. Attacks on "some basic conception of the American way of life," for example, "freedom of speech, freedom of worship, etc.," had to be reconciled by the end of a show. Nothing could be mentioned which might offend any group, including minority groups, lodges, political organizations, fraternal organizations, college or school groups, labor groups, business organizations, religious orders, civic clubs, and athletic organizations.[30]

Writers for General Mills shows were also instructed to stay away from controversial issues and not slur any occupation. Regional differences could not be satirized, with "no ridicul[ing] of manners or fashions that may be peculiarly sectional." Although it had occurred a century ago, the Civil War had to be mentioned carefully in order to be sensitive to Southern viewers. No material potentially offensive to our Canadian neighbors or to British royalty could be presented. Not surprisingly, General Mills was especially concerned about the presentation of food, particularly baked goods. "Food subjects commercially treated can not be presented with program content that is unappetizing or tends to effect nausea upon the listener or viewer," company policy went. Because General Mills sponsored a Western, writers were not allowed to reference other cowboy stars such as Gene Autrey or Hopalong Cassidy, or even "competitive horses such as 'Trigger'; 'Silver,' et. al."[31]

Miles Labs and its agency, Ted Bates, outlined in their program policy that no character in *The Flintstones,* the show it sponsored, could ever be stricken with either a headache or stomachache. The marketer of Alka-Seltzer (and loser of several FTC battles) also insisted that no bromides or sedatives be part of an episode of *The Flintstones* (just in case a writer wanted to try his hand at prehistoric pharmacy). To be sure not to offend important customers, no derogatory or embarrassing representations of doctors, dentists, or druggists could be made on the cartoon show. Coca-Cola and its agency, McCann-Erickson, focused on how the bubbly beverage was mentioned or depicted on the show the client sponsored, *Adventures of Ozzie & Harriet.* "One does not serve 'Cokes' or 'Coca-Cola,'" program policy made clear, "one serves 'bottles of Coke.' Think of Coke as the fluid, liquid product of the Coca-Cola Co." Coca-Cola also insisted that no half-consumed bottles or glasses be shown for any length of time, afraid of conveying the idea that one could resist downing a whole portion of the pause that refreshes. Mars, sponsor of a show with the unfortunate name *Circus Boy,* demanded that no sweets other than its own be seen by viewers, including "ice cream, soft drinks, cookies, [and] competitive candy." Viewers of the show must have been left with the impression that circus goers had a maniacal fondness for chocolate-and-caramel confections.[32]

Liggett & Meyers and its agency, McCann-Erickson, had similar competitive concerns, demanding that no pipes, cigars, or even messy ashtrays be shown in shows it sponsored. The company did, however, want characters to smoke its products on a regular basis. "While we do not want to create an impression of one continual, smoke-filled room," policy went, "from time to time in the shows we feel 'natural' smoking action is a requisite by the cast. It should never be forced." "Incidental" shots of cigarette machines, posters, and display pieces were encouraged, as was the "end of a [cigarette] carton sticking out of shopping bag." Liggett & Myers also had something to say about the age of smokers, stating that, "obviously, a 12-year-old should not be shown smoking. . . . [but] on the other hand, the high school and college market is extremely important to Liggett & Myers as future longtime customers." Future cigarette company executives would regret the paper trail consisting of such statements made by their predecessors, suggesting a clear and dedicated attempt to bring younger people into the tobacco fold.[33]

The Surrogate Salesperson

The makers of Lucky Strike cigarettes were also intent on keeping Americans puffing, and were in no hurry to break away from their winning formula, centered around *The Jack Benny Program,* which they continued to sponsor through the spring of 1959. During a show in March 1959, Benny resumed his fondness for performing the Luckies jingle in ethnic-oriented settings, when he and his cast did a "ceremonial" song and dance in Native American headdresses. In another March show, the Luckies commercial was performed by Don and Benny as a magic act, while two weeks later, the product was again given a key role in the show's major sketch. Within a courtroom drama, Benny introduced into evidence a pack of Luckies found in guest star Genevive's purse and another pack found at the scene of the crime. The other guest star, Ed Sullivan, however, got her off the hook by stating that the entire audience smoked Lucky Strikes. With the beginning of the 1959–1960 television season, however, television history was made when Lux (bar soap and liquid dish detergent) replaced Lucky Strike as the sponsor of *The Jack Benny Program.* "The biggest dish washing news in 12 years," Lux's campaign slogan, was intended not only as advertising puffery but to indirectly reference the brand's ending Lucky's amazingly long association with Jack Benny, dating back to radio. The end of Lucky's sponsorship was a sign of the times; Americans' concern about smoking was continuing to rise, sparked by a July 1954 article in *Reader's Digest* linking cigarettes to cancer. Benny found a way to even make this advertising fodder, however, referring to the changeover in an October 1959 show by having the Sportmen Quartet keep performing the old Lucky jingle rather than the new Lux one. After Don complained that the switch was a difficult one to make, Benny replied, "Well, stop smoking and start bathing." Dennis Day joined in, exclaiming that he did not want to work for a man "who couldn't hold a sponsor." In just a couple of weeks, however, the new sponsor's brand was firmly entrenched in the show's routine, with Benny insisting that the group present the Lux commercial as a "minute waltz" (but in forty seconds).[34]

The cast's antics with Lux continued through the remainder of the television season. In February 1960, Don read the Lux liquid spot as a Shakespearean soliloquy, accompanied by Benny on his famous violin. On an April show featuring the Beverly Hills Easter Parade, Don presented the Lux commercial while dressed as an old woman in an Easter bonnet. Two weeks later, Dennis Day read the Lux soap commercial in a Chinese accent while wearing traditional Chinese clothing. Benny had supposedly just returned from Hong Kong, having been carried on stage by rickshaw previously in the show. On a show in May, Benny's "sponsors" refused to renew his contract, deciding to use instead a mechanical dummy (which eerily reproduced the star's unique slow turn of the head). As the 1960–1961 season began, however, Lux was out as sponsor, replaced by co-sponsors Lipton Tea and State Farm Insurance. The biggest dish-washing news in a dozen years hadn't, apparently, moved enough soap. Undaunted, Benny and crew continued to use their show as a sustained commercial. On an October 1960 episode, with the Nixon-Kennedy election just three weeks away, Don presented the Lipton Tea commercial in political campaign speech style. Just days after the Kennedy victory, Don surprisingly did not use a political theme for the State Farm spot, instead performing it accompanied by a seal named Oscar. A couple of weeks later, Benny introduced Howard K. Brawley, the creator of the current State Farm advertising theme song, to the studio audience and the millions of viewers at home. Benny then spoke in the song's rhythmic style, as pure as integrated advertising could get. Just thinking that viewers would care who wrote the State Farm song reveals the degree to which advertising was a part of *The Jack Benny Program*. In the last episode of the year, Harlow belted out the Lipton Tea jingle Sophie Tucker–style, a fitting season finale for the show with the loudest commercial voice in commercial television.[35]

As discussed earlier, not all stars were as willing as Jack Benny to frame their show around advertisers' products. Garry Moore, now host of *I've Got a Secret,* would integrate ads but was one of the few stars who refused to submit his copy to sponsors for approval. Moore would receive advertising copy from sponsors' advertising agencies, then rewrite it to fit his less hyperbolic style. "Sponsors should be made to realize that a can of peaches is not the Holy Grail," said Moore. Jackie Gleason and Jimmy Durante went further by refusing to deliver full commercials on their shows, only doing the lead-in and then passing the message off to an announcer or as a segue to a filmed spot.[36] These were unusual cases, however; stars typically continued to cater to industry pressure to use their power as spokespeople. In BBDO executive Arthur Bellaire's book, *TV Advertising,* he expressed how important a spokesperson was to a company at the time:

> The person chosen to represent the advertiser becomes a corporate personality who, over the course of a single season, has 1,000 — perhaps 1,000,000 — times more contact with the consumer than the president of the company, chairman of the board, sales manager, or any individual salesman.[37]

Bellaire accurately captured the idea that a cooperative television host was, quite simply, the single most important tool in a large marketer's toolbox circa 1960.

Many in the industry considered Polaroid's use of spokespeople to sell its cameras a textbook example of how to use the medium. By the 1959–1960 season, the company was spending around 75 percent of its $2.5 million advertising budget on television by having Jack Paar and other show hosts, including Garry Moore and Dave Garroway, take snapshots of their guests. Neil Schreckinger, account executive for Doyle Dane Bernbach, stated that "we can reach millions of people who can see the results of a picture taken in seconds," although those were nervous seconds for Polaroid executives. If the Land Camera malfunctioned or the star took a bad picture, viewers would likely be left with a less than positive image of the product. Mr. Schreckinger, however, was not about to allow even this possibility take away from his agency's brilliant use of television advertising's product demonstration abilities. "If the picture isn't good," he explained in classic account management logic, "you don't have to wait weeks to find out. You can tell right away, and take another shot 60 seconds later."[38]

With brand reputations on the line, sponsors remained as conservative as ever regarding a spokesperson's public image. By 1960, advertisers had tired of the wholesome Dinah Shore type and were now looking for a "young Donna Reed" or a "young Jane Wyatt" as a spokesperson for their product. Patricia Harris, casting director of Cascade Pictures, "the MGM of television commercials," insisted that not much had really changed, with advertising agencies wanting a woman who was young but not too young, pretty but not too pretty, and shapely but not sexy. As far as casting men in commercials, the trend in 1960 was toward the more genteel sort, specifically a Van Johnson type circa 1950. This "boy-next-door" look had displaced the previous year's demand for rugged, tattooed blue-collar workers with chest hair poking from open-neck shirts. Hal Humphrey was puzzled by advertisers' fixation with the boy and girl "next-door" type, noting that "the people who have lived next door to me never have looked anything like those I see in the movies or on TV commercials. I've got to do something about getting out of these lousy neighborhoods."[39] Humphrey also satirized advertisers' intense selection process in choosing a spokesperson, offering a series of "Humphrey's Handy Image Hints" as a tongue-in-cheek guide. Tips included the following:

Loretta Young—Whistler's Mother in capri pants. A happy combination of sanctity of the home and a little harmless sex. She can sell soap, home permanents and Beverly Hills real estate.

Walter Brennan—Homey, reliable and a throw-back to our pioneering forefathers. A sure-fire hit for farm machinery, arch support shoes and Beech-Nut chewing tobacco.

[Mike] Nichols and [Elaine] May—Typify youth and sophistication with just a trace of beatnik. Pair would be great for sports cars or a mild deodorant with a name like "Zoom!"

Lawrence Welk—A bit of old world charm emanating from giddy Hollywood. He rocks—like in rocking chair, man! Wunnerful for Dr. Scholl's foot pads.[40]

As it turned out, General Electric, rather than a sports car or "mild deodorant" manufacturer, hired Elaine May and Mike Nichols to endorse its products. The comedy team represented cutting edge entertainment in 1960 America, an interesting choice to reach young marrieds furnishing their new suburban homes with appliances. In "Major Appliances," a 1960 spot created by Young & Rubicam, May played an elegantly dressed woman, Nichols an appliance salesman dressed in a tuxedo. May approaches Nichols, asking to see a refrigerator. After Nichols, apparently her lover, shows her the newest GE model, May whispers to him that she has really come to end the relationship. She describes the refrigerator's features and then tells him she is unable to ask him to "give up all this to become the son-in-law of a viscount." The quirky commercial is in the Clio Hall of Fame.[41]

Although celebrity testimonials were pervasive, virtually everyone was surprised when Eleanor Roosevelt turned up in a television commercial for Good Luck margarine in 1959. Eager to make money for her various charities, Mrs. Roosevelt told her agent at the time, Thomas L. Stix, that "with the amount of money I am to be paid I can save over six thousand lives. I don't value my dignity that highly. Go ahead and make the arrangements." In addition to promoting the Lever Brothers brand in the spot, the ex-First Lady expressed the hope that "America could lead the way in helping to feed the starving people of the world." Despite Mrs. Roosevelt's good intentions, most critics were appalled at her decision to send a message of social responsibility alongside an endorsement of a condiment. Jack Gould, television critic for *The New York Times,* considered Mrs. Roosevelt's "linking her concern for the world's needy with the sale of a food product at a retail counter disquieting in the extreme." He conceded that Mrs. Roosevelt was "entitled to a lapse in judgment," but criticized Lever Brothers and its agency, Ogilvy, Benson & Mather, for a lack of "discretion and guidance." Mrs. Roosevelt defended her decision to appear in the spot, correctly stating that through commercials, "one reaches far more people than can possibly be reached in any other way." Lever capitalized on what *Advertising Age* deemed "by far the biggest name snared by radio-tv admen," running radio spots with Mrs. Roosevelt's voice and displaying point-of-sale posters of her televisual image in grocery stores. This actually was not the first time Eleanor Roosevelt appeared in an advertisement; she was occasionally featured in print ads for Otarion hearing aids. The Good Luck spot, however, launched Mrs. Roosevelt into a new orbit of commercial potential. Weeks after the airing of the campaign, Frank Sinatra asked her to appear on an upcoming spectacular. With a huge appearance fee waiting for her, Mrs. Roosevelt was off to Hollywood.[42]

The greater reliance on and smarter use of advertising spokespeople could be correlated with a drop in the number of actual field salespeople. In 1939, before television, there was one salesperson for every thirty-nine Americans, while in 1956 there was one for every eighty-five. Television advertising was assuming some of the responsibilities of the traditional salesperson by laying a foundation of brand awareness and building a brand's identity among consumers. Some companies were even opting to drop their sales forces completely as television advertising reshaped the structure and operating methods of business. Super-Anahist, the second leading brand of antihistamine, used television advertising in lieu of a sales force, as did Lewis-Howe, maker of Tums. Bristol-Myers's television budget was three times that of its sales budget, while the maker of Lestoil used television — not salespeople — to introduce its brand to a new market. As others had done before, executives observed that television advertising seemed to be taking on some of the responsibilities of retailers. Ed Graham, co-creator of the Piel Brothers campaign when he was at Young & Rubicam, believed that "supermarkets [were] becoming more and more impersonal," opening a window of opportunity for commercials to assume a greater role in personal selling. "The shopping housewife will choose, all other things being equal, the product sold by a friend, such as the Piel Brothers or Emily Tipp, the lady of the Tip Top [bread] commercials." (The voice of Emily Tipp was that of Margaret Hamilton, the actress who played the Wicked Witch of the West in *The Wizard of Oz*, not a particularly "friendly" voice but an increasingly familiar one in commercials). Still, it was clear that television advertising had altered and was continuing to alter the DNA of American consumerism by redefining and seemingly diminishing the roles of both company salesperson and local retailer.[43]

The ever-widening influence of television advertising was readily apparent by its impact on the nation's cultural geography. For defining a geographic market, advertisers had traditionally used a federal government measure, the Standard Metropolitan Statistical Area (SMSA). For advertisers who used a lot of spot television, however, media coverage had become a more important criterion than demographic data, redefining a market as an area within the range of a television signal. Broadcasting systems even had terms for these new geographic areas, recasting cities into advertising terms. Westinghouse Broadcasting called a television market a "Megatown," while Corinthian Broadcasting called one a "Tele-Urbia," making television coverage the chief determinant of where marketers' products would be distributed. Television advertisers including Heublein (the new owners of Maypo hot cereal), Ralston Purina, and Anheuser Busch, for example, all reorganized their distribution systems based on a 50–60 mile radius of each broadcasting area. Retailers whose markets received advertisers' commercials often demanded distribution, as consumers would come into their stores wanting to buy the advertised products. With broadcast coverage naturally a principal concern for spot television advertisers, the national map was effectively being redrawn based on commercial interests versus physical geography. The relative strength of a television signal to carry advertising into Americans' homes had become, at least from the view of business, what constituted a city.[44]

Of course, automobile manufacturers relied heavily on television advertising to get people into local showrooms for a test drive. Despite the tighter economy of early 1959, Chevrolet pulled out all the stops to persuade Americans with wanderlust to see the U.S.A. through its windshields. Chevrolet's advertising agency, Campbell-Ewald, recommended that the automobile manufacturer spend a whopping $25,000 to produce a commercial called "Chasing the Sun." Because advertisers such as Chevrolet were investing so much money in producing and airing shows, the agency believed it was logical for sponsors to spend a proportional amount on the commercials which would air on the programs. With Chevrolet spending about $100,000 a week on time and talent for its half-hour *The Pat Boone Show,* spending $25,000 on a two-and-a-half minute color commercial to reach the program's 55 million viewers did not seem too exorbitant to Campbell-Ewald executives. "Chasing the Sun" would prove to be one of the most elaborate commercials produced to date, with locations in two small towns in New York and a beach in Florida. The spot featured a couple driving from their snow-bound New England home in their brand new Chevrolet toward Florida, with the view through the car windows showing the changing weather.[45]

Chevrolet's arch rival, Ford, went in a different direction by licensing characters from the comic strip "Peanuts." In his commercial debut, Charlie Brown challenged Lucy to think of another station wagon that was easier to own, park, load, or drive than the Ford Falcon. The announcer then explained to Linus that the Falcon was the nation's least expensive six-passenger wagon. After the announcer described the Falcon's standard features, Linus replied that he thought it was very beautiful, not one to waste words. In a commercial for other models, Ford traded on the mystery of the final frontier and exploited the nation's growing fascination with space travel. In front of an astronomical observatory, an announcer told viewers that they would soon see something never seen before. Three meteors then appeared in the sky and landed near the observatory. As a crowd of well-dressed people gathered to look, the meteors were transformed into shiny new cars, specifically a Galaxy, Thunderbird, and Falcon. With its slogan, "A wonderful new world of Fords," the car company parked itself on the leading edge of science and technology.[46]

Rather than look forward, Buick decided to look back by plopping spokesperson Bob Hope in a number of historic models, including those from 1904, 1910, and 1924. The announcer told viewers that Buick had been a leader in manufacturing automobiles for fifty-seven years, and that the car company was meeting the challenge of the 1960s with "the best Buick yet—the turbine-powered Buick 60." By featuring Bob Hope and classic cars, Buick was, however, only resurrecting the past, as the heydays of both star and automobile were from an earlier era. Mercury too relied on the appeal of a familiar personality, George Burns, to pitch its new line. Burns told viewers that he had "two of the most gorgeous girls" he had ever seen in his two-car garage—two new 1960 Mercury station wagons. Beside the attractive "hardtop styling," Burns continued, the wagons were equipped with a feature that Gracie loved—a back window which rolled down, serving as "a cigar-smoke eliminator." The announcer then joined Burns to list the wagon's many other standard features and emphasize that the price was just slightly more than "one of those dolled-up cars riding around under a low-priced banner."[47]

Edsel's last advertising gasp was, however, much more pitiful than such fuddy-duddy campaigns employing ex-vaudeville stars. Although John Cameron Swayze was insisting that the 1959 Edsel was "built to be the most distinctive car on the road," consumers were figuratively and literally not buying it. In one convoluted spot, an Edsel was parked under a circus tent. The announcer explained that riding a horse bareback is one way to get around, but it is harder than it looks. A simple way to travel in style, this logic continued, was to buy an Edsel. In another 1959 spot, a woman told John Cameron Swayze that she had owned a new Edsel for an entire month but had yet to put a drop of gas in the tank. Ford was desperately trying to position the car in the shrinking low-priced segment dominated by Plymouth, Chevrolet, and itself, but the Edsel's fate was sealed. The company had sold about 50,000 cars in the last few months of 1957, 29,000 in 1958, and 20,000 through May 1959—numbers far smaller than Ford was used to. By July 1959, all original members of the Edsel marketing and advertising team had resigned, retired, or had been transferred to other Ford divisions. The Edsel itself would soon be retired, earning its cultural status as arguably the biggest marketing blunder of all time.[48]

Rather than trod such familiar terrain, Doyle Dane Bernbach was breaking new ground in its revolutionary ads for Volkswagen. In the 1960 "Rear Window," for example, a few Volkswagen representatives visit an Italian car designer in Milan and ask him what he would change on the Volkswagen. After thinking for some time, the designer says that he would make the car's rear window a little larger. In "Box," produced the same year, an announcer tells viewers that a simple cardboard box was the inspiration for the design of the new Volkswagen station wagon. "Suppose you had a lot to carry," he reasons. "You'd get a box." After describing some of the wagon's features, the announcer states, "Put it on wheels, and you've got the whole idea behind the Volkswagen station wagon." As with the vehicle itself, Volkswagen's focus on simplicity and functionality in its advertising ran totally contrary to post-war American automobile manufacturers' emphasis on power and styling, foreshadowing a new paradigm of marketing communications.[49]

The coming revolution in marketing communications could also be de-tected in the 1960 presidential campaign, as the two candidates eagerly used television advertising to get their messages across to the American people. With the Cold War a political hot button, both parties focused on the interna-tional scene. In one spot for the Republican presidential ticket of Vice Presi-dent Richard Nixon (R-California) and former Senator Henry Cabot Lodge (R-Massachusetts), Nixon was asked, "What is the truth, can we keep the Communists from taking over in Africa?" Nixon replied, "I believe we can if we keep working through the United Nations." Supported by the campaign slogan "They understand what peace demands," the Republican candidates softened their more hawkish image. In another spot, Nixon firmly declared, "Only strength and firmness can keep the peace," an eerie foreshadowing of his political position regarding a future attempt to slow the spread of com-munism in Southeast Asia.[50]

Democratic presidential candidate John F. Kennedy (D-Massachusetts) also ran commercials in the fall demonstrating his grasp of Cold War politics. In one spot, Kennedy sent a warning note, declaring, "The relative strength of the United States, compared to that of the Soviet Union and the Chinese Communists together, has deteriorated in the last eight years and we should know it." Other commercials, however, referenced the variety of domestic and personal issues that surrounded his candidacy. In one such spot, a woman in a crowd addressed Kennedy's Catholicism, asking him, "Do you think you would be divided between two loyalties, to your church and to your state, if you were elected president?" Kennedy answered, "I would not. . . . I would fulfill my oath of office, as I have in Congress for fourteen years." In another spot, a reporter asked Kennedy, "What legislation do you have in prepara-tion on the civil rights issue?" Kennedy responded, "The President could compel all companies which do business with the government to practice open, fair hiring of personnel without regard to race, creed, or color." By touching on issues of religion and race, Kennedy broadened his support and positioned himself as a more multidimensional candidate than Nixon. He also, as we all know, looked exponentially better than Nixon on television, which would ultimately make the difference in the election. A new era in the televisual packaging of political candidates had begun.[51]

As the first year of the new decade ended, the television industry had survived its worst crisis and anticipated the new frontier that lay ahead. Within the universe of television advertising, 1959 and 1960 had been turning point years as the quiz show scandals formally ended the founding modus operandi of commercial television. The cacophony of commercial clutter, obsession with efficiencies, and sponsor "rating-itis" were all the result of advertisers' attempts to keep up with the Joneses, leading to their eviction from the entertainment side of the business. In addition, the FTC's concerted attempts to force advertisers to tell the truth in TV commercials revealed the thickness of the mist that had settled on the televisual pond. Still, there was hope that commercial television could rise above its past transgressions, as a new age of Camelot promised that the American Dream could be shared by all.

PART THREE

The New Society

*

Chapter Five

Think Young, 1961–1962

Now it's Pepsi for those who think young.
Pepsi-Cola's new advertising theme, 1961

In January 1961, executives of Pepsi-Cola decided that the time was now right to make a full-scale launch into television advertising. Pepsi was one of the great icons of American consumer culture, but the company had only sporadically used network television through the 1950s. With a newly elected, youthful president in office and the biggest generation in history hitting their teens, advertisers like Pepsi-Cola were confident that most Americans were ready to "think young." Pepsi had recently switched advertising agencies from Kenyon & Eckhardt to BBDO, and saw the New Frontier era as an opportunity to link its star brand to youth culture. Philip H. Hinerfeld, vice president of advertising, explained why his company decided to think young:

Today, all America thinks young . . . less than three weeks ago America inaugurated the youngest elected President in its history. The average age of his cabinet is also the youngest ever. Why, at Pepsi-Cola Company the average of our top management team is under forty-six years of age.[1]

Pepsi went all out for its new campaign, hiring photographer extraordinaire Irving Penn to supervise the commercial shoot. Pepsi was after Penn's simple but dramatic visual look, what *Life* magazine referred to as "realistic elegance." As music, the company bought the rights to Eddie Cantor's hit song of 1928, "Makin' Whoopee!"—an anthem of youth of a previous generation. By substituting new lyrics and calling it "The Pepsi Song," the company could retire its current jingle, introduced in 1958, "Be Sociable," which now seemed rather dated. In combination, Pepsi believed the Penn-inspired visuals and suggestive music would further link the brand to life's "real pleasures" and make the brand a powerful symbol of youthful joie de vivre.[2]

Pepsi's new campaign marked the revolution that had begun to bubble up in advertising and, in a much larger sense, American society. The American torch was clearly passing to a new generation, evident to all as seventy-year-old Dwight David Eisenhower handed the keys to the White House to a forty-three-year-old. In addition, few could ignore the demographic bulge that had dramatically brought down the average national age. Other signs of the times, such as the FDA's approval of the first birth control pill in 1960, signaled that it truly was the dawn of a new era. The New Society was expected to make real the postwar mythologies of entitlement and limitlessness, and grant more Americans more of everything. Although many believed the new Kennedy administration would be anti-business — reflected by a skittish stock market and cabinet official Arthur Schlesinger's suggestion that advertising should be taxed — the business community remained bullish on advertising until proven otherwise. The number of advertisers that used network television in 1960 hit an all-time high of 376, up from the previous high of 341 in 1956. The average American was now being exposed to an average 10,000 television commercials a year according to *Broadcasting* magazine, and the $12 billion a year that businesses spent on advertising exceeded the gross national products of Austria and Norway together. Americans would spend more time watching television than pursuing any other pastime in 1961, with sets turned on one-third of the day in the 90 percent of households with televisions. With faith in the unlimited possibilities of the American economy, however, most people in the business world expected advertising revenues to double over the course of the 1960s, just as they had over the 1950s.[3]

The Cone Plan

Before such a feat could be achieved, however, the television and advertising industries would have to get their respective houses in order. As it had on the West Coast a year before, the FCC brought representatives of the biggest advertisers together for a summit in October 1961. The hearings, held in New York, were largely in response to the new FCC chair, Newton N. Minow, blasting what was being broadcast over America's airwaves. Before the National Association of Broadcasters (NAB) in May 1961, in a speech that transcended industry dynamics to strike a cultural chord which reverberates to this day, Minow called network television a "vast wasteland" and characterized commercials as "screaming, cajoling and offending."[4] At these FCC hearings, company executives were asked to reveal their own particular corporate policies regarding inappropriate subject matter. Procter & Gamble, at $100 million a year the biggest television advertiser, quoted from its written policy regarding the presentation of business in shows it sponsored. Wanting to keep the public perception of business as the deliverer of the American Dream, Procter & Gamble mandated that

there will be no material on any of our programs which could in any way further the concept of business as cold, ruthless, and lacking all sentiment or spiritual motivation. If a businessman is cast in the role of a villain, it must be made clear that he is not typical but is as much despised by his fellow businessmen as he is by other members of society.[5]

Brown & Williamson, makers of Kools, Raleighs, and Viceroys, was not surprisingly sensitive to how cigarettes were portrayed in shows it sponsored. The company explained that no actor could be shown aggressively stamping out a cigarette in an ashtray or under his or her foot, and that actresses could not be shown smoking on the streets, an act apparently considered to be charged with sexual, immoral overtones.[6] Further corporate policy stated that

whenever cigarettes are used by antagonists or questionable characters, they should be regular size, plain ends, and unidentifiable. But no cigarette should be used as a prop to depict an undesirable character. Cigarettes used by meritorious characters should be Brown & Williamson brands.[7]

Representatives from other leading television advertisers, such as Prudential insurance and Revlon, also appeared at the FCC hearings, offering their editorial policies. The Prudential spokesperson explained that the company considered shows which "cast a little doubt on financial institutions" as inappropriate for them to sponsor. Prudential was true to its word, having once refused to sponsor a documentary about the bank holiday of 1933. The Revlon representative told the commission that the company objected to one scene in an *Alfred Hitchcock Presents* script in which a woman was cut in two, which the network agreed to drop. The company's objections to a scene in another Hitchcock show in which a woman was strangled, however, went unheeded by the network (apparently strangling was considered by CBS to be family entertainment, bisection otherwise). In one stage of the hearings, advertisers pointed out to the commission the critical difference between television and print media. While newspapers and magazines offered a guaranteed circulation at a fixed price, they argued, there was no such guarantee in television— cause enough for sponsors to have input into the presentation of the material.

Douglas L. Smith, vice president of advertising at S. C. Johnson & Son, cut to the chase, declaring that "since we pay the bill, we have a right to insist on changes." Corporate America was making it clear to all that when it came down to ultimate responsibility in commercial television, the real and metaphoric buck stopped there, allowing them decision-making power when it came to content.[8]

Although he did not get a chance to speak at the FCC hearings, Fairfax Cone, the outspoken chair of Foote, Cone & Belding, believed he had the answer to television's programming dilemma. Before the Broadcast Advertising Club in Chicago in 1961, Cone emphasized that his version of the "magazine concept" was the only viable way to raise the standards of television. Rather than buy time for a specific program, he argued, advertisers should buy time that would be distributed across a network's schedule, the way it worked in British commercial television. Just as advertisers contracted for a designated number of pages in magazines without say over the surrounding editorial matter, Cone believed, advertisers should do the same in television. Such a plan would free advertisers from responsibility for program content, the single source of censorship and editorial manipulation. Additionally, because advertisers could no longer choose shows on the basis of ratings, Cone pointed out, the overall quality of programming would improve. Cone was convinced the plan would serve both of what he termed were "two publics," one consisting of the "gum chewers and lip movers and the no-opinion holders," the other "the sensible and sensitive Americans." Cone, hopefully, employed more sophisticated market segmentation techniques when working for his clients.[9]

Cone's idea was a twist on the original magazine format, whereby advertisers simply bought time on shows rather than producing them, more and more the industry standard. Interestingly, Cone's proposal suggested that the means to improving television's program format was changing its advertising format, that is, for advertisers to give up their preferred positions for the sake of the medium as a whole. The "Cone Plan," as it soon became known, created hot debate in the television and advertising communities, with some big advertisers threatening to pull out of television completely should the plan go into effect. Even most network executives disapproved of the proposal, recognizing that advertisers' identification with specific programs was analogous to their right to choose particular magazines in order to reach a designated target audience. Others feared that if spread across an entire day's or week's schedule, commercials promoting products intended for adults (such as automobiles) would be aired during children's shows, and vice versa. Cone countered that with the trend toward multiple sponsorships, his concept or something like it was an inevitability. The fundamental problem with television, according to Fairfax Cone, was that it, unlike newspapers or magazines, "set out to be a medium to make money instead of a medium of expression," again reflecting his belief that fixing television required fixing advertising. The trend toward alternate sponsorships was also wreaking havoc with some standard television practices, such as the custom of promoting the following week's show at the end of each program. Announcers found themselves in the awkward position of having to say things like, "And now a word from last week's sponsor for next week's show." [10]

The principal flaw with the Cone Plan was, as some noted at the time, that comparing television to print was like oranges to apples because magazines and newspapers were purchased by advertisers to reach specific markets. It was true that advertisers typically did not dictate the location of an ad in a print medium, but they selected the magazine or newspaper for the kind of audience it reached. Taking away advertisers' ability to sponsor or place commercials during particular shows would be like saying they could no longer target demographic groups via print media. "Unless networks or local stations are themselves conceived as "magazines," *Harvard Business Review* correctly observed, "the analogy fails to hold." Furthermore, Cone's proposal to even the playing field by removing advertisers' power to choose specific shows ran counter to the natural instincts of big business. "The one thing competing advertisers desire to buy above all else is a clear advantage," the journal concluded. Cone seemed to be ignoring that the limited supply of prime time hours in which to advertise (only twenty-eight hours a week) was itself a reason marketers with the biggest promotional budgets would never agree to the plan, wanting to keep smaller advertisers at bay. [11]

Further, advertisers' control of television had seriously eroded since the quiz show scandal of 1959. By raising their interest in the production side of the business, networks had increased their power to the point where they, not sponsors, determined what shows would be produced and aired. Thomas M. Garrett, writing in *America* magazine in January 1962, estimated network's control of shows as 85 percent, and warned that giving them control of the remaining 15 percent through the Cone Plan would be a mistake. Instead, Garrett believed, it was up to the general public to be more discriminating, for each viewer to become what he called an "apostle of the possible." "The most feasible way to reform television is to reform its audiences," Garrett argued. [12]

Babes in Toyland

As televisual sponges, however, children required additional protection from soaking up information that could prove harmful in some way. Under pressure from Washington, the NAB made new provisions in its code regarding advertising to children, an area in which marketers proved they could not self-regulate. One provision, for example, stated that "commercials directed to children should in no way mislead as to the product's performance and usefulness," a measure specifically addressing the problem of toy advertising. The NAB's new guidelines addressing toy advertising were the result of actions being taken not by the FCC but by the FTC. As the baby boom created a new, mammoth market, toy advertising on television was deservedly becoming a primary area of concern to the FTC. Toy manufacturers, not surprisingly, considered television an ideal medium by which to advertise as, perhaps more than any other product, toys benefited from the small screen by appearing larger than life. Children, unable to determine how big the toys really were or what exactly they could do, were enthralled by the sights and sounds of airplanes, rockets, and missiles. Although the FTC's own codes banned all deceptive advertising on television, a special effort by the NAB to protect children (and their parents) from fraudulent or misleading toy commercials was clearly warranted. The FTC had in fact never cited a toy manufacturer for any violation until September 1962, when it charged Ideal Toy with deceptive commercials. Until then, advertisers took free advantage of children's inability to separate puffery from reality, routinely lying to them and building commercials around claims which the toys could never deliver. The 1960 holiday season was plagued by a number of commercials that either misrepresented products or attempted to unfairly coerce children into buying products.[13]

Before the 1961 selling season, the NAB had its Television Code Review Board clear all toy commercials before they aired, and successfully persuaded the industry association, the Toy Manufacturers of the USA, to adopt some basic guidelines regarding advertising on television. Toy marketers were urged to avoid a number of objectionable practices, including fictitious demonstrations and dramatizations, the use of the words "only" and "just" when describing the toy's cost, and implying that by owning the toy a child would be better than his or her peers. The new guidelines hardly deterred the nation's largest toy marketers from investing in television at all-time highs. Aware that their target audience might never again be this large, toy marketers were planning to spend about $10 million on television for the holiday season alone during 1961. Louis Marx and Company planned to spend six times the amount it had in 1960, all of it during shows scheduled in the mid-afternoon. Mattel, Inc., sponsor of *Matty's Funday Funnies* on ABC, announced a 20 percent increase in television spending in 1961. Remco Toy Company planned to advertise aggressively on the two shows it sponsored, *Captain Kangaroo* on CBS and Shari Lewis's puppet show on NBC. "With television," Saul Robbins, president of Remco said, "we sell as much of an item in one year as we used to in three." Lionel Corporation decided to expand beyond trains by introducing a line of science toys backed by "heavy outlays" of advertising.[14]

Even Maxwell House, a brand not at all associated with children, decided to market toys, albeit as a promotional technique. In April 1961, the division of General Foods partnered with Amsco Toys to create the Maxwell House Coffee Time Set, advertising the set on such shows as *Captain Kangaroo* and *The Shari Lewis Show*. The set included a percolator that actually perked, a toy stove, and cups and saucers. Such efforts were designed, of course, to have children influence their parents' purchasing decisions, and to start building brand preferences at an early age, a long-time, enduring advertising strategy. "Because they accompany and influence mothers on shopping trips," Ellen Seiter has observed, "children constitute an especially appealing market." Citing the three reasons that marketers love kids, Seiter explains that "children influence adults (on cheap items and on major consumer durables, such as appliances and cars), they will soon spend a lot of money themselves, and they provide an opportunity to inculcate brand loyalty at an early age, thus ensuring future markets." (Not even General Foods could predict, however, that these children would ultimately forego Maxwell House for something called Starbucks.)[15]

Despite the firmer NAB guidelines, many toy commercials being aired in the holiday season of 1961 were still using what could be considered deceptive techniques. Some advertisers continued their use of "only" in describing a toy's price, while others exaggerated the capabilities of their products. The video portion of a commercial for a toy airplane turret gun, for example, employed actual jet-plane footage, while the audio portion of a spot for a tabletop baseball game included crowd noises, stadium sound effects, and commentary by a professional play-by-play announcer, none of which came with the game. Those in the toy business blamed intense competition for tempting them to commit their advertising sins, as marketers battled to sell products to the millions of baby boomers in the prime of their toy consumption. Ironically, it was television that had created the higher level of competition, as the toy industry grew from a $1.6 billion business in 1959 to a $2 billion one in 1961, largely as a result of heavy television spending. Television was even taking much of the seasonality out of the industry, leveling out the huge holiday sales peak via relatively even advertising support throughout the year. It was clear that toy advertising had reached a fever pitch, fueled by the demographic pig-in-a-python combined with the war for sales, market share, and profits.[16]

Also benefiting from such levels of toy advertising, big retailers had come to expect that toy manufacturers would maintain constant and heavy television advertising throughout the year. Montgomery Ward, for example, looked first at marketers' media schedules when deciding if it should take on a new product. John Snow, toy division manager of the retailer, demanded that manufacturers' television support be nothing less than "saturation, on the screen every day." Trade ads directed to retailers focused on the advertising support toys were getting on television in 1961. "Get ready for action," one such ad read, "when kids coast to coast see the sensational Sok-Ker Pitch Back in action on TV!" Some marketers, swayed by this kind of competitive pressure, adopted a do-or-die attitude toward advertising on television, even if commercials occasionally bordered on deception. Mel Helitzer, advertising director for Ideal Toy, believed that criticism of such commercials would cease because children became "indoctrinated by effective advertising" and were "a strong, demanding voice in household marketing." Bold and shocking comments such as these reflect the Wild West nature of the toy business in the postwar era, revealing television advertising's role and complicity in the process.[17]

More than just investing in higher levels of television advertising, however, the toy industry was using the medium to license and cross-promote other forms of entertainment. Walt Disney toys were promoted in television commercials for the new Disney film *Babes in Toyland,* for example, seeding Disneymania among mini-baby boomers. Going one step further, the maker of Tinkertoys was developing its own network program, *Tinker's on TV,* featuring, in the company's words, "the country's best known, best loved kid star!" The crossing of toy marketing with entertainment was a powerful blend of consumer and popular culture, creating synergies that multiplied the effects of advertising toward children. This kind of multidimensional, cross-pollinating strategy, originally found in radio and the comics, would become the standard formula for marketing to children, an almost irresistible force directed to the most vulnerable group of consumers.[18]

Visual Poetry

Just as toys benefited a great deal because of television's small screen, products consumers would otherwise give little thought to gained most from being advertised on television. It was difficult for print media to create much consumer excitement about scouring pads, for example, but television was remarkably capable of achieving such a feat. Television advertising's power, Fairfax Cone brilliantly recognized, was its ability to "win an argument [viewers] didn't know they had the slightest interest in," a perspective not unlike that of critics who claim that advertising creates needs only to satisfy them. Indeed, others outside the industry had a significantly more critical view of television advertising's particularly intrusive character. *Newsweek* believed that viewers had little interest in engaging in the sort of constructed argument Cone had faith in. "The television commercial is the most scorned and ridiculed of all American institutions, not excluding the outdoor privy," the magazine boldly stated. "More energy is expended each week to avoid TV commercials than is spent each year to harvest rhubarb." Arnold Toynbee, the famed British historian, went even further. "The destiny of our Western civilization turns on the issue of our struggle with all that Madison Avenue stands for more than it turns on the issue of our struggle with Communism," Toynbee warned in 1961.[19]

Despite such criticism, the advertising industry itself rejoiced in its success. In May 1961, the second American TV Commercials Festival was held at the Hotel Roosevelt in New York, bigger and better than the first. *Time* magazine's reporter had major qualms about attending the festival, writing that "at first thought, and at second thought too, a festival of TV commercials is as appealing as a festival of anthrax germs." (*The New Yorker* also sent a representative to the festival, who was nearly as leery about what would transpire. This reporter likened the event to something out of Sartre, a "Television Nightmare—being trapped in a room with a set on which the programs consist solely of commercials, with the volume kept, immovably, all the way up.") Upon watching the hundred best commercials of the past year, as determined by the festival's jury, however, the *Time* reporter's doubts quickly faded. "What was remarkable about the parade of commercials," the journalist wrote, "was that they had been made with so much more imagination, humor, photographic skill and musical talent than the programs they were designed to interrupt." At times, the reporter got positively gooey about the artistry of the spots, describing the cinematography of a Prell shampoo commercial to "visual poetry." After determining that a commercial for Metrecal, a diet aid, captured the "pathos of Willy Loman," the writer concluded that the best commercials were "pound for pound, a great deal better than *Gunsmoke.*" The big winner of the award show was BankAmericard, with its "Conductor" spot created by Johnson & Lewis. In the animated commercial, a conductor led an orchestra as words appeared over his head, declaring that BankAmericard was the credit card for all types of purchases.[20]

The use of animation to promote such a "serious" product as a credit card was another indicator that television commercials were on the cusp of a new era. The creative renaissance in television advertising had begun, ironically, just as governmental agencies were calling for more "truth" and literal representation. Advertisers were finding ways to reduce the puffery in their commercials while at the same time expanding the boundaries of creativity and imagination. In the 1961 "Driver's Seat," for example, Norman, Craig & Kummel broke all rules of reality (and gravity) for its client, Hertz. A couple was shown vacationing in New Orleans as an announcer told viewers that a rental car from Hertz was a great way to have fun on one's next vacation. As a chorus sang "Let Hertz put you in the driver's seat," the couple flew through the air and landed in the front seat of a moving car. As in subsequent spots of the campaign, the flying actors were actually in a Hollywood studio, yanked out of a car by thin wires. The film was then run backward and superimposed on another film of highway traffic, high-tech special effects in these cut-and-paste editing days.[21]

The new generation of television commercials had much to do with the new wave of comedy sweeping the entertainment business. Stand-up comedy of the early 1960s was a world away from the 1950s slapstick style of television (think Lucy and Ethel on the assembly line of chocolates), often employing a more subtle, sophisticated approach and rooted in social or political commentary. With few topics sacred to comics like Nichols and May, Mort Sahl, and, of course, Lenny Bruce, American humor was becoming much more witty, satirical, and ironic, qualities which infiltrated advertising. Some major voices in advertising, however, most notably David Ogilvy, subscribed to no form of humor when it came to selling products. *Television Magazine* agreed in a February 1961 article: "A too-funny commercial runs the risk of obliterating the sell with its hilarity."[22]

Despite those who pooh-poohed humor, television advertising was getting distinctly funnier and more irreverent, due to new breed agencies like Doyle Dane Bernbach, which put creativity first. (The agency further distanced itself from most others by refusing to submit its ads to quantitative research before they ran, anathema to subscribers to the test-anything-and-everything school of advertising.) In one of a long series of commercials starring Jack Gilford (a former blacklisted leftist, rather ironically), DDB used humor in a way unheard of in the 1950s. In "Train," a 1962 spot created for Borden's Cracker Jack, Gilford was shown walking through the corridor of a sleeping car. After seeing a box of Cracker Jack passed repeatedly between two berths, Gilford grabbed the box, ate some of the snack, and then continued the passing process. Gilford's ploy was finally discovered by the owners of the box at the end of the spot. That same year, Doyle Dane Bernbach used a much less subtle form of humor to advertise another snack food, Frito-Lay's Laura Scudders potato chips. In the Clio Classic Hall of Fame spot "Old Lady in Rocker," an elderly woman was shown sitting in a rocking chair in a Victorian parlor. The announcer told viewers that Laura Scudder created her own potato chips after being unsatisfied with other brands. After he mentioned that Laura Scudder's chips were "extraordinarily crunchy," the Whistler's mother look-alike bit into a chip, producing an effect of seismic proportions as the entire parlor quakes. Each of these commercials would be considered funny by today's standards, forty years after they were conceived.[23]

The most irreverent comedian creating television commercials in the early 1960s was Stan Freberg. Freberg was hired by Chun King and its agency BBDO to get Americans to think more about and buy more chow mein, given the charge to use his offbeat, iconoclastic view of the world to plant the Chinese dish in America's gastronomic consciousness. In one 1961 spot created by Freberg, a couple was shown eating Chun King chow mein from the can rather than popcorn in a crowded movie theater. In another, a man discussed Chinese food in an elevator, not noticing that all the other passengers were of Chinese heritage. Chun King's commercials broke a number of advertising rules, including the first one, to never be "negative." In its effort to get canned chow mein into more households, the company told viewers that "95 per cent of the people in the U.S.A. are *not* buying Chun King chow mein." (The claim was not actually true; more than half of American households purchased chow mein, the bulk of it Chun King.) In one animated spot, the company broke another major rule of advertising when it never mentioned the brand—the product's name appeared only visually in a few different scenes. Freberg's commercials were credited with increasing Chun King sales by 30 percent, but the comedian was willing to go beyond the call of duty to move even more product. As his television spots drove up consumer awareness of Chun King chow mein, Freberg helped merchandise the brand by personally calling food brokers and retailers and asking for greater distribution and shelf space.[24]

On an (egg)roll, Chun King further raised its television advertising profile by producing its first fully sponsored show, "The Chun King Chow Mein Hour Starring Stan Freberg." For the special, aired on February 4, 1962 (the eve of the Chinese New Year 4600), Freberg asked Saul Bass, the renowned theatrical and industrial designer, to create the sets. Chun King used the special to kick off another venture, a planned worldwide chain of Chinese food drive-in restaurants called Riksha Inn. The first such store opened in February ten miles outside of Orlando, Florida, its menu consisting entirely of the Chun King line of heat-and-eat Oriental foods. Although grocery sales of the products continued to grow, Chun King was biting off, in retrospect, more water chestnuts than it could chew with its restaurant concept. With Freberg, however, Chun King continued to push the television advertising envelope until a network and another sponsor felt they had gone a bit too far. In the spring of 1962, Freberg outdid himself by creating commercials for Chun King that satirized those of other advertisers and the industry's self-importance. One spot made the outrageous claim that "nine out of ten doctors recommend Chun King chow mein," a twist on Bufferin's main copy point, while another asked, "Does she, or doesn't she, use Chun King chow mein?" a reworking of Clairol's famous, risqué advertising question. A third spot suggested that Chun King provided "FAST FAST FAST relief," a reference to Anacin's well-known claim. While ABC's West Coast office approved the spots for airing, the network's East Coast office turned them down, under pressure from the sponsors whose valuable equities Freberg was trading upon. Freberg responded that by tinkering with the television commercial canon, he was performing a public service. "My commercials give the viewer the chance to live vicariously," he stated. The viewer "always wanted to answer back to those unctuous announcers. In a way, I answer back for him." By assuming the role of an outsider, Freberg was a great fit for the Chun King brand, which was itself a relative underdog in the world of packaged goods dominated by huge corporations (analogous to the respective roles of DDB and Volkswagen in their own industries). Undaunted, Freberg continued to appropriate icons of popular and consumer culture and use them as Chun King fodder. By fall 1962, Freberg had turned his attention to jingles, more specifically yodels by the "Chun Kingston Trio."[25]

The increasing wackiness of television opened up a window of opportunity for the return of television advertising's beloved brothers, Bert and Harry Piel. From 1955 to 1960, Young & Rubicam's campaign for Piel's beer (then the fourth best-selling beer in New York City) was regarded as among the wittiest and most entertaining. The animated commercials with the voices of Ray Goulding and Bob Elliott took viewers to a strange land which often had little to do with beer. In 1960, however, Piel's dropped the campaign because its popularity simply did not translate into beer sales. "A thousand people would talk about Piel's because of Bert and Harry," said advertising director Stephen J. Schmidt, "but only fifty would buy the beer." (Forty years later, the Taco Bell chihuahua would be retired for the same reason.) After Bert and Harry disappeared, however, sales fell even further, causing the company and Young & Rubicam to bring them back from the advertising dead. As a teaser for the new campaign, the agency created a "people's choice" movement, the "Citizens Committee to Bring Back Bert and Harry Piel." One-and-a-half million New Yorkers voted to resurrect Bert and Harry, an outpouring of support bestowing nearly iconic status to the fictional characters.[26]

The seemingly exponential leap in television advertising creativity was also due to advancements in the production side of the business. By the summer of 1962, there were more than 450 production companies making commercials, taking in a total of $75 million a year. Eighty percent of all commercials were shot in New York, with West Coast firms specializing in animation. The production of a commercial was much like that of a feature film, with the same type of personnel required, including grips, propmasters, electricians, painters, costumers, set designers, film technicians, and sound technicians. With this many specialists involved, the effort was, as someone termed it, "an epic in labor relations." In the preproduction stage, agencies had to deal with the Screen Actors Guild, the Screen Directors Guild, the Screen Extras Guild, and, possibly, the Screen Writers Guild. During the shooting of a spot, technicians from as many as thirteen locals of IATSE, the film union alliance, could be present. An agency account executive touching anything on the set risked the wrath of union representatives, an even scarier proposition than anything clients could dish out. (Even burly Teamsters, however, could not prevent Joyce Hall, chair of Hallmark Cards, from occasionally rearranging his cards to prevent dreaded "corner clipping" during the shooting of his commercials.)[27]

Sing Along with Mitch

Better production values had much to do with a heavier emphasis on and smarter use of music. By 1962, the broadcast commercial music industry had grown to be an $18 million business. In 1957, just 5 percent of all musical television commercials used original music; five years later, almost all did. Over this same stretch of time the total number of commercials that used any music multiplied about five times. The rise in musical commercials was due to the greater effort by advertisers to capture the attention of viewers, an increasingly precious commodity. Research showed that music, either as a jingle or under the voice-over, boosted commercial recall and helped viewers remember the brand being advertised. According to Mitchell Leigh, president of Music Makers, a producer of commercial music, "Music gives a product emotional memorability. It also helps give an image of a company." Music directors at large agencies kept their Roledexes filled with the names of some fifty musical producers, each one known for a particular sound or style. For U.S. Steel, for example, Leigh wanted a commercial with something he referred to as "big" music. "It says, 'Sure we're big, and fat, and rich, but we love you,'" he explained.[28]

The rising popularity of rock'n'roll also had a significant impact on the role of music in television advertising. Critics of rock'n'roll believed the exodus of leading songwriters from traditional musical genres and Broadway had made singing commercials superior to popular music. In addition to music publishers pushing their existing catalogs to Madison Avenue for licensing royalties, many notable songwriters looked to advertising for work as rock'n'roll squeezed other kinds of music to the margins. Richard Adler, who had previously written music for such Broadway shows as *Pajama Game,* was now writing tunes for Newport and Kent commercials. "They kept asking me," Adler explained, "and I finally decided 'Why the hell not?' Rock'n'roll was eating up all the air time anyway, and I was offered a good piece of money." Even the likes of Cole Porter and Leonard Bernstein partnered with advertisers, the former licensing his song "It's Delovely" for a DeSoto commercial, the latter composing a score for a deodorant spot. In addition to Adler, Porter, Bernstein, and Frank Loesser (who after writing the music for *Guys and Dolls* was now composing ditties for Piel's beer), Harold Rome (*Destry*

Rides Again) and Charles Strouse and Lee Adams (*Bye Bye Birdie*) entered the advertising game. Heightening the temptation to try one's hand at commercial work was the industry policy of not revealing authorship until a song had been sold. While famous songwriters were not above composing songs for commercials, word getting out that their work fell short of advertising standards was simply unacceptable.[29]

Notable newcomers to the world of commercial jingles took the work seriously, approaching television advertising as a legitimate artistic genre. Adler and some others who moved between Broadway and Madison Avenue preferred the term "advertising musical" over "jingle," as the former elevated the process to an art form. "I look forward with enthusiasm to writing more compositions for the Madison Avenue literature," Adler said in April 1962, only partly tongue-in-cheek. Adler recognized a distinction between art and advertising when it came to some of his songs, however. Lucky Strike had once offered Adler a large sum of money to use his song, "Everybody Loves a Lover," which the cigarette company wanted to convert into "Everybody Loves a Lucky." The songwriter turned down the offer, saying, "I didn't write the song for that purpose." As a composer of "advertising musicals," Adler commanded a unusual degree of respect among radio people, with some disk jockeys crediting him after a commercial for which he wrote the music was played on the air. Joe Stone, a vice president at McCann-Erickson in 1961, credited Mitch Miller with making it acceptable for people of Adler's stature to do commercial work. Stone first started working with Miller in 1955, three years before the music producer hit the big time with his "Sing Along with Mitch" record album. As Miller (who disliked rock'n'roll) continued his commercial work, other music performers, writers, and producers became convinced that advertising could help advance their own careers through greater exposure and cross-promotion opportunities. Miller himself brought in Rosemary Clooney and Frankie Laine to sing jingles for Ford.[30]

Although some believed that commercial music would eventually "cross over" and become part of the popular music canon, most of those involved in its production thought otherwise. Stuart Ostrow, vice president of Loesser's Frank Music Corporation, predicted that television advertising songs would not "become part of the literature," while Harold Rome was even more dubious. Rome, who had written commercial music for Sanka, admitted that "I can't get any emotion into Sanka coffee." (Perhaps because it was de-caf.) Ostrow and Rome were being proved wrong, however, by instances of commercial music creeping into the orbit of everyday life. Lester Lanin, a bandleader popular within society circles, noted the increasing number of requests by teenagers at debutante parties for the Mr. Clean song and for the Newport cigarette "cha cha cha" jingle. Recognizing an opportunity, Lanin revealed the title of his next record album — *Lester Lanin on Madison Avenue* — a compilation of television jingles without the words.[31]

Other entrepreneurs had interesting ideas regarding how to make advertising jingles a more ubiquitous presence, and make money doing so. In 1961, John Pearson, head of the Audio Ad Company, created a concept he termed "semi-subliminal advertising." Pearson's scheme was to integrate familiar commercial jingles into the musical programs used as "background" by stores and restaurants (best known then and now as the brand "Muzak"). When the jingles were played without their lyrics, Pearson hypothesized, shoppers and diners would recognize them at a subconscious level, and "mentally add the name of the company or product." Even without words, his theory went, the music would reinforce a company's commercials and brand equities. In fact, Pearson claimed, because they operated at the subconscious level, the lyricless jingle would be even more persuasive than the original. Pearson tested his "semi-subliminal" concept at a store in Beaumont, Texas, finding that the technique increased the sale of Wrigley gum by 250 percent. The Wrigley jingle was broadcast every fifteen minutes, played in a variety of genres including a waltz, samba, foxtrot, and march. Upon hearing the results, other advertisers, including Pepsi and Schlitz, became intrigued with the idea. Although the test was successful, Pearson knew that more research was required to accurately determine how frequently lyricless jingles should be played to produce the "highest recognition and lowest irritation." Another of his goals was to find an FM radio station which would broadcast music twenty-four hours a day, integrated of course with semi-subliminal commercials.[32]

Alongside music, voice-over talent had progressed significantly beyond television's early days of "radio-style" commercials. The best voice-over talent in the business in the early 1960s was Allen Swift, known in the trade as "the man of 1,000 voices." Swift was capable of creating or reproducing virtually any sound, accounting for his unsurpassed popularity among producers of television commercials. By 1962 Swift had recorded 10,000 commercials, been the spokesperson for more than 350 sponsors, and had used 100 different voices to plug 35 different brands of beer. His forte resided in the ability to reproduce animal sounds, alter voice quality, instantly change accent and dialect, and go from child to geezer without missing a beat. Instructed once to create the sound of a pencil for a commercial, Swift asked whether it was lead or mechanical, round or hexagonal, and if it had an eraser.[33]

The importance of vocal talent in television advertising was reflected in a landmark decision reached by the U.S. Circuit Court of Appeals in Boston in June 1962. Three years previously, actor/comedian (and ex-Cowardly Lion) Bert Lahr had sued the maker of Lestoil cleaner for invasion of privacy, defamation of character, and unfair competition. The suit revolved around a Lestoil commercial in which an animated duck said, "I never felt so emulsified in my life or so clean," in a voice remarkably similar to Lahr's. Lahr charged Lestoil with "misappropriation" of his "creative talent, voice, vocal sounds, and vocal comic delivery," and further accused the company of "trading upon his fame and renown." The suit was thrown out of a Boston district court but reversed by a higher court, the latter ruling that Lahr was entitled to have two of the three counts heard by a jury. What bothered Lahr most about the "Lahrceny" of his voice was that an established star's performing anonymous commercial voice-overs was considered the bottom of the Hollywood barrel. Lahr's personal and professional reputation was at stake, with his friends, according to the actor, asking, "What'sa matter, you need the money?" If Lahr won the suit, he planned next to take action against the Kellogg Company, sponsor of the cartoon show *Yogi Bear*. Lahr believed one of the main characters in the show, Snagglepuss, had also borrowed his distinctive voice. Lahr was hardly the first actor to seek damages for vocal plagiarism by animators. In the fall of 1961, for example, Red Skelton threatened to sue the creators of *The Bullwinkle Show*, whom he claimed had stolen the voice of his Clem Kadiddlehopper character for that of the irreverent moose.[34]

Volume Control

The heightened intensity surrounding ownership and legal entitlements in television advertising was directly related to increased concern over advertising clutter. As advertising on television approached the $2 billion mark in 1962, there was a growing belief that consumers were becoming desensitized to individual messages. Experts in such things estimated that the average American was exposed to some 1,600 promotional messages every day (now it's believed to be around 3,000), and that the cost of advertising in both actual terms and relative to sales had risen sharply due to television. In 1962, one study reported, the average marketer realized $70 in sales from each dollar invested in advertising, compared with $100 generated in 1947, adjusted for inflation. There was additional evidence of and rationale for the idea that viewers had gotten much better at screening out commercials. The Center for the Study of Audience Reactions, a market research firm, found that 20 percent of the average adult television audience had become "more or less impervious to the blandishments of television advertising." Ernest A. Jones, president of MacManus, John & Adams Agency in Detroit, concurred that viewers were developing self-defense mechanisms against television advertising. "The American consumer is undergoing a self-protective evolution," Jones believed, "developing a mental screen against all advertising." [35]

Part of the increase in advertising clutter was due to a rise in the non-entertainment announcements that were inserted between network shows. More program promotions and credits and public service announcements, according to John W. Burgard, vice president of advertising at Brown & Williamson Tobacco Company, were "detrimental to the sponsor and irritating to the viewer." Mr. Burgard was joined by other advertising executives in an attempt to persuade the networks to cut back on this material, less to ease viewer irritation than to make advertisers' own commercials stand out that much more. CBS was quite clear about the length of commercial time and the times in which programs could be interrupted, but less firm about the number and length of its own messages. Network policy clearly stated that commercials could not account for more than three minutes per half hour, that the main entertainment portion of program could not be interrupted more than twice, and that programs had to open and end with noncommercial elements. Advertisers believed that the networks should be as rigid regarding their own commercial messages. [36]

As the pressure to be heard above the commercial din grew, agencies and advertisers picked another fight with the networks. The dispute concerned "product protection," the time between commercials for competitive products. After Westinghouse Broadcasting, which now owned and operated television stations in five large cities, announced it was going to reduce the amount of product protection from fifteen to ten minutes, executives at Ted Bates rebelled. The agency declared it would move all of its commercials scheduled with Westinghouse to other stations unless the fifteen-minute product protection policy was restored. Benton & Bowles soon joined Bates in the protest, as did the industry trade group, the AAAA. The association claimed that with the shorter time between competitive commercials, "the value of television for advertisers would be vitiated," a function of "blurring and confusion." Advertisers apparently did not mind if viewers confused their commercials with entertainment, but had a major gripe if viewers confused commercials with other commercials. In August 1962, the two main protagonists in the product protection issue, Westinghouse and Ted Bates, reached a compromise. Broadcasters could run directly competitive commercials within a ten- to fifteen-minute period, but had to notify advertisers if such an event was likely to occur. Advertisers could then cancel the spot or request that it be moved to a noncompetitive time slot.[37]

To counter clutter, advertisers were looking for any and all ways to make commercials work harder. Some advertisers filled their spots with as much information or emotional energy as possible. *Time* magazine applied a culinary analogy to television advertising, observing that "commercials are stuffed with a vigor that would astonish even a sausage maker." Advertisers' fear that their commercials were not being heard by viewers pushed some to desperate measures. A manufacturer of sound-testing equipment decided to test the volume of commercials in the Boston area and found that many were louder than the programs during which they aired, proving what many believed. Two-thirds of the forty shows tested, in fact, aired commercials at a louder volume than the program material. Joy and Dynamo detergents were found to be 78 percent louder than the shows they ran on, while Zest soap, Ivory soap, and Anacin were recorded as 59 percent louder than their respective programs. Twenty percent of the commercials were broadcast at the same volume as the shows themselves, while 15 percent (including Goodrich Tire, Kraft, and Lestoil) were actually quieter.[38]

Looking for more innovative ways to make commercials stick in the viewer's mind than simply turning up their volume, many clients and agencies again turned to research. Of particular interest to advertisers was determining "scientifically" whether or not testimonials by celebrities were worth their usually sizable investment. Not atypically, two different studies revealed very different findings about the value of celebrity endorsements. Gallup & Robinson found that television advertising was far more memorable and persuasive when somehow linked to the star of the sponsored show. When the host participated in the commercial, or better yet, presented the entire commercial alone, levels of recall and comprehension jumped. The data, based on a sample of some 9,000 commercials, showed that when a star of a show did in fact take part in a pitch, viewers' responses were a whopping 48 percent higher than the average commercial's. The study thus showed that Arthur Godfrey's folksy appeals for Lipton tea, soup, and desserts, or Jack Benny's integrated commercials for cigarettes or insurance were as effective as long believed to be. From a marketing standpoint, this research indicated, the mix-

ing of entertainment and selling articulated in a host's personal product endorsement was a perfect hybrid of popular and consumer culture, a strategic
application of a celebrity's inherent trustworthiness and believability.[39]

Findings from a study done by Schwerin Research, however, offered a
different take on the use of celebrities in advertising. Schwerin found that
there were only half as many television spokespeople in 1960 as in 1958, and
that commercials using spokespeople were less effective than they once had
been. In reporting Schwerin's findings, *Broadcasting* magazine suggested
that there had been a "vitiation of the authority, reliability, and believability
these representatives were hired to engender," probably because they were
simply overused in the late 1950s. The trend toward "participation spots"
versus program sponsorship also contributed to the drop in celebrity testimonials, as did the greater use of animation and humor and pure "wearing-out"
or overexposure of some veteran stars. (As a sign of the times, Betty Furness
and Westinghouse finally parted ways after their eleven-year partnership.) It
was particularly ironic that just when celebrity testimonials were receding,
Rod Serling performed his first. Serling, who loudly protested sponsor interference in many of his scripts and shows, found himself in the uncomfortable
position of plugging Schlitz beer during the 1962 telecast of the Emmy awards.
Serling immediately regretted his prerecorded endorsement of the beer that
made Milwaukee famous, saying he "didn't realize how wrong it was until I
sat down in the Palladium among 3,000 of my peers, and saw myself 90 ft. tall
on that screen selling beer." Hal Humphrey believed that such stars' willingness to sell products on television was directly responsible for the general loss
of glamour in the entertainment business. "The star holds no special magic
. . . any longer," Humphrey declared in May 1962. "If our idols drink beer,"
he wrote, referring to Serling, "they're no better than we are." [40]

Brand Identification

The disparity between the two research studies on the power of celebrity testimonials could likely be explained by the relative fit between star and brand.
Overuse of testimonials had apparently diluted their strength as an advertising technique, but when celebrity and product meshed seamlessly, the technique was as strong as ever. Indeed, rather than hiring a star purely on the
basis of degree of fame, most companies were becoming more selective about
finding one who matched their own corporate identity. Perhaps the best coupling between client and television host in the early 1960s was that of Dutch
Masters cigars and Ernie Kovacs. Kovacs, himself an avid cigar smoker, was

one of the handful of more edgy comedians now working in television. Kovacs had hosted series for both NBC and CBS in the early 1950s, but his style and temperament seemed a better fit for television a decade later. Until January 13, 1962, when Kovacs was killed in a car accident, Dutch Masters cigars had enjoyed a successful, rather unusual relationship with the television star. The maker of Dutch Masters, the Consolidated Cigar Corporation, first hired Kovacs in the spring of 1959 for a panel show called *Take a Good Look*. Although not a ratings success, surveys indicated that the show and Kovacs were a good fit for the brand.[41]

Recognizing Kovacs's genius, the sponsor gave the host free rein in its commercials. Kovacs applied the same type of sketch comedy to the advertising as he did for the rest of the show, once developing a series of spots using pantomime. In one, a man took his seat in a concert hall and proceeded to light his cigar, a politically incorrect act even in those publicly smoky days. After others around him did not react, the camera panned to the orchestra, revealing that all the musicians were smoking cigars as well. After just one season, Consolidated Cigar found that its Dutch Masters brand had become strongly and positively identified with Kovacs. To further link star and product, the company put Kovacs's picture on the Dutch Masters package with the phrase, "Have one on me — Ernie Kovacs." Although the relationship between Kovacs and the network was a tenuous one, resulting in a demotion from his regular series to monthly specials, Consolidated Cigar remained a big fan. For the fall 1961 season, the company continued its association with Kovacs through sole sponsorship of these half-hour "Ernie Kovacs Specials," which ran until his untimely death.[42] *Printer's Ink* eulogized Kovacs, noting his unique contribution to television advertising:

Ernie's commercials . . . prove that the gap traditionally supposed to exist between the businessman and creative talent can be bridged. They prove that pioneering in TV sponsorship can pay off and that ratings aren't the final yardstick.[43]

Other sponsors were working overtime to find programs and spokespeople offering optimum "brand identification." Geritol and Sominex, understandably, sponsored *Art Linkletter's House Party*, a show reaching a predominantly older audience. Some advertisers had less luck in finding a perfect match between personality and product. To promote its 1961 Lark, Studebaker settled for Alan Young, star of the show *Mr. Ed*, which featured the eponymous talking horse. The car company was, however, also able to land Young's equine co-star, who horsily explained that the new Lark offered "big car comfort at compact prices." The makers of Winston cigarettes now sponsored *The Flintstones,* even having Fred and Wilma Flintstone and their animated neighbors, the Rubbles, light up during commercial breaks. Although it eventually became a show targeted to children, *The Flintstones* was originally presented as "the first animated cartoon series for adults," with its debut broadcast on September 30, 1960, indeed occurring during prime time. While this can explain the show's sponsorship by a tobacco company, one could still wonder about Winston's very existence in prehistoric times. Such an anachronism proved, perhaps, that the Flintstones truly were the modern Stone Age family.[44]

Other marketers seemed almost as anachronistic in their attempts to boost their brand image. American Motors Corporation (AMC), for example, tried to link its brand to old-fashioned patriotic values when it sponsored the special "Let Freedom Ring" on New Year's Eve 1961. During the special, actors Richard Boone, Howard Keel, and Dan O'Herlihy sang hymns from colonial and frontier days, backed up by the Mormon Tabernacle Choir. Portions of speeches made by Abraham Lincoln and Thomas Paine were recited, with a brief appearance by AMC chair (and soon to be Republican governor of Michigan) George Romney topping off the festivities. With its focus on the nation's past rather than its future, AMC and America seemed to be going in opposite directions. Two months earlier in its own salute to America, Westinghouse did indeed venture a stab at what the future might look like. The company sponsored a show called "The Sound of the Sixties," a special which predicted what music and comedy of the later 1960s might be like. A chorus sang "futuristic" commercial jingles for Winston and Chevrolet, and parodied commercials for Soviet propaganda by presenting them as they might appear on American television. (Westinghouse would likely have picked another theme if it actually knew what late 1960s America was going to be like.) Whether by focusing on America's past or future, nationalistic pride was clearly not the best choice for advertisers trying to rally consumers around its brands in the early 1960s.[45]

Still Ticking

Savvier marketers were finding more innovative and progressive ways to increase brand awareness in television's more expensive, more competitive advertising climate. One such way was the documentary film designed specifically for television, a technique that had been effectively used by advertisers in the past. Here companies produced a film showcasing some aspect of its activities, and television stations, hungry for material to air during non-sponsored hours, ran them at no cost. The films were, of course, peppered with subtle or not-so-subtle plugs for the company and its products or services. For just a few thousand dollars, then, a marketer could realize as much as $100,000 worth of media time and, moreover, deliver a promotional message to a consumer in a format not likely to be recognized as advertising.[46]

Wallace Laboratories, for example, produced a "documentary" about drug research that was integrated into many local stations' news programs. Only four seconds into the film, however, the company's name was mentioned, as was its new product, Capla, which "safely and effectively reduces high blood pressure." Other marketers, such as Goodyear Tire & Rubber, took a more soft-sell approach. The company produced a film about speed tests of custom cars on the Bonneville Salt Flats, without ever mentioning the Goodyear name. An inordinate amount of camera time, however, was spent focused on the cars' tires, which were clearly labeled Goodyear, as well as on the participants' shirts, also prominently bearing the company's brand. Other documentary films which could be seen on television in 1962 included "A Visit with Betty Crocker" (produced by General Mills), "Introduction to a Champion" (a thirteen-minute story about Delta Air Lines' new jets), and "The Romance of Cheese," produced by Kraft Foods. As more scrutiny continued to be directed to plugola, the practice of entertainers name dropping advertisers' brands, marketers increasingly looked to documentary films as an alternative means of entertainment-based, low-cost promotion. The documentary form of advertising had the effect of further colonizing television entertainment for commercial purposes, yet one more way the boundaries between content and commerce were intentionally corroded.[47]

The documentary format went beyond corporate films in television of the early 1960s, morphing into a *cinema verité* or realism-based commercial technique. During its 1961 sponsorship of *An Age of Kings*, Standard Oil of New Jersey ran brief commercials showing the uses of oil in everyday life. The following year, during its sponsorship of the *Festival of Performing Arts*, the company used a documentary style to show viewers some of its research and development activities. Timex, one of the originators of the realism school of television advertising, found new settings to demonstrate the durability of its watches. In "Still Ticking," Warwick & Legler sent John Cameron Swayze to Acapulco for the most torturous torture test yet. In the 1962 commercial, Swayze watched as Raul Garcia, a high diver, leapt into the ocean from the La Perla cliffs with a Timex watch attached to his wrist. Garcia survived the jump, as did the Timex. "Is it any wonder," Swayze asked viewers, "that more people buy Timex than any other watch in the world?" The commercial ran a full two minutes and twenty seconds, adding to the mini-documentary effect.[48]

Other agencies appropriated the documentary style and found new, creative ways to promote their clients' products on television. For its client Sunbeam, Foote, Cone & Belding created a commercial in which actual commuters were asked to use a Sunbeam electric razor to see if they could shave off more whiskers than they had earlier in the morning. The spot was shot in lower Manhattan, using the then popular "man-in-the-street" approach to convey a sense of pure truth and believability. For its client Liberty Mutual Insurance, BBDO produced a series of documentary-style commercials focusing on how to prevent industrial accidents. One spot, shot on location at the company's Rehabilitation Center in Boston, showed how Liberty Mutual helped rehabilitate injured hands. These types of commercials, many in the industry believed, were superior to the hard-sell approach of traditional commercials, capable of breaking through the barriers viewers had built up as a result of advertising clutter. Casting director Patricia Harris, however, was somewhat taken aback by the trend toward stark realism in television advertising. The demand for what she called "Ma Kettle" types had led to the unlikely situation where every character actor in Hollywood seemed to be finding work. Used to casting better-than-average looking people, Harris believed that the search for "real-life" types had gone too far. "It could begin to look like Halloween, if this keeps up," she mused. Hal Humphrey agreed, stating that "after a large dose of the scratch-and-grunt commercials so prevalent this year, most of us . . . must be ready to go back to the illusion that we are all handsome, young and already full of Anacin."[49]

Rooted in a gritty form of realism, the documentary style was obviously well suited for public service announcements ([PSAs] which, more often than not, seemed to run in the middle of the night when media time was cheapest and most likely to be unsold). For the Keep America Beautiful project, Dancer-Fitzgerald Sample used a documentary approach in a 1962 spot, "It Happens in the Best Places." In the commercial, "Susan Spotless" was shown criticizing her father for littering while on their trip to the Statue of Liberty. The announcer then explained that littering happens in the best of places and in the best of families. Viewers were then asked to "please, please don't be a litter bug, 'cause every litter bit hurts." Young & Rubicam also used the documentary style in a PSA produced that same year for the newly created Peace

Corps, with a voice-over contributed by none other than President Kennedy. Through the genre of realism, and specifically PSAs, the Great Society of the early 1960s was beginning to creep into the universe of commercial television, imprinting the American Dream with much more of a democratic spirit and a social conscience than seen before in the postwar era.[50]

In the Public's Interest

The trend toward greater realism spread into other avenues of commercial television as news and public affairs began to garner legitimate respect from advertisers in 1961 and 1962. News and other programs "in the public's interest" had throughout the history of the medium been television's ugly duckling, lacking the sexiness (and ratings) of entertainment shows. Despite intense efforts by the networks to push news and public service programming (partly to fulfill its official civic mission but mostly to make money), only about half of such shows found advertiser sponsorship through the 1950s. In 1961, however, the situation began to turn around, driven in large part by networks' price cutting and some creative packaging. According to the Television Bureau of Advertising, advertisers purchased $38 million in time on news shows in 1961, up 48 percent from 1960. They also bought $5 million worth of other special events in the public interest (ranging from the presidential inauguration to the Miss America pageant), almost twice that of 1960. The Metropolitan Life Insurance Company, for example, made its first venture into television, attracted by the chance to sponsor "extraordinary, fast-breaking news events" on CBS. Gulf Oil had a similar arrangement with NBC, sponsoring thirty-five such special announcements in 1961. Xerox Corporation became a first-time advertiser on television when it started sponsoring the public affairs program *CBS Reports* in November 1961. Xerox's agency, Papert, Koenig, Lois, one of the new generation of shops, considered documentary or public service programming to be an excellent opportunity to advertise its client's new photocopier. Wanting to show business people how easy the Xerox 914 duplicating machine was to operate, creative director George Lois had a monkey make copies in his 1962 spot, "Chimp." Although some executives' feathers were ruffled by such a portrayal of their profession, Corporate America had begun to recognize news-based programming as an excellent vehicle for business-to-business advertising.[51]

Even Martin Marietta Corporation, an aerospace company that sold no consumer products, decided to advertise during important news events by sponsoring a televised interview with the cosmonaut Gherman Titov and astronaut John Glenn in May 1962. Advertising sponsorships of the first space orbits were risky propositions, considering the lack of viewership history. Recognizing the opportunity to be part of a historic event, however, Colgate chose to sponsor the *CBS News Special Report* broadcast of Glenn's *Friendship 7* flight. Colgate even produced and ran a space-oriented commercial for the broadcast, "Space Man," with copy telling viewers that "more future spacemen and their families help stop bad breath, help fight decay by brushing after eating with Colgate Dental Creme." Being America's first orbital flight, the broadcast attracted a sizable audience, bringing down its cost per thousand viewers to only $1.50. The broadcast of the second such flight, however, with astronaut John Carpenter, received much less media attention, and could not attract any sponsors. True to form, the broadcast did not realize nearly the ratings of the first, making the event a poor buy in terms of television efficiency. More savvy executives had predicted the second orbit would bomb as an advertising vehicle, with one noting that "if Joshua made the sun stop twice, the audience would be smaller the second time." Rather than having no sponsors of the flight's coverage, NBC sold the media portion of the event to Gulf Oil but paid the half-million-dollar production costs itself. Picking up the production cost tab was the typical way networks sold off the distressed merchandise of unsponsored news events.[52]

The networks' concerted attempts to cut their losses on news and public affairs was a function of these shows' expanded coverage on television. From 1958 to 1962, television hours of news and public service programming increased over 60 percent, as networks fulfilled the mandate of their licenses and appeased the FCC by offering viewers an alternative to the "vast wasteland" of Westerns, sitcoms, and crime stories. During the FCC hearings, James C. Hagerty, vice president of ABC, admitted that news was a loss leader, that "entertainment, if you will, subsidizes the news." Advertisers had historically shied away from sponsoring news shows because of their notorious fear of controversy, and the belief that their brands would somehow be associated with the tragedies that were being reported. Further scaring away advertisers were lower ratings and an unfavorable cost per thousand compared to entertainment programs, although there were some notable exceptions. The cost per thousand of the Huntley-Brinkley news broadcast on NBC was $2.50 per household in 1962, an excellent buy (accounting for its heavy sponsorship). Howard K. Smith's news show on ABC cost $9.00 per household, in media terms a white elephant for the sponsor, Nationwide Insurance. The president of Nationwide, Murray D. Lincoln, however, had political connections with

Smith, making the sponsorship more a patronage than an objective business decision.[53]

The relationship between politics and sponsorship would soon become truly newsworthy, foreshadowed at a meeting of the Washington Roundtable in New York City in May 1962. The agenda of the speaker, Donald I. Rogers, financial editor of the *New York Herald Tribune,* was to urge businesspeople to avoid sponsoring shows with liberal hosts. One of Rogers's primary targets was Jack Paar, who had once criticized William F. Buckley, editor of the conservative *National Review.* Calling Paar "Fidel Castro's buddy," Rogers objected to the $25 million a year advertisers were spending on the show to reach its audience of 30 million viewers. Business was, as Rogers saw it, underwriting a liberal agenda by supporting Paar and other television personalities he considered to be leftist. On the news side, Rogers saw Chet Huntley and Howard K. Smith as direct political descendants of Edward R. Murrow, the latter, according to Rogers, not only liberal but an "advertisers' darling." Rogers saw many of the news and public affairs shows of the day as "antibusiness, antifree enterprise propaganda," an enemy which should be fought rather than supported by advertising. To make his point perfectly clear, Rogers made the rather startling claim that "American businessmen probably would have done less harm to the American institutions if they had paid all of these millions of dollars right into the Communist Party."[54]

Mr. Rogers must have had a premonition of sorts, as just six months after his speech, an alleged Communist sympathizer did indeed appear on a network show. During a broadcast of a show called "The Political Obituary of Richard M. Nixon" (remember this was 1962), Howard K. Smith ran a two-minute taped interview of Alger Hiss. Hiss had served prison time for perjury after denying Whittaker Chambers's allegation that he supplied Soviet agents with classified United States documents while Hiss was a State Department official in the 1930s. Chambers, an ex-Soviet agent himself, was now a virulent anti-Communist and editor of *Time* magazine's foreign affairs section. The network, local stations, the FCC, and the show's sponsor, Nationwide Insurance, all were deluged by phone calls, telegrams, and letters protesting Hiss's appearance on television. What made the situation particularly incendiary was that the show ran in place of "The American Fighting Man" (which was originally planned to air on Veterans Day). Millions of viewers thus expecting to enjoy a documentary which would have made John Wayne proud instead got the chance to see a liberal present an uncritical piece on an apparent Communist. In Cold War America, this did not make good television. Many viewers considered Smith's show to be "unpatriotic," while some stations with advance knowledge of the interview refused to run the show (in violation of FCC policy). The episode turned out to have a ripple effect through the advertising community. Schick Safety Razor attempted to cancel its advertising contract with ABC, with the company saying it did not want its products associated with a network that would broadcast such a program. Hardly coincidentally, the chair of Schick's parent company, Eversharp, was Patrick J. Frawley Jr., a principal figure in California's anti-Communist campaigns. Although politics and advertising were supposed to stay in opposite corners, commercial television was hosting a juicy ideological battle.[55]

The issue continued to domino, in fact, as another company soon joined Schick in protesting Hiss's appearance by attempting to cancel its contract with ABC. Kemper Insurance, sponsor of the *ABC News Report,* told ABC it no longer wanted to advertise on the show, but the network would not honor its request. As James S. Kemper, chair of the company, explained, "Our own people in the office do not feel it was cricket to advertise the Hiss performance at the conclusion of the Kemper Insurance show." As in Schick's case, however, there were more than business issues at work here, as political interests and affiliations provoked a sponsor to try to take back some of the control the networks now held. Mr. Kemper, in fact, happened to be the former national treasurer of the Republican Party. Nationwide Insurance, the sponsor of the show on which the Hiss interview ran, had no intentions of trying to escape from its contract with ABC, also due to personal politics. Murray D. Lincoln, president of the company, happened to also be president of the Cooperative League of the U.S.A., a political coalition with distinct leanings toward the left. Smith's own political agenda seemed clear enough as well, having recently spoken supportively at one of the Cooperative League meetings. With nothing less than First Amendment rights at stake, those in the media took sides. WMCA, a New York radio station, supported ABC's position, stating in an editorial that the network "has been the target of a punitive campaign unmatched since the McCarthy era." All things considered, Schick's and Kemper's attempt to not honor their advertising contracts because of network policy was a truly rare event in television history. Only an appearance by Fabian in an ABC broadcast of "Bus Stop" and, on another occasion, raising the issue of abortion on an episode of CBS's *The Defenders* got sponsors' hackles equivalently raised.[56]

Given the anti-Communist climate of the early 1960s, however, it should not have been too surprising that the Hiss issue touched such a collective nerve. Some critics, in fact, used the Cold War as the very lens through which to view television's woes. One writer compared television to "lethal dust from the sky," creating "polluted waters," something which "rejoices [America's] enemies." "Hand[ing] over the greatest educational mass medium of the day to the Bowel Pill Men," the critic believed, was analogous to "comic books in the library, bingo in the classrooms and beer cans behind the alter." Like juvenile delinquency—an obsession with postwar conservatives—advertisers were responsible for debasing the nation's standard of values, showing an "ultimate contempt for art" by the shows it produced and through its commercial interruptions of quality shows. (The critic had a valid point; on December 7, 1961, the twentieth anniversary of the bombing of Pearl Harbor, a news announcer on a local Boston television station said, "Channel 7 will remember Pearl Harbor—after this word from Downyflake.") After watching Jane Austen's "Persuasion" degraded by commercials, one writer concluded that "maybe the country is ripe for a 50 megaton bomb after all." Interestingly, some advertisers actually used the vernacular of an atomic apocalypse in their commercial campaigns. Mobil gas, for example, reworked the generic idea of octane into a proprietary ingredient called "Megatane," a reference to the megaton bomb.[57]

With political ideology and the Cold War bumping into sponsorship decisions, viewer attitudes, and the language of commercials, television advertising was, as usual, fully engaged in America's civic arena. What had clearly changed over the last couple of years, however, was that television advertising, like the nation as a whole, had begun to "think young." In addition, sponsorship of documentaries, news, and public affairs programming and advertising "realism" were efforts by Corporate America to surround itself with as much "truth" as possible. Although many of the problems inherent in commercial television—clutter, loudness, and misdeeds against children—remained, television advertising appeared to have had turned a corner in its evolution by addressing social and political themes of the New Frontier. More "quality" shows were also being staged, an attempt to revive the spirit of television's golden age of a decade past, and an entirely new style of advertising was gradually emerging, reflecting a growing sense of irreverence and iconoclasm across the cultural landscape. The nation was on the brink of major cultural change, but commercial television was still being looked to as the messenger of the American Dream.

Chapter Six

The Psychic Air We Breathe,
1963–1964

And now a word from Anacin.

Walter Cronkite in June 1963, immediately after a report on the Cuban missile crisis

As America entered the final years of the baby boom and what I believe to be the postwar era, television advertising was in the midst of a major transition. The single-sponsor system and live format of commercial television were all but extinct, replaced by the more efficient and formulaic prescription of Hollywood videotape and media time for hire. A different form of advertising was bubbling up, smarter, riskier, and more self-referential than anything before. Like the nation as a whole, television advertising was in the process of reinventing itself, shedding the skin of its past in order to cope with new opportunities and new challenges. Change was in the air, and television advertising was about to prove that it could adapt and even thrive in a different cultural climate. As the postwar era drew to a close, television advertising would evolve into a more mature, advanced organism, and equip itself with the tools necessary for a new age.

Freedom in a Free Land

What had not changed was the intimate relationship between commercial television and the American Dream. In fact, both television and television advertising appeared to be still growing as cultural forces. In March 1963, Dr. Gary Steiner, associate professor of psychology at the University of Chicago, published the results of a three-year study of television and its role in American society. Steiner's major conclusion was, simply, that being without television was "the new American tragedy." As evidence for this bold proposition, Steiner noted that one-fourth of those with broken television sets had their sets repaired in half a day, and close to half had them repaired in one full day. Norman Cash, head of the Television Bureau of Advertising, an industry trade group, also found significance in Americans' panic when their television sets went on the fritz. "The caveman's fear of his fire dying out was nothing compared to the crisis in the home today when the set breaks down," Cash wrote a year after Steiner published his findings.[1]

If, judging by speed of repair, television had for most become a vital part of daily existence in America by 1963, television commercials had become an integral part of national identity. "Mass consumer advertising makes up a very large part of the psychic air we breathe," announced *America* magazine in January 1963.[2] Psychologists, political scientists, and sociologists were increasingly recognizing the value of advertising as a window into American society, a key set of symbols by which to decode the national zeitgeist. Neil Hurley, a political scientist at New York University, observed that

in the postwar era, advertising has grown into such an instrument of social control (by conditioning people to new purchasing habits) that it provides the social scientist with a window from which to view the value system of contemporary America. . . . The TV commercial, as all mass consumer advertising, does more than mirror the country's values; it also molds them. The commercial is both an agent of change and an index of national values.[3]

A survey of current commercials, Hurley noted, suggested that the dominant national values being mirrored and molded were pleasure (via advertising for cigarettes, cigars, beer, chewing gum, and soft drinks), status (automobiles), "super-hygienic attractiveness" (soap, cosmetics, and toiletries), and security (motor oil and tires). Advertising to teenagers, Hurley concluded, reflected and promoted the values of athleticism, popularity, sexuality, and "datability." Should we wonder why the sexual revolution lay just around the cultural corner?[4]

Other observers of the scene, such as NBC personality Hugh Downs, looked to television advertising as an exercise in freedom and democracy. In August 1963, already an industry veteran, Downs told four hundred Alberto-Culver salesmen that television advertising might be propaganda, but it was a vital part of America's freedom. "Nothing can be a fairer or more moral or more a manifestation of freedom in a free land than exhorting people to purchase and try a product when they are free to purchase and try others," Downs told the audience at their annual sales meeting. Perhaps borrowing upon Vice President Nixon's comments to Premier Khrushchev in the famous 1959 "Kitchen Debate," Downs argued that the major flaw of communism was its "attitude toward buying and selling," while "the plurality of persuasions that make up diverse advertising propaganda" was a proud symbol of American democracy. Downs also told the shampoo salesmen that their cause was a noble one, claiming that consumers' ability to choose among many brands was an integral part of the American Dream. "Nothing Jefferson, or Tom Paine, or Patrick Henry ever dreamed of is freer," he preached.[5] Norman Cash also saw television advertising as essential to the freedom of the marketplace, good for the American economy and the nation's interests in general. "As long as television can be supported by advertising revenues," Cash argued,

commercial freedom must be exercised, or you automatically place a ceiling on the growth of the most valuable communications device modern man has known. This is not a time for any industry to think about setting limits on sales and profits. . . . Advertising gains reflect the nation's business health because advertising, sales and profits are inseparable companions.[6]

Downs and Cash had tied television advertising to the nation's fundamental values of pluralism and freedom, a metaphor and exercise of the founding principles of the American experiment.

Even government officials, not a particularly enthusiastic supporter of the televisual liberties taken by marketers, considered advertising to be an extension of American freedoms. U.S. Secretary of Commerce Luther H. Hodges was ideologically aligned with advertisers, stating that

America in the 1960s does not have to choose between schools and soap, between missiles and consumer products and services, between progress and freedom — we can have them all, and advertising can help us get them. . . . Consumer spending alone accounts for about two-thirds of our gross national product, and in this area the influence of advertising is direct and potent.[7]

As others had done since around the turn of the century, Hodges was tacking advertising onto the American jeremiad, part of our divinely inspired mission for individuals and the nation as a whole. In the New Frontier years, however, this sort of rhetoric held special power, as Americans looked to consumerism and its agents as one of the main avenues leading to the promised land of abundance and prosperity for all.

Pronouncing advertising as a particularly American idea was more than just Cold War rhetoric. The United States in 1963 accounted for 77 percent of the world's expenditures on television advertising, a figure that did not include spending by American advertisers in other countries. Almost twenty years after the rise of television advertising, the U.S. remained one of the few countries in which advertisers could select shows for commercial placement. Many countries, such as The Netherlands, had yet to even introduce commercial television, while other countries, such as Israel and the Union of South Africa, remained completely television free. Television advertising was still totally forbidden in France in 1960, while in Italy, commercials were allowed but were stacked into three designated time periods each day. Both British and German television allowed scattered commercials throughout the day but no program sponsorships. Where permitted, American advertisers exported commercials to foreign countries, translating their spots into other languages in order to both save money and maintain a consistent brand image. One production company, Round Hill International, in fact, specialized in translating commercials from English into foreign languages. The company, whose clients included General Motors, Seven-Up, and IBM, had 150 translators on call, charging $90 for a translation into a common language like French and $125 for a more unusual language such as Persian. Round Hill was also familiar with the linguistic do's and don'ts of particular cultures. For German commercials, for example, Round Hill recommended a Hanover accent, while avoiding at all costs a Castillian accent for any commercial to air in Latin America or a male voice in Thai or Tagalog. The translating and exporting of American television advertising around the world was helping to make real Henry Luce's vision of the "American century," defined by global economic and cultural dominance.[8]

Black and White

Despite the popular vision of television advertising as a fair reflection of national identity and a noble expression of American freedom, it was clearly not color-blind. Throughout its almost twenty-year history, television as a whole had essentially ignored African Americans, allowing them precious few opportunities to be seen and heard. Although the Supreme Court had ruled a decade earlier that "separate but equal" status for blacks was illegal, television executives had apparently not heard the news. With the exception of a few isolated examples—Amos'n'Andy, Nat King Cole's short-lived show, the role of Rochester on Jack Benny's show, and guest appearances by Sidney Poitier, Ossie Davis, and Marian Anderson—blacks were almost nowhere to be found. The Jim Crow nature of television contrasted with other arenas of popular culture—particularly sports and music—where blacks had a significant presence. Baseball, for example, had witnessed a gradual parade of blacks into the major leagues after Jackie Robinson's breakthrough in 1947, while the pop charts had been filled with African Americans ever since Chuck

Berry's big success in 1955. As African Americans' profile in popular culture grew even more in the early 1960s, their absence in consumer culture was that much more apparent. This was about to change.[9]

As the civil rights movement escalated in the summer of 1963 with the March on Washington, the New York City chapter of the Congress of Racial Equality (CORE) led a campaign to get more African Americans cast in television commercials. Working with the local chapter of the NAACP, the Urban League, and other groups, CORE sought a "better general representation" of American life in advertising. The discrimination that existed in television advertising was "bad for America," CORE announced, and should end, lest the organization lead a boycott against offending advertisers. Although CORE's goal was to have more blacks on television shows as well, the organization focused first on commercials, as "the sponsor has full control here." CORE wisely understood that it was advertisers that brought television to viewers, and thus had the most to lose (and gain) when it came to economic pressure and consumer dissatisfaction. Lever Brothers was the first advertiser CORE approached, and the company quickly responded by producing six "bi-racial" commercials. The first integrated commercial on network television was for Lever's brand Wisk, airing on *Password* on August 14, 1963 (exactly two weeks before the Washington march). "We informed our agencies of our desire to take affirmative action because of our conviction that a broader cross-sectional representation of Americans in advertising today is good business," a Lever spokesperson claimed. One of the first businesses to advertise on television, Lever had suddenly decided, after two decades, that "affirmative action" was good business. Immediately after its success with Lever, CORE approached Colgate-Palmolive and then Procter and Gamble, each of whom also responded positively to the organization's demands. Within six months, the CORE committee reached agreements with thirteen major television advertisers, and had begun negotiations with thirty-six others to provide for African Americans to be featured in commercials and on sponsored programs. Advertisers who planned to cast African Americans in commercials included Nabisco, Gillette, Kellogg, Beech-Nut Life Savers, Schlitz, Campbell Soup, Bristol-Myers, Falstaff Brewing, and Brown & Williamson.[10]

Before beginning its successful campaign, CORE had done its homework. To raise public awareness of the dearth of blacks on television, CORE installed a set on the sidewalk in front of the Theresa Hotel in Harlem and offered passersby a silver dollar for every African American who appeared on the screen. The publicity stunt, of course, cost the organization very little money. Clarence Funnye, director of programs and community organization for New York's CORE, explained that the group's goal was simply to have television advertising accurately reflect what America looked like. "Wouldn't it be nice if now and then on television a little Negro girl came running in shouting, 'Look, Ma, no cavities,'" Funnye asked, referring to the popular line in Crest toothpaste commercials.[11] NAACP Labor Secretary Herbert Hill joined Funnye in noting the absence of blacks in television advertising. On an NBC special called "The American Revolution of '63," which aired in September, Hill stated that

Negroes in America use detergents and they eat meat and they drive automobiles, and they buy all the products of every sponsor on radio and television, and yet I have never seen a Negro used on a commercial in a major television program, nor have I ever heard of a Negro used in a major promotion on radio.[12]

By focusing on the racial dynamics of television advertising, CORE and its colleagues were fighting segregation in one of America's largest and most important public arenas. This battle of the civil rights movement has not received the attention and respect it deserves, as significant perhaps as the parallel attempts to defeat segregation in housing, education, and public transportation. As a window of society which reached millions of Americans everyday, shaping cultural attitudes and opinions including those of race, television advertising can be considered one of the front lines in blacks' struggle for equal rights. Regrettably, this same struggle exists today via a "race gap" in network television, with broadcasters still reluctant to provide African Americans with an equitable presence on their shows.

In addition to leaders in the African American community, some in academic circles were increasingly recognizing the contradictions between television advertising life and real life, that inequalities based on the social divisions of race, gender, and class were embedded in the medium. The issue became the focus of the 1963 International Conference on General Semantics, held at New York University just as CORE led its summer campaign. In the opening address of the conference, S. I. Hayakawa, professor of English at San Francisco College, argued that American advertising was democratic in theory but not in practice. Although commercials implied that the marketplace was color-blind, Hayakawa posited, "the culture is not willing to live up to its advertising." Hayakawa pointed to commercials for amusement parks that did not mention the fact that African Americans would not be allowed admission and those for new homes that were in red-lined neighborhoods. Even commercials for products as democratic as soda pop, Hayakawa told the audience, did not mention "that if you are Negro you will have to drink it standing on the sidewalk outside the cafe." The freedoms of the American marketplace, so eloquently captured by important people within the television and advertising industries, apparently did not apply to blacks. Seeing an opportunity for positive social change, however, Hayakawa proposed that as a "revolutionary communications instrument," television in general could help bring about racial equality, and he called for a closing of the gap between the medium's rhetoric and America's undeniable prejudices. As a Japanese American (and fierce critic of the misrepresentations and false promises within popular culture), Hayakawa was pointing out the inconsistencies between America's democratic principles and its real practices in consumer culture.[13]

CORE's concerted effort to desegregate the airwaves and the public discussion of the issue spurred advertisers who were not on the organization's target list to voluntarily include African Americans in their commercials (precisely as CORE intended). American Motors, for example, promptly ran a commercial on *The Danny Kaye Show* featuring an integrated group of assembly line workers praising the craftsmanship going into the new Ramblers. The integration of television advertising obviously had a positive effect on the careers of African American actors and singers. Laura Greene, a Cleveland-based vocalist who sang jingles when not working the supper club circuit, initially faced discrimination in commercial work, as when a Florida power company pulled its business from the producer of its commercials upon learning that an African American was the singer. As blacks gradually became assimilated into television advertising, however, the company came full circle by requesting that Greene record most of its commercials.[14]

One year after CORE's campaign and Hayakawa's address, the American television commercial landscape was relatively more racially diverse. Ajax commercials featured a new hero, "Wax-'em Jackson," an African American professional flooring expert. Procter and Gamble, which only reluctantly integrated a commercial for Tide, was pleased to find "no adverse reaction from white viewers and an upbeat in good will from Negroes." Commercials for Vitalis, Gillette, and Desenex all featured African American athletes, and white and black children played happily together in commercials for Handi-Wrap. From a purely economic standpoint, the inclusion of African Americans in television commercials was, of course, long overdue. According to research published in *Sponsor,* a leading trade journal for the television industry, 90 percent of black households owned at least one television set (preferred brand, Admiral), and blacks watched more television than whites on a per capita basis. *Sponsor*'s research also showed that in addition to representing a $25 billion market, African Americans spent more of their disposable income than whites. According to the journal, blacks were also more status conscious, more brand loyal, more likely to buy on impulse, and less likely to bargain than whites. Despite these purported compelling factors, Corporate America was still not yet prepared to extend to African Americans the full privileges of the consumer paradise of the American Dream. H. H. Webber, vice president of consumer relations for Lever Brothers, explained that his company's efforts were simply an attempt to keep up with the social revolution sweeping the country. "We are not trying to create change," Webber said in August 1964, "we're trying to reflect it." Webber's explanation was a classic dodge, refusing to confront the social consequences of advertising. Although Lever Brothers was considered a trailblazer in desegregating television commercials, portraying images of full equality was out of the question.[15] Even though mixed neighborhoods were actually not that uncommon, Webber explained that

We probably wouldn't show side-by-side housing with Negroes and whites, or social situations that arise from it. . . . Showing a Negro housewife chatting over the back fence about the family wash just isn't a natural situation in most of the country.[16]

Like many if not most white Americans, the Lever Brothers executive was not prepared to extend people of color full equality, a sentiment which ran counter to two major victories of 1964, the Freedom Summer voting rights drive and the Civil Rights Act. The American Dream had always been the exclusive domain of whites, and allowing blacks to share it demanded, at minimum, a reconsideration of its core values. The times they were a'changin', as Bob Dylan told us that year, but not overnight.

The Wonderful World of Color

The issue of color was playing out in an entirely different sense as the medium itself became more technologically colorful during these years. By the beginning of 1963, about thirty major advertisers were shooting their spots in color with some companies, such as AT&T, Chevrolet, Ford, Kodak, Kraft, and RCA. Innovators in color commercials believed the additional expense of 20–30 percent was worth reaching the mere 2 percent of viewers who had color sets at this time. Chevrolet and its agency Campbell-Ewald were early subscribers to color television, having already produced some two hundred color spots since 1957. Led by its agency, J. Walter Thompson, Ford had experimented with color commercials even earlier, in 1955, when the number of color set owners could hardly form a quorum. Aware of the business maxim that innovators of technology tend to retain industry leadership, the agency advised some of its other clients to use color, incorporating color commercials into the first *Kraft Theatre* way back in 1953 and shooting color footage for Kodak in 1955. Knowing firsthand of the liabilities of viewers seeing their delicious products in televisual black and white, Kraft wisely recognized the importance of color to its business. Kodak, an advertiser that could perhaps benefit more than any other by this technological advancement, quickly dropped sponsorship of the monochrome *The Ed Sullivan Show* on CBS to NBC's *Walt Disney's Wonderful World of Color* in 1963.[17]

Most packaged-good marketers were slow to adopt color, opting to wait until more households owned color sets, but NBC's embracing of the innovation sped up the process. NBC was broadcasting three-fourths of its evening network shows in color in January 1963, prompted if not dictated by the interests of its parent company, Radio Corporation of America (RCA). RCA sold more color television sets than any other manufacturer, and retained a virtual monopoly in the production of color picture tubes. Embarrassed to run black-and-white commercials during an NBC show broadcast in color, many advertisers rather suddenly found themselves having to convert to color. By April of that year, 60 percent of all commercials during NBC's prime time color shows were also in color, with the network already flaunting its pioneering in color television through its peacock symbol.[18]

For marketers in the early 1960s, the move to color commercials was probably the most exciting development in advertising since that of television itself. Research studies completed by Schwerin Research in 1956 and 1957, Burke Research in 1960, and the Advertising Research Bureau (ARB) in 1962 definitively proved that color commercials were more impactful and persuasive than those in black and white. Verbatim comments from viewers such as "Seeing the commercials in color was the same as shopping in a store," an observation made by a housewife during the 1960 study, were the stuff of marketers' dreams. Advertisers looked to color as an alternative, fully legitimate way to "turn up the volume" of their commercials. "It offers a means of overcoming the general clamor of advertising in the market place, without adding to the noise," said a Kodak spokesperson. Consumers considered a color television set to be a status symbol, similar to what a black-and-white set had been in the 1940s or what a high-definition set is today. For some unknown reason, Cincinnati had the highest per capita ownership of color televisions in 1963, with citizens proud to have their city nicknamed "Colortown, U.S.A." The industry, however, still had a ways to go in terms of understanding viewers' appreciation of color. Warning broadcasters about issues to consider in reproducing colors, *Sales Management* advised readers that "in the far West where suntans are a way of life, flesh tones on the warm side are most acceptable, while in the North a peaches-and-cream look is more popular."[19]

Not surprisingly, advertisers quickly fell in love with color television, shifting buying schedules around to shows that were broadcast in color. The idea of television as a surrogate salesperson was revived, although now its selling skills were new and improved. Color television, proponents argued, made it possible for the consumer at home to see the advertised product as he or she would at the time of purchase. Car companies especially appreciated the technology's ability to bring their products to life on the screen. As interest in international travel grew through the 1960s, automobile advertisers increasingly set their products in foreign locales to project romance and mystique. In a 1963 color spot, Chevrolet set its car in Venice, Italy, floating the automobile down one of the city's canals. As real-life Venetians registered true surprise at the sight, the announcer explained that even in Venice, "Chevrolet's jet smooth look of luxury attracts attention." Rather than use trick photography to achieve the effect, Campbell-Ewald placed a "neutral buoyancy device" under the car to allow the Chevy to actually "drive" down the canal. The commercial then moved from exotic Venice to a generic American suburb, as the announcer told viewers, "You'll be on solid ground with the truly beautiful value of Chevrolet."[20]

In another 1963 Chevrolet color spot produced by Campbell-Ewald, the automobile company stayed closer to home, setting its 1964 model on top of a bluff in the American west. The dramatic visuals were complemented by equally powerful symphonic music, as an announcer explained that Chevrolet "stands alone because it's in a class of its own." Chevrolet and Western iconography went together like the Lone Ranger and Tonto, as the car company added values of freedom, adventure, and escape to a brand (and a country) grounded in practicality and restraint. Chevrolet executives were particularly excited about their 1964 models, introducing the line in full color during a special edition of *Bonanza*. For the show, which aired September 29, 1963,

Chevrolet had Lorne Greene, the actor who played Pa Cartwright, announce that the sponsor would not interrupt the program for any commercials. What Pa did not mention was that the entire last five minutes of the hour would be devoted to a "grand opening" of the 1964 line of cars.[21]

The Only Way to Fly

The swing toward color commercials in 1963 was a major factor for another travel-based industry, the airlines, to become television advertisers. That year, in fact, a dozen different airlines made major commitments to television as an advertising medium, quadrupling their collective spending from $2.2 million in 1962 to $8.5 million. Airline marketing executives had until 1963 been reluctant to advertise on television for efficiency reasons, thinking that the price of a ticket was too high for the average American, especially when there was no "money-back guarantee." Many Americans were also still afraid of flying, reflected in part by the fact that 80 percent of long-distance travelers went by car. Further dampening airline executives' enthusiasm about television advertising was the strict fare regulation by the Civil Aeronautics Board, outlawing any price competition. With as many as eighteen airlines going to the same place in the same type of airplane at the same price, however, it was clear that image was going to separate the industry's winners from the losers. The "businessman" market was simply too small to keep the industry aloft, forcing airlines to exploit the burgeoning vacation market to fill empty seats. Spurred by color technology and the 1962–1963 New York City and Cleveland newspaper strike, KLM and other airlines jumped into television with both feet and were pleased with the results. Seymour J. Frolick, senior vice president and director of television and radio for Eastern Airlines' agency, Fletcher, Richards, Calkins & Holden, became convinced of television's ability to promote travel. "Television brings movement, life, activity and variety to the Florida vacation sell," he observed, aware that Florida in moving color was as real as it could technologically get. In contrast to the static quality of magazines, the monochrome of newspapers, or the uni-dimensionality of radio, color television was the ultimate medium for travel marketers.[22]

Other airline executives quickly became convinced that television advertising was the means of persuading those who had never flown to take to the air. Airlines quickly chose their respective strategic turfs. Eastern told viewers to "be the man with the Florida tan," resting any safety concerns by adding, "You don't fly—the experienced pilot flies—you just sit." Many advertisers went after the less pleasant aspects of automobile travel by emphasizing the time savings of flying, and reminded viewers that they could rent cars at their destination. (Hertz's own advertising featured its "fly-drive plan," a partnership program it held with more than twenty airlines.) Some airlines, most notably BOAC, focused on the sights and sounds of exotic locales such as the Caribbean. BOAC's hurdle was to lessen people's reluctance to travel to foreign countries, a function, BOAC reasoned, of many Americans' fear and embarrassment of not knowing other languages or customs. National Airlines adopted hedonism as its principal theme, casting attractive blond women as stewardesses in its spots, even putting some in bathing suits amid sand, surf, and palm trees. "Mix business with pleasure," the National stewardesses cooed, squashing any hint of indiscretion by telling men to "bring your wife." National also boasted of its "magic meal," which included gourmet foods like African lobster piquant, filet mignon, and French pastry. Western Airlines also focused on luxury, using an animated bird (dubbed "VIB" for Very Important Bird) which anticipated a party animal of a subsequent generation, Budweiser's Spud MacEnzie. In Western's spots, VIB held a glass of champagne in one claw and a long cigarette holder in the other, chirping that Western was "the *only* way to fly." VIB soon became a minor cultural hero; the fictitious bird not only received loads of fan mail but became the official mascot of a number of Air Force flying squadrons. Some television comedians were also attracted to the bird's *je ne sais quoi,* incorporating "the only way to fly" into their acts.[23]

Other airlines used equally effective if less daring advertising approaches. Northeast Airlines seduced Northerners by announcing the exact temperature in Miami in its commercials, cleverly recording all possibilities and inserting the correct one live at airtime. Through its agency, J. Walter Thompson, Pan American World Airways translated its conservative print campaign to television, claiming it was still "the world's most experienced airline." In its spots, Trans World Airlines showed slides of exotic locations as an off-camera announcer offered a running narrative, replicating what many vacationers would do when they returned from their trip of a lifetime. Delta Airlines shot all of its commercials in color, reasoning that owners of color sets were more likely to be able to afford an airline ticket. Northwest Orient also tried television advertising in 1963, but planned to continue using radio and newspapers as its primary media. In February 1964, a Northwest official predicted that it "doubt[ed] that it will ever use television as a heavy advertising medium," a short-lived prophecy. As had already occurred in most product and service categories, all major airlines would in fact adopt television advertising as their primary medium, a key factor in changing Americans' preferred mode of domestic long-distance travel.[24]

Slice-of-Life

The technological innovation of color dovetailed perfectly with the still popular trend of realism. Realism in television advertising was evidence of the broader shift away from focusing on the product (feature-based advertising) toward showing the user's enjoyment of the product (benefit-based advertising). By May 1963, realistic commercials had morphed into a subgenre consisting of "unrehearsed" interviews or interviews with "real-people," alternatively called true-to-life, slice-of-life, actuality, or believability. As Patricia Harris had noted a year earlier, attractiveness had once been the primary qualification for being cast in a commercial, but now, according to Maxine Anderson, another one of Hollywood's top independent casting agents, "the trend is to real people."[25] Advertisers' attempts to present their commercials as improvised documentaries was met with a level of skepticism among consumers, however. Schwerin Research found that most viewers disliked the approach, never believing for an instant that the documentaries were spontaneous. One housewife was particularly critical of a spot for "new improved" Tide detergent, in which a woman purportedly did not know she was part of a commercial:

There she sits in a kitchen with more lights than a night baseball park, telling a complete stranger how dirty her husband's T-shirts were before she used "New Improved Tide," and then when this stranger says, "You're on television," the gal looks stunned and replies, "Oh, I'll be darned!" If she were that dumb, she wouldn't know about "New Improved" anything. She'd still be beating her clothes on a rock.[26]

This same housewife greeted another "unrehearsed" detergent commercial, in which a woman claimed that her clothes smelled like the "outdoors" after using the advertised product, with equivalent doubt. "She never lived in my old neighborhood in the Bronx," the woman commented. "If her clothes smelled like that outdoors, she'd have to burn them." Some industry professionals agreed with viewers that realistic commercials were pretentious and obviously phony. Steve Frankfurt, vice president and executive director of art for Young & Rubicam, insisted that the very term "realistic commercials" was oxymoronic, and that "slice-of-life" was an illusory pursuit. "The average commercial aiming for credibility just isn't life — no matter how you slice it," he sneered at the 1964 AAAA annual meeting. Realistic commercials with music were an especially sore spot to Frankfurt. "If a man comes into your living room to sell you something," he concluded, "then you have a right to ask him how come he brought his orchestra."[27]

If female viewers detected an air of insincerity around realistic commercials, male viewers had major reservations about them for much different reasons. When asked, many men complained that the women being cast in commercials for household products looked, to put it bluntly, too much like their wives. Instead of gowns and high heels, actresses were wearing slacks, aprons, and flat shoes, taking much of the sex appeal out of television advertising. Knowing that women were more educated than they had been when television was a new medium, however, advertisers of household products were convinced that women—by far the primary shopper for a household—would see through a disingenuous presentation of glamour. Fortunately for men at least, categories steeped in fashion and style remained realism free. Most advertisers of cosmetics, shampoos, clothing, and cigarettes continued to cast women who looked much different from how most wives did while washing floors. "If women are to buy such personal products," one casting director stated, "they must feel they are going to make her beautiful like the woman in the commercial."[28]

As the realism trend continued, however, the careers of thousands of anonymous commercial actors received a shot in the arm. There were about six thousand "unknowns" working exclusively or almost exclusively in television commercials in August 1963, with the busiest 1 percent earning $100,000 or more. More than 70 percent of television commercials were still being made in New York, as producers tapped the wealth of Broadway and off-Broadway talent. Then as now, landing a role in a television commercial was a windfall for an out-of-work actor. In the 1950s, leaders of both the Screen Actors Guild (SAG) and the American Federation of Television and Radio Artists (AFTRA)—the two unions representing television advertising talent—had insisted that residuals be paid to members if commercials were repeated. Although not known at the time, this condition was proving to be one of the smartest decisions in advertising history, as the industry standard shifted to taped commercials from the live format. Interestingly, actors and announcers who made their principal living through commercial work looked down on celebrities who entered the field. Commercials were perfectly legitimate for anonymous specialists like them, they felt, but stars from Hollywood or professional sports stars were considered greedy carpetbaggers looking for an easy buck.[29]

Indeed, a contingent of well-established actors, previously reluctant to do commercials, were proving to be a thorn in the sides of less-than-famous ones. Attracted by the money and exposure, movie stars of yesteryear were now eager to appear in commercials, reflecting the ascendancy of television and decline of film. Edward G. Robinson, Barbara Stanwyck, and Claudette Colbert all promoted instant Maxwell House coffee, for example, seduced by the $50,000 for a single day's work. "I hesitated about accepting the offer at first," said Robinson. "I had never done anything that commercial . . . but I saw nothing wrong with it—as long as the ad was in good taste and I believed in the article that was being sold." Robinson appeared to be following in the footsteps of Henry Fonda, who as a television commercial virgin did a beer spot to pay his taxes. Some ex-stars decades past their heyday, such as Joe E. Brown and Buster Keaton, were doing their selling "unbilled," that is, without their names being mentioned. Others, eager for the publicity, not only wanted their names mentioned but also whatever movie or television show in which they were currently appearing. A parallel trend in the industry was the hiring of ex-radio announcers as commercial voice-over talent, perhaps the first instance in advertising history when recycling the past was considered progressive.[30]

Like the celebrity endorsement, however, the realism trend in television advertising became a victim of overuse and began to wear out its welcome in 1964. The casting of "plain-Jane" types had become so pervasive that individual advertisers no longer felt they were breaking through the clutter by running against the "glamour" stream. One of the subtexts of the realism approach was advertisers' belief that through their casting of less-than-gorgeous women, men would perceive their wives to be that much more beautiful, thereby creating a positive predisposition to the advertised brand. As this rather strange, psychology-derived theory was not proven valid in the marketplace, advertisers began to move back to the more traditional use of attractive male and female performers. Pepsodent toothpaste led the charge back to glamour, running a campaign featuring a number of women seemingly chosen from a Broadway chorus line. As in the use of once-famous radio announcers, the production values of television's golden age had returned as retro chic.[31]

The Muse of History

As more recognizable and good-looking actors returned to television screens, shorter length commercials also rapidly came into vogue. Thirty-second commercials were fast replacing sixty-second ones, with twenty-second and ten-second spots also gaining ground. Shorter spots were advertisers' response to stations' looser policies regarding "piggybacking," the running of consecutive commercials. Different research studies bore out advertisers' move to shorter spots, showing that more commercials, even if shorter, had in aggregate a bigger impact than fewer longer commercials. Schwerin found that a thirty-second spot garnered 93 percent of the recall of a sixty-second spot (at significantly less cost), while Gallup & Robinson found no difference at all in recall between shorter and longer commercials. Some advertisers applied some of their media time savings to production and research, with some deciding to shoot five or six commercials but air only the one or two that pretested best. Another trend in the industry, long overdue, was the greater use of television advertising by local retailers. Perhaps due to the popularization of color, retailers were investing more in television advertising in their local markets. As is the case today, however, production values of local retail television advertising were somewhat less sophisticated than those used in commercials for national marketers of consumer goods. One Jacksonville, Florida, car dealer, in fact, managed to produce a commercial for $21, less than a thousandth of what Chevrolet had forked out to create its "Chasing the Sun" spot four years earlier. Rather incredibly, the spot won first prize in a local award show, proving perhaps that big budgets and good advertising did not necessarily go hand in hand.[32]

A much larger awards show, the fourth annual American TV Commercials Festival, was held in May 1963, with the first "Clios" handed out. The name of the statuette was determined by the festival's founder and organizer, Wallace A. Ross, who explained,

We want[ed] to distinguish it from Oscar, Emmy, and Tony. We thought about Addie for advertising; Minnie for the minute commercial; Telly for television; Fanny because that's where most commercials fall; Selma for "sell more"; and Shirley because it's a nice name. Some of the judges wanted to name it after me — the Wally — but I declined. Finally, we called it the Clio. After Clio the Proclaimer, the muse of history.[33]

Ross's choice of names not only reflected his reasonable view that television advertising had assumed the role of public proclaimer for the twentieth century, but also his desire for the Clios to be a historical repository of the best commercials. In keeping with this grand vision, the fourth awards festival was bigger, more extravagant, and more profitable than the ones that preceded it. Admission to the show was $25 per person, with tables at the

Waldorf-Astoria Hotel priced at $250. Each of the 1,367 commercials entered in the competition carried a $20 fee. By day's end, the festival had grossed $85,000, a tidy sum for Ross. Prior to the one-day event, 135 judges from five cities had selected winners in fifty-six categories. Winning spots tended to be of the realism school, with live action favored over studio setups. Again, members of the press were surprised at the quality of the industry's cream of the crop. Alan Levy of *The Reporter* believed a commercial for Excedrin pain reliever featuring real people with real headaches had "a documentary quality reminiscent of Robert Flaherty," while a Cracker Jack spot offered "social comment, poignance, wit, and a message." Levy also found "epic grandeur" in a Hertz commercial, and thought that "the singing commercials that won Clios were more melodic than the songs in several of the better musicals on Broadway." As the festival grew in stature, winners of Clios were more apt to use the honor for self-promotion. The week after the fourth festival, in fact, BBDO took out a full-page ad in *The New York Times,* proclaiming it had received the most Clios. BBDO actually had a long history of patting itself on the back; in the 1920s the agency took out an ad in *Printer's Ink* after winning the Harvard advertising awards, more or less the Clios of their day.[34]

Interestingly, gender dynamics played a part in determining which commercials would receive the treasured Clio award. Seventeen of the 135 judges were women, who, according to Ross, tended to react distinctly differently to the commercials. Ross believed the women to be less reserved, not concerned with maintaining a front of objectivity:

There is no cautious restraint, lest emotion or non-objectivity be revealed, as in the case of men. The women will laugh and sigh and moan and cry and turn their nose up or their lips down as the case may be. The reactions are spontaneous, forthright and openly expressed and it is often necessary to remind them that the more conservative men judges prefer not to be influenced by the reactions of their compatriots.[35]

Ross also stated that women tended to rate commercials at either end of the one-to-ten scale, less likely to "play it safe with 'sevens,'" as the men often did. Gender differences also played out through the kind of product being advertised. Men scored a demonstration-type commercial for a Sarong girdle very high, for example, appreciative of being shown how such a device actually worked. Women, however, rejected the spot completely, believing such a demonstration to be unnecessary. Men also rated soap and deodorant featuring beautiful, scantily clad women quite high, while the women judges "turned away in disgust." When it came to issues of gender and sexuality, the professional judges were displaying much the same sort of attitudes and behavior expressed by lay viewers.[36]

Sexuality was a particularly sensitive issue for some viewers when it came to the casting of male models and actors in commercials. In a column in *Printer's Ink* called "A Woman's View," an anonymous woman criticized what she believed to be the large number of homosexuals in television advertising. "Last night's survey, from 8 P.M. until 1:15 A.M.," she noted, "netted six sure homosexual models . . . , eight probables and three maybes." How the woman determined who was homosexual was not mentioned, but the writer did make it clear she was disturbed "at the number of beautiful, terribly effeminate young men who dot our TV screens daily." She longed for more "real, honest-to-God, masculine heterosexual male[s]" in commercials, and wondered why marketers and their agencies consciously cast so many allegedly homosexual actors. Even the woman's ten-year-old child had developed the ability to spot homosexuals on television, she claimed. Upon seeing one of the "sure homosexuals," the child purportedly declared that the actor was "not a real man, like Daddy, he's just one of those pretend men." Amazingly, the anonymous writer maintained she had not "really formed any opinions about homosexuals one way or the other." The more homophobic were undoubtedly very pleased to see "Erik is Here," a 1964 spot produced by Grey Advertising for Lorillard. In the commercial, a handsome, "real" man was shown sailing a Viking type ship into New York harbor, a visual mnemonic for the American arrival of the Erik cigar. The announcer described the cigar's "bold new shape," declaring that the product was the "most interesting idea from Scandinavia since blondes." At the end of the commercial, a beautiful woman (with blonde hair, of course) joined Erik on the ship, completing the phallic metaphor and charging the spot with a heavy dose of sexuality. The spot foreshadowed the much more overt sexuality that would soon sweep through advertising in the latter half of the 1960s, as marketers turned counterculture lifestyle into commercial fodder.[37]

Art for Art's Sake

The sexualization of television advertising was part and parcel of its growing recognition as an authentic art form. Despite the industry's historical obsession with research, creativity—versus rational argument—was now broadly seen as the key to advertising success and, ultimately, increased brand sales and profits. Research could help determine good advertising from bad advertising, but only through creativity could good advertising come forth in the first place. This idea, most in the industry believed, was especially true for the medium of television. Television, wrote one critic, "is an industry dedicated to . . . the proposition that all soaps, cigarettes and toothpastes are not created equal," implying that creativity in advertising was the big non-equalizer. Although some critics still resented the mere presence of advertisers (one calling them "unwelcome toll collectors at the gates of television pleasure"), others argued that if there was an art form on television, it was the commercials rather than the programs. "Only the ads make a strong aesthetic appeal, sensual and passionate," claimed Paul Goodman in *The New Republic* in February 1963. Citing the eroticism embedded in commercials for Thrill liquid detergent and Ban deodorant, Goodman suggested that advertising was inherently more interesting because it was intended to cause an effect (sales), while programs were designed simply to hold attention. Programs were thus tactical and passive, commercials strategic and active. It was thus in advertisers' interest, Goodman pointed out, to further exploit the possibilities of the television medium via such technical elements as speech, music, noise, graphics, and montage.[38]

In a survey of Americans' attitudes toward television advertising, Social Research Inc. found that many viewers also believed that commercials had reached the status of art. "More and more the commercial is coming to be seen as a unique television art form," the 1964 survey reported. Television advertising had arguably reached true artistic status in the spring of 1963, when the Museum of Modern Art in New York included fifty-four commercials in its exhibit, "Television USA: 13 Seasons." Funded by the three networks, the exhibit showcased what a group of judges considered to be the best commercials from 1948 to 1961. Not all considered the escalating emphasis on creativity a particularly good thing, however, as too much art might get in the way of plain old salesmanship. "Advertising may be getting dangerously close to art for art's sake," warned Emil Mogul, president of the agency Mogul Williams & Saylor. Although no one could foresee it, the emerging creative revolution signaled a much greater threat to traditionalists. The classic postwar American Dream centered around domesticity, family life, and the privileges of a consumer paradise was on the cusp of a major reformation as the counterculture loomed ahead. Even if more stylistic than political, the much more irreverent, iconoclastic values of the "new creativity" would help turn the American Dream on its head over the course of the next decade.[39]

Just about everyone in the industry, however, would agree that effective television advertising still combined creative innovation with a sound reason-for-being or point-of-difference. A number of the best commercials of 1963–1964 did just that, as advertisers went to new lengths to bring together left- and right-brain thinking. For a 1963 commercial for Maxwell House coffee, for example, Benton and Bowles spent fourteen months figuring out a way to visually represent its physics-defying claim of offering "a cup and a half of flavor." In the spot, a cup of coffee is filled and then, magically, another half a cup rises over the rim in thin air. As in the Hertz "flying" commercial and the Dreyfus lion spot, the agency superimposed two films to create the illusion, a state-of-the-art special effect in the early 1960s. DDB continued its break-through campaign for Cracker Jack, again putting Jack Gilford on a train for comic effect. In a 1964 spot for the snack, Gilford sneaks a few handfuls of Cracker Jack from a sleeping child sitting next to him. "When it comes to Cracker Jack," the announcer told viewers, "some kids never grow up."[40]

Even laundry detergent and cleaning products were now being presented with a creative spark, not an easy task. In "White Knight," a 1963 spot produced by Norman, Craig & Kummel for Colgate-Palmolive, a knight on horseback demonstrated the amazing cleaning power of Ajax laundry detergent. Medieval mythology met suburbia as the knight aimed his lance at a woman mowing a lawn and a man painting a house, their dirty clothes instantly whitened. The powerful (and allegedly sexual) imagery suggested to viewers that Ajax detergent was indeed "stronger than dirt." For its sister product, Ajax All Purpose Liquid Cleaner, Colgate-Palmolive again used fantasy to demonstrate whiteness of epic proportions. In response to Procter and Gamble's highly successful campaign for Mr. Clean, Norman, Craig & Kummel used the visual metaphor of a "white tornado" in commercials for Ajax cleaner. With white representing cleanliness and a tornado power, the brand successfully fought back the upstart genie. In addition to Mr. Clean and Ajax, other brands of cleaning products such as Salvo, Dash, Joy, Cheer, and Action employed fantasy and surrealism to turn the drudgery of cleaning into moments of grandeur. New York-based writers, art directors, and producers of television advertising may have been inspired by the new pop art movement or perhaps the new wave of cinema being imported from Europe, which each drew heavily upon symbolic imagery and mythic iconography.[41]

Unfortunately, not all marketers and agencies could turn out such stuff of creative genius. In the spring of 1963, the newly formed League against Obnoxious TV Commercials claimed five hundred members in twenty-one states, spreading its gospel via a monthly newsletter. The league polled its members each month to determine which advertisers would receive its "Seal of Obnoxiousness," although the league did find time to praise decent commercials as well. More statistically reliable studies showed that viewers generally liked food and beverage commercials and disliked health and beauty and cleaning product commercials. According to Schwerin Research, for example, the ten most popular commercials in June 1963 in the New York City area were those for, in alphabetical order, Alka-Seltzer, Ballantine Beer, Chevrolet, Gravy Train, Hawaiian Punch, Ivory Snow, Oreo Cookies, Piel's Beer, Schlitz Beer, and StarKist Tuna. The ten commercials considered most objectionable were those for Action Bleach, Anacin, Bayer Aspirin, Bufferin, Crest Toothpaste, Dash Detergent, Excedrin, 5-Day Deodorant, Salvo Detergent, Secret Deodorant, and Tide Detergent. *Consumer Reports,* an occasional commentator on the television advertising scene, also found health-related commercials to be typically the most objectionable. The magazine named a campaign for Anacin its "Worst Ad of the Month," annoyed by such spoken copy as, "Please, Mother. I'd *rather* do it *myself.*" *Consumer Reports* not only considered the commercials "painful vignettes," but also misleading by implying that Anacin was "unique and a tranquilizer, neither of which was true." Completely coincidentally, Anacin won the "Most Obnoxious TV Commercial" contest staged by the *Oregon Journal* and determined by the newspaper's readers. One reader wrote that "it seems they are trying deliberately to give the viewer a headache so he'll buy Anacin," while another declared that "I would not buy a cure that was a cause of my headache and nervousness in the first place." Rosser Reeves, head of Ted Bates, the agency that created advertising for Anacin, recalled rather proudly after his career that these "were the most hated commercials in the history of advertising" and were "written between cocktails at lunch."[42]

Despite being at the bottom of the television advertising barrel, over-the-counter remedies accounted for a disproportionate share of commercial time. Pharmaceuticals, applied toiletries, and cosmetics, in fact, had the highest advertising-to-sales ratio of any product category. Drug companies spent 30 cents on advertising—more than 80 percent of it on television—of every dollar of sales. Bristol-Myers, the manufacturer of Anacin, spent even more, roughly 40 cents of the brand's sales, on advertising. A generic product with no research and development costs to recover, aspirin offered marketers like Bristol-Myers huge profit margins. Such profits in turn made available the huge media budgets, ultimately driving up sales. (Aspirin consumption increased four times as fast as population growth through the 1950s, a clue perhaps that the decade was indeed not as carefree as pop culture typically tells us it was.) Manufacturers of aspirin were essentially forced to advertise on television versus in print because, as one drug company executive asked, "Who wants to read about a headache?" Because drug advertising necessarily dealt with illness, bodily functions, or pain, however, it was inherently at an aesthetic disadvantage. Complicating matters was that actors could no longer portray doctors in commercials, and advertisers' idea of using real doctors as spokespeople had not succeeded, mostly because actual physicians resisted such offers. To attract viewers' attention in such an unpleasant product category and under such constraints, copywriters magically transformed medicalese into more understandable but clearly fraudulent advertising language. In a classic Geritol spot, "iron deficiency anemia" was redubbed "tired blood," arguably the best (or worst, depending on your view) dumbing down of a medical condition in advertising history.[43]

Besides the ever-present batch of bad TV commercials, there was often just too many. Many stations were airing more than the NAB's allotted six minutes of commercials per hour, leading FCC chair Minow to declare that "the American public is drowning [in television commercials] and calling for help." There was little doubt that many if not most television stations were consistently violating the code's recommendation regarding commercial time. In a random monitoring of Los Angeles stations, for example, the NARTB found that all three network stations frequently exceeded eight to twelve minutes of commercials per hour. One independent station averaged fifteen minutes of commercials each hour, on one occasion running twenty-one minutes of advertising in a single hour. Cramming as many spots as possible into a finite period of time was of course driven by greed, but it was also an attempt to squeeze in the rising number of commercials being produced. In 1962, 44,000 television commercials were produced in the United States, with a commercial aired somewhere in the nation every 1.7 seconds. Goodman Ace described overcommercialization in more experiential terms, claiming that within a single sixty-minute period of watching television, he was "sprayed, shaved, shampooed, deodorized, smeared, bathed, fed, medicated, Supp-hosed, sedated, refreshed, brushed, Saran-wrapped, plastered, and insured." Art Buchwald satirized the ratio of program to commercial time by stating that each time he tuned in to a commercial, it was interrupted by a program. "Just when the commercials get interesting," Buchwald wrote, "somebody like Ben Casey or Perry Mason comes on and spoils the show."[44]

Dream Consumers

The worst television commercials, however, were those that were not merely offensive but posed potential harm to consumers who could not defend themselves. After outlawing the terms "only," "just," and "suggested retail prices" in television commercials, the FTC was hot on the trail of advertisers of dangerous toys. Two toys the FTC had serious misgivings about were the Arch-A-Ball and Puncherino. The Arch-A-Ball was an ophthalmologist's nightmare, consisting of an inflatable plastic ball attached by a rubber string to a transparent plastic visor or headpiece worn over the upper face and eyes. The user would punch the ball like a punching bag, making the ball crash into the plastic visor (a toy apparently intended for junior masochists). In January 1964, the FTC ordered the maker and distributor of Arch-A-Ball to drop its allegedly invalid safety claims in its commercials, and instead mention the more interesting news that the visor or eye shield "may break or shatter and thereby cause injury to the user's eyes or face." The similar Puncherino, made by the aptly named Stupell Originals, consisted of a seven-inch plastic ball attached by a rubber string to plastic goggles with spaces between bars. The company defended its product by saying that if Puncherino had to carry a warning, so should all toys, devices, and athletic activities as they too carried some risk. Despite the Socratic wisdom of Puncherino's legal team, the FTC's order prevailed.[45]

Prodded by the FTC's actions, the NAB adopted a new set of toy advertising guidelines in March 1964 with an expanded scope, stating that toys should not be set in an "unrealistic wartime atmosphere," that dramatizations should not encourage a harmful or unsafe use of the advertised toy, and that commercials should not frighten children. Even with these tighter guidelines, toy manufacturers remained bullish on television advertising, however, and stations took advantage of their ability to reach large numbers of children in a single swoop. Local television stations had doubled their 1961 rates and jammed in as many spots as possible into shows, sometimes as many as fourteen in a single hour. Study after study showed that under this barrage of commercials, children had become "dream consumers," being highly brand conscious and displaying deft recall abilities.[46]

With 41 million Americans in 1964 under the age of ten—a figure which exceeded the nation's entire population a century earlier—cereal marketers too glommed onto the unprecedented power of television advertising to reach children. Cereal marketers had spent about $55 million in television advertising in 1963, most of it directed to children. Cereal television advertising to children was a direct legacy of radio advertising of the 1930s, when cereal companies sponsored heroes like Jack Armstrong, Tom Mix and his Ralston Straight Shooters, the Lone Ranger, Superman, the Green Hornet, and Terry and the Pirates. Recognizing that children were often the "gatekeepers" for which brand of cereal would be purchased for the household, the "big six" cereal marketers—Nabisco, Post, General Mills, Quaker, Ralston, and Kellogg—maintained a constant presence on television by sponsoring shows popular with children and advertising heavily. Premiums, of course, were also carried over from radio days, an indelible part of cereal consciousness for children. By 1963, cowboy-related premiums such as Tom Mix six-shooters and Lone Ranger silver bullets were out, considered relics of America's past. In their place were symbols of America's future—interplanetary and nuclear regalia such as space helmets and atom-bomb rings. Rather than giving away premiums for free by packing them into or onto the box, cereal marketers developed the self-liquidating premium. A couple of box tops and 25 cents not only covered the cost of a premium but ensured multiple purchases, a huge advantage in a category in which novelty reigned over brand loyalty.[47]

Although sponsoring shows guaranteed a means of reaching large numbers of children, actually creating children's shows was an even bigger opportunity. Cereal advertising ran against the grain, so to speak, of marketers' general exit from the entertainment or production side of the business, with programming designed for purely commercial purposes. Ellen Seiter has observed that Hanna-Barbera's creation of new limited or "streamlined" animation techniques in the late 1950s made it possible for networks to turn a profit on thirty-minute cartoon shows. The new style led to nothing less than the establishment of Saturday morning as a solid block of kid-oriented programming, a demographic dream to marketers of children's products. Kellogg, through its agency, Leo Burnett, developed a number of animated programs starring adventure-prone, kid-friendly critters like Yogi Bear, Huckleberry Hound, and Quick Draw McGraw. General Mills, via Dancer-Fitzgerald, Sample, countered Kellogg's bear, dog, and horse with shows featuring a lion (King Leonardo), skunk (Odie), chipmunk (Rocky), and bull moose (Bullwinkle). Animal animation was carried over into the brand identity and advertising for many cereals like General Mills's Trix (featuring the puckish Trix rabbit) and Quaker's Cap'n Crunch (featuring the lovable captain). Even for adult-oriented brands, cereal marketers occasionally used humor and irreverence in commercials to differentiate products from their look-a-like competitors. General Mills once hired Stan Freberg, for example, who took time off from his Chun King duties to spoof a popular show, David Susskind's *Open End,* for a campaign for Cheerios. In the "Open Oat" commercials, Freberg moderated a panel of experts who held different opinions regarding the symbolism of a Cheerio.[48]

Although the baby boom was in its final year in 1964, only its first wave was passing into young adulthood, heading off to college to create a culture much different from the one in which they had been raised. Millions of teens and preteens remained, a target audience that could not be ignored regardless of consumer product category. The postwar baby boom had redirected the trajectory of advertising, forcing marketers to consider how their businesses related to the wants and needs of children. What was different about advertising to children in the postwar era versus the prewar era was much more than the jump from radio to television. In the 1930s, marketers advertised products intended for use by children to children. Cereal marketers, most notably, sponsored afternoon radio shows to capture the attention of their target audience. While marketers of the 1950s and 1960s continued to advertise products intended for use by children to children, they were now also targeting children to influence the purchase decisions of their parents. With the average child watching twenty-four hours of television a week, marketers across product categories — cars, shampoos, pet foods, soups, and insurance — actively targeted children to shape the consumer habits of the family. Knowing that all consumers showed brand preferences when seeing people like themselves in commercials, advertisers like Texize and Ford cast children in their campaigns to form an affinity with kids. The "nag" factor was less than scientific, but any executive with kids knew its power in the home. Children's influence on buying decisions could actually be quantified; one survey found that 94 percent of mothers reported that their children demanded products they had seen advertised on television.[49]

With children increasingly recognized as the family's "gatekeeper" — a first in the history of consumerism — a number of firms specializing in the art of communicating to kids sprang up. The Gilbert Marketing Group specialized in research services for the youth market, helping advertisers and marketers effectively reach children with communications and products. Each year the firm held "Youth Market Clinics," attracting hundreds of agency and corporate executives wanting to learn the secrets of marketing to children. Eugene Gilbert, president of the firm, estimated that $50 million was being spent on advertising directed to children in 1964. One advertising agency, Helitzer, Waring & Wayne, also positioned itself as an expert in marketing to children. The small firm was reportedly growing faster than any other advertising agency in the business, doubling both its billings and its office floor space annually. Interestingly, the agency was not pursuing "children's accounts" but rather "adult accounts" over which children had influence, specifically airlines, cameras, automobiles, gasoline, and moving companies. Mel Helitzer, the agency's founder, was the same Mel Helitzer who, as advertising director of Ideal Toy, had basically endorsed deceptive advertising to children. He now gleefully explained that children became legitimate consumers at age three, when they were first able to be persuaded by television advertising. The agency spent 85 percent of its clients' media dollars on television as, according to Helitzer, "the right kind of a commercial really sinks into their [children's] subconscious. They'll hum it, sing it, repeat it for days." Helitzer did not consider this brainwashing, however, claiming that kids had significant reasoning abilities. "There are do-gooders who feel that advertising to this young group involves exploitation," Helitzer made clear, "but these kids are discriminating consumers even at this early age."[50]

Helitzer's observation of children's dual role while watching television commercials — engaged, even delighted, yet critical viewer — has been documented in subsequent, more formal studies, notably those of David Buckingham. Like adults, Buckingham's research has shown, children are able to keep one foot in and one foot out of television advertising, simultaneously accepting of and resistant to commercial motives. For marketers, of course, the "trick" is to create advertising which kids do not reject.[51] A firm believer in kids' ability to reject bad commercials, or see through what he called "the shoddy sell," Helitzer and his colleagues subjected all elements of a children-directed marketing proposition to the same rigid research tests as one directed to adults. The agency pretested a product's name, packaging, and advertising at private nurseries willing to exchange some classroom time for cash or free toys, just the beginning of the encroachment of consumer culture into America's educational system. Nursery school students were exposed to different commercials and then asked what they liked and disliked, or asked to choose the best looking package from a product line-up. The agency would also ask children to wander through a mock store, wanting to see which products the kids gravitated toward (most often those with yellow or red packages). Despite the sophisticated research techniques, Helitzer admitted that "getting information out of the kids after testing is not always easy." "This is virgin marketing territory," he explained, "and we're still breaking new ground." Still, Helitzer was confident that his agency offered a valuable service to marketers wanting to capitalize on children's influence over family purchases. To attract such marketers, the agency placed an ad in *The New York Times* with the title, "How to Woo the World's Most Misunderstood Consumer." Borrowing from children's verse, the ad stated:

> Whoever says children just rule over toys
> Should add up the spending of our girls and boys.
> They influence spending of fifty billion dollars
> So don't estimate juvenile hollers.[52]

Producers of television programs were also eager to tap the collective spending power of the most children in any single time or place in history. *Daniel Boone* made its debut on NBC in September 1964, designed primarily not for its televisual values but for its merchandising potential. Television merchandising was now a $200 million industry, as clothing, toy, and other manufacturers licensed television programs or characters for product development. The trend toward using television shows as a merchandising strategy, one critic wrote, "reflects the thickening blur in the line between broadcasting's advertising context and its non-advertising content." This blurry line has also been documented by Buckingham, who, after interviewing 124 children in the early 1990s, concluded that "films or programmes that cross the boundaries between fact and fiction are likely to generate problematic and ambivalent responses." Problematic or not, *Daniel Boone* was a clear attempt to duplicate the incredible success of the *Davy Crockett* craze of a decade before, which had been a merchandising bonanza (and itself a reworking of the Hopalong Cassidy mini-craze of 1950). Mel Helitzer, not surprisingly, remembered the *Davy Crockett* phenomenon with particular fondness, saying that "those were the days when a stray cat had to worry about cars, dogs, and coonskin-cap manufacturers." Without any caps to sell, Helitzer, then at Ideal, took all the stuffing of his company's plush bears, laid the bear stuffing out like trophy skins, and stuck on a label saying "The Bear That Davy Crockett Shot." The bear sold well.[53]

For the role of Daniel Boone, NBC brought back Fess Parker, who had played Davy Crockett in the three-part 1955 series. The network's Manager of Merchandising Enterprises was happy to report that even before the first episode aired, Boone-inspired products were selling beyond expectations. Forty licenses had already been signed, including those for T-shirts, pajamas, sweat shirts, frontier jackets and trousers, frontier trading cards, toy wagons and canoes, and toy forts with soldiers. Future products included a Daniel Boone doll, a frontier-style lunch kit, and a comic book with an application form for membership in Trail Blazer Clubs. Executives of Log Cabin Syrup were especially excited about the synergies between its brand and the show, envisioning Daniel Boone-themed log cabin packages and a number of Boonesque self-liquidating premiums. Kids all over America would soon be putting extra syrup on their pancakes and breaking into their piggy banks to get a Log Cabin Syrup Indian teepee, pioneer cabin (perfect as a Trail Blazer Clubhouse), Daniel Boone knapsack, and birch-bark canoe. Sponsors may have lost control over program content, but they were having the last laugh by using television advertising as the hub for highly profitable merchandising.[54]

The Sponsor's Kitchen

The full emergence of television as a merchandising vehicle for alternative forms of entertainment-based products also helped pave the way for Hollywood's entry into television advertising. After almost a decade and a half of blaming television for its woes, the motion picture industry decided that if it couldn't beat television, it would join it. Television first started to seriously hurt the movie business in 1949, certainly a major factor in bringing down attendance numbers in the 1950s. Hollywood executives, understandably upset, condemned the upstart medium for keeping audiences at home. Movie studios refused to supply the television industry with films, serving only in a production capacity. In the emerging entertainment world of cross-promotion and media synergies, however, movie moguls realized television could be an ally rather than an enemy. The biggest motion picture producers and distributors, including Columbia, Paramount, Warner Brothers, Universal, MGM, and Twentieth Century Fox, now began to spend significant amounts of money on television advertising to promote their new films. In contrast to the traditional medium used to promote a film—newspapers—television's sight, sound, motion, and, most recently, color, could replicate cinematic storytelling and emotion. Television commercials were particularly effective, Hollywood producers believed, for horror films, children's movies, and potential "blockbusters." Viewers could now witness scenes like Natalie Wood doing a striptease in *Gypsy* and Joan Crawford kicking Bette Davis in *Whatever Happened to Baby Jane?* from the comfort of their Barcaloungers and Lay Z Boy recliners.[55]

Although the industry put a positive spin on it, Hollywood's promotional switch from newspapers to television came when earnings in the film industry were going decidedly south. Angry about paying the higher "amusement" rates that newspapers often charged entertainment marketers, and desperate to fill seats, movie producers looked to television advertising as a means of possibly reviving their own golden age. As in the airline industry, the spark was the fourteen-week New York (and Cleveland) newspaper strike during the winter of 1962–1963, when television advertising more than ably filled in for print ads for films. New York audiences flocked to Radio Music Hall to see *Days of Wine and Roses* despite the newspaper strike, impetus for Hollywood to continue to invest in television advertising after the strike ended. Heavy television advertising for *Bye Bye Birdie, Lawrence of Arabia, To Kill a Mockingbird,* and *Hud* helped turn the films into big box office. The film industry soon recognized that television advertising was also ideally suited for merchandising peripheral products. In one notable 1964 partnering of television and movies, advertisers such as Kraft chocolates, Jack Frost sugar, and C & H sugar tied in to Walt Disney's new movie, *Mary Poppins,* with clips from the film integrated into commercials. The two sugar companies (which distributed their products in noncompeting geographic territories) included a segment of one of the movie's songs, "A Spoonful of Sugar" in their commercials, telling viewers that their brand "helps the medicine go down in a most delightful way." C & H even offered a Mary Poppins spoon (for one proof-of-purchase and 50 cents), produced by Oneida and bearing the likeness of Julie Andrews in full Poppinalia. *Mary Poppins* represented a new level of media and marketing synergy, as television advertising became seen as the logical bridge between movies and brands. Disney had long been an innovator when it came to cross-promoting its own products, most recently in the mid-1950s when it used its show *Disneyland* as one long commercial for its theme park.[56]

The rise in cross-promotions, tie-ins, and joint ventures was directly related to the decline of the single-sponsorship system in television advertising. The virtually complete adoption of the multiple-sponsorship system diluted the strength of both agencies and advertisers themselves, effectively taking each out of the key decision-making loop. This opened up the opportunity, perhaps the need, for marketers to actively seek out business partners. By the early 1960s, the vast majority of shows were sold directly from production companies to the three networks, which, in turn, sold one-minute spots to advertisers. Local stations too found themselves at the mercy of network executives in New York. "All power rests with the networks," claimed Sam

Rolfe, producer of the show *Eleventh Hour.* Bert Granet, producer of *The Twilight Zone*, concurred, joking that "all agencies have to do now is see that the commercials aren't upside down." The shift toward multiple sponsorships was having a positive effect in the censorship arena, however, as no longer exclusively owning shows, advertisers were much less likely to interfere with the creative process. "The advertiser . . . is less concerned with taboos and . . . knows that the stifling of ideas eventually must lead to mediocrity," observed George Polk, vice president of television programming at BBDO. Another leading television producer believed in 1963 that "80 percent" of the "phobias" sponsors had regarding program content had dissipated. With few exceptions, such as partisan politics, sponsors were no longer afraid of controversial topics, aware that Americans had developed much more sophisticated televisual tastes. "Sponsors no longer appear to be cast in the role of blue-penciling menaces," noted *Sponsor* magazine in July 1963.[57]

In this more tolerant climate, some writers attempted to sell scripts that had previously been rejected because of their controversial content. In 1960, DuPont rejected Eliot Asinof's "Eight Men Out" script, the story of the Chicago Black Sox scandal, which was originally planned for *The DuPont Show of the Month.* Baseball commissioner Ford Frick protested, however, and the company dropped the story. Asinof eventually turned the script into a book, which he was shopping around for television production three years later. Although most of sponsors' "phobias" had evaporated, witchcraft apparently was one fear too great to completely conquer. Quaker Oats, one of the sponsors of the new series *Bewitched*, quite naturally had co-star Dick York eat a bowl of Puffed Wheat in one of its commercials which aired during the taped show. Curiously, however, the star of the show, Elizabeth Montgomery, who played the witch Samantha, did not appear in any of Quaker's spots. Robert Lewis Shayon of the *Saturday Review* noticed Montgomery's absence, wondering why she was excluded from the commercials. It appeared that the cereal company did not want its brand linked too directly to sorcery, even if the show was televisual fantasy. Shayon appealed to Quaker Oats to put Samantha in the commercials, declaring that although a witch, she was a good, even delightful witch. "Quaker Oats ought not to withhold from her its ultimate benediction," Shayon insisted. "Samantha must be allowed to eat in the sponsor's kitchen." Shayon's comment was tongue-in-cheek, but he made a valid point considering that when it came to domestic tasks, Samantha's powers were strictly off-limits, at least according to her husband.[58]

For the few remaining advocates of single-sponsorship television, brand naming a show remained a prestigious albeit costly strategy. *Kraft Music Hall* and the *Bell Telephone Hour* were ideal but expensive vehicles, a means for elite advertisers to own a block of network time and leave a solid imprint of consumer goodwill. Such shows, however, were becoming relics of a different age of television. With the beginning of the 1964–1965 television season, almost all "quality" shows patronized by large corporations had disappeared. *The U.S. Steel Hour, Alcoa Presents, The DuPont Show of the Week, General Electric Theater, Armstrong Circle Theater,* and the Bell & Howell-sponsored "Closeup" specials were gone from the airwaves, as sponsors bowed to network pressure. Such shows, the networks told sponsors, simply did not draw enough audience, bringing down the ratings for an entire evening of prime time. Sponsors of the shows moved their television budgets to news or left the medium entirely, choosing magazines to reach an educated, affluent, and influential audience. The success of television advertising was, ironically, causing some advertisers to leave television.[59]

In any case, for advertisers with many different brands under their corporate umbrellas, like General Foods, a shotgun approach made much more strategic sense than patronizing a single show. Over the 1963–1964 television season, General Foods sponsored the shows of many of the leading stars of the day, including Jack Benny, Danny Thomas, Garry Moore, Lucille Ball, Andy Griffith, and Phil Silvers. Before each of these stars' first show in the fall of 1963, however, General Foods decided to bring them all together for a one-hour comedy special. Such a special, company executives believed, would help boost the ratings of each of the six shows, as well as serving as an excellent advertising vehicle itself. Although it was a wonderful idea in theory, General Foods and its agency, Benton and Bowles, underestimated the degree to which egos would play in putting such an ensemble on one stage. Ms. Ball, for example, believed her part to be subservient to Phil Silver's, and insisted on some changes to the script. This power play, which bumped up her role at the other stars' expense, caused Jack Benny to demand further revisions which gave him more lines. The show ultimately went off without a hitch, but served as a telling reminder that too many celebrity cooks could spoil a televisual dish.[60]

Like star conflicts, sponsor conflicts would arise occasionally. During the summer of 1963, for example, Bill Cullen was scheduled to fill in for the vacationing Johnny Carson on *The Tonight Show* until NBC realized a sponsor conflict would result. Cullen was a spokesperson for Frigidaire refrigerators on his *The Price Is Right,* while Hotpoint sponsored *The Tonight Show.* Industry rules went that once a star became associated with one company or brand, he or she could never be a spokesperson for a competitor within the same product category. There were, however, some rare exceptions to the rule. Bob Hope was for many years a spokesperson for Buick, but in fall 1963 switched to Chrysler. Even superstar Hope found himself at the center of a sponsor conflict, having to withdraw from hosting the 1963 Oscars because of his association with one brand of toothpaste after a competitive brand decided to sponsor the broadcast. (Frank Sinatra ably filled in.) The flood of new products into the marketplace in the 1960s made it a liability for stars to be exclusively associated with one brand. Survival as a spokesperson was fast becoming dependent on foregoing loyalty to one advertiser and retaining "free agent" status.[61]

What's Wrong with Men?

Interestingly, the major transformation of television programming and advertising in the early 1960s was completely lost on a small segment of Americans who considered their sets furniture. Indeed, the overt commercialization of television was a surprise to some who switched on their sets for the first time in years during the newspaper strike of 1962–1963. Devout newspaper readers, not familiar with how television had changed, were amazed to see newscasters mention a brand or sponsor before a commercial break. Newscasters had once simply introduced a commercial with the generic "and now a word from our sponsor," but were now tacitly personally endorsing products. On CBS, for example, Walter Cronkite regularly introduced commercials after reading a story. One night in June 1963, Cronkite introduced a spot for a "pushbutton window spray" right after reading a particularly tragic news story, an unfortunate segue in terms of journalistic integrity. The odd juxtaposition was hardly a random incident; the following evening Cronkite followed a report on the Cuban missile crisis with the coincidentally appropriate words, "And now a word from Anacin."[62]

Critics from the print medium were, not surprisingly, most bothered by this mixing of objectivity and salesmanship. The practice was yet another instance of how television, as an expressly commercial medium, blended entertainment with advertising while newspapers and magazines typically kept them apart. Richard L. Tobin of the *Saturday Review* suggested that by naming products, reporters' "capacity as unbiased newscasters has somehow been profoundly shaken." There was in fact no FCC or NAB rule regarding television newscasters introducing (or even performing) commercial messages. News programs had previously used a designated announcer to tell viewers the name of the sponsor in the beginning of each show and to segue into commercial breaks, but Madison Avenue was now pressuring networks to have their anchors personally deliver these commercial announcements. Some advertisers were going further by placing company- or product-labeled signs behind anchors, or even incorporating their names into the news shows. All these efforts were, of course, intended to extend advertisers' time on the air and create further brand identification with a particular show and star.[63]

With its "breaking news" arrangement with NBC, Gulf Oil did not have to sneak its brand name into news shows. Since 1961, Gulf Oil had sponsored some eighty "instant specials" on NBC, including the sinking of a prominent ship named the *Thresher,* the launching of *Saturn I,* an Alaskan earthquake, and the verdict in the Jack Ruby trial. As both the space race and Vietnam War escalated in the early and mid-1960s, the company found itself sponsoring an increasing number of events as they happened to occur. In August 1964, for example, the first close-up pictures of the moon (from *Ranger 7*) were "brought to you by" Gulf Oil, as were two reports of crises in Vietnam. Through its unique venture with the network, Gulf Oil, in effect, "branded" many of the seminal events of the frenetic and turbulent 1960s. Other advertisers found innovative ways to have their brands stand out on television. Shell Oil went against the industry trend of shorter commercials, opting to air two-minute commercials beginning in fall 1964 to ensure its spots would run in isolation. E. F. Loveland, Shell's advertising manager, justified the expense for more than "protection" reasons, saying that the two-minute spot would "tell our story more thoroughly . . . [and] convincingly." Shell's commercials adopted the look and tone of public affairs programming, thus blurring the distinction between news programming and advertising.[64]

Purex Corporation also looked to public affairs to win over its target audience of housewives. While television clearly favored large advertisers, Purex proved that the medium could be used as part of a guerilla marketing strategy for smaller ones. The soap/cleanser/detergent category was dominated by three huge companies that spent heavily on television, Procter and Gamble, Colgate-Palmolive, and Lever Brothers. These three companies collectively spent $269 million on advertising in 1963, making Purex's $10 million in spending seem like pocket change. To maximize brand awareness, Purex used the unorthodox tactic of sponsoring hour-long historical and factual programs designed to stir up controversy, such as a reenactment of the Sacco-Vanzetti trial and a program on sexual frigidity. Although the latter program was originally aired on a weekday afternoon, according to *Business Week,* "so many women told Purex they wanted their husbands to see it that it was repeated during prime evening time." In sexual dysfunction, it was clear that Purex had struck a nerve at the dawn of the 1960s women's liberation movement, perhaps even tapping into some of the ideas expressed in Betty Friedan's breakthrough new book, *The Feminine Mystique.*[65]

As suggested by its slogan, "You'll find the woman's touch in every Purex product," Purex went beyond issues of sexuality to position itself as an ally of the postwar woman. The company was sympathetic to contemporary women's issues, producing television specials bound to draw an interested female audience. Through the early 1960s, Purex aired such shows as "The Single Woman," "The Cold Woman," "The Trapped Housewife," "The Working Mother," "Mother and Daughter," and "Change of Life." The company followed these up with a series on feminine "perplexes," including such shows as "The Indiscriminate Woman," "The Lonely Woman," "Glamour Trap," "Problem Child," and "What's Wrong with Men?" In addition to addressing personal issues, Purex sponsored public affairs programs designed for a female audience, such as a news show hosted by ABC reporter Lisa Howard and a series called "What Every Woman Should Know about Communism." Purex's biggest advertising coup, however—its sponsorship of the 1961 Kennedy inauguration ceremonies—had nothing to do with gender issues and was, in fact, pure luck. Because of heavy snows in the northeast, millions of people stayed home to watch the event, making it one of the best television advertising bargains in history.[66]

Xerox Corporation had a novel idea regarding how to both stand out on television and promote its interests abroad via public affairs programming. In the spring of 1964, the company announced it would spend $4 million to produce and air six ninety-minute fictional films intended to "create a greater understanding of the many activities and global services of the United States." The dramas would be shot on location in emerging nations, and aired on both ABC and NBC. Xerox hired some of the best talent in the entertainment business to write, produce, direct, and score the series, including directors Stanley Kubrick, Joseph L. Mankiewicz, and Otto Preminger and composers Leonard Bernstein, Richard Rodgers, Henry Mancini, and André Previn. The big names agreed to receive only scale wages for work, and the company's agency, Papert, Koenig, Lois, waived its media commission. Xerox wanted and received only a one-sentence credit line during each show, but realized corporate goodwill in other ways. By aligning with the United Nations, the company gained a much greater international presence, particularly in the countries in which the films were shot (and would potentially air). The president of Xerox, Joseph C. Wilson, stated the project's objective as to "help men better communicate with each other," but added that "it is all-important for Xerox to be favorably known throughout the world." What better institution to partner with than the United Nations to achieve such a goal and establish Xerox as a global brand?[67]

Hey, Look Him Over!

Influenced by the greater presence of and respect for public affairs on television in the early 1960s, political advertising became a more important factor in elections at all levels. A 1963 Clio-winning commercial for Birch Bayh (D-Indiana) called "Hey, Look Him Over!" was widely credited for Bayh's upset defeat over incumbent Homer Capehart, who had served in the Senate for eighteen years.[68] The spot included a jingle sung by a group called the "J's with Jamie," a quartet which performed jingles in commercials for Marlboro cigarettes ("You get a lot to like with a Marlboro"), Campbell's Red Kettle Soup ("The Campbells are coming with pork and beans"), Pillsbury ("Nothin' says lovin' like something from the oven"), Alka-Seltzer ("Relief is just a swallow away"), and Wrigley Gum ("Look for the spear and get chewing enjoyment"). *Time* magazine made the fascinating observation that the J's with Jamie had "probably been heard by more people more times than any other group in the history of sound." To the tune of the popular song "Hey, Look Me Over," the group sang:

> Hey look him over, he's your kind of guy
> His first name is Birch, his last name is Bayh.[69]

While politicians had been sold like products for some time, the televisual packaging of Bayh along the lines of the Marlboro Man, the Campbell Kids, the Pillsbury Doughboy, Alka-Seltzer's Speedy, and Wrigley Gum's Sprite represented a new approach to marketing senatorial candidates.

Commercials for the 1964 presidential election also reflected the sophisticated tactics and competitive tone of consumer packaged goods marketing. "To an almost overwhelming degree," *The New York Times* observed, "American political campaigns are being fought on the tv channels of this country through the use of advertising." The Democratic National Committee hired the hottest agency in town, Doyle Dane Bernbach, to create its campaign for candidates President Lyndon B. Johnson (D-Texas) and Senator Hubert H.

Humphrey (D-Minnesota). The Democrats began meeting with Doyle Dane Bernbach executives in September 1963—about six weeks before the assassination of President Kennedy—to discuss the president's reelection campaign. Originally drawn to the Doyle Dane Bernbach's humorous work for Volkswagen, the committee retained the agency to help reelect LBJ. In one Johnson spot, part of a model of the United States was shown being cut off as an announcer stated, "In a *Saturday Evening Post* article for August 31, 1963, Republican presidential candidate Senator Barry Goldwater said, 'Sometimes I think this country would be better off if we would just saw off the Eastern seaboard and let it float out to sea.'" In the age of television, gaffs such as Goldwater's could spell instant doom to a political candidate. In another spot for Johnson, hands were shown taking a social security card out of a wallet and tearing it up. Over this visual, the announcer informed viewers, "His running mate, William Miller, admits that Senator Goldwater's voluntary plan would destroy your Social Security. President Johnson is working to strengthen Social Security." Directly competitive commercials such as these positioned Johnson as the kinder, gentler candidate, and leveraged the president's attempts to forge a liberal consensus.[70]

As in previous elections during the Cold War, international affairs and specifically the looming fear of atomic war entered the discourse of political television advertising, with Johnson casting Goldwater as more likely to engage in militaristic conflict with the Russians. One very controversial commercial depicted a little girl sitting in a field of flowers, counting the petals of a daisy. As the girl reached the number nine, the camera zoomed in to the girl's pupil and the screen darkened, upon which the image of an atomic bomb explosion appeared. Johnson himself assumed the role of voice talent for this spot, telling Americans, "These are the stakes: to make a world in which all of God's children can live, or go into the darkness. We must either love each other, or we must die." The powerful spot (which ran only once before Johnson pulled it) was an indirect barb at the hawkish Goldwater, and furthered Johnson's image as the voice of military reason (in spite of the escalating Vietnam conflict).[71]

Fighting fire with fire, the Republican National Committee also used television heavily to market presidential candidate Senator Goldwater (R-Arizona). Party officials considered Goldwater to be ideally suited for the medium, believing that commercials were instrumental in the senator's winning the California primary. The committee first hired Leo Burnett to create its television campaign, but soon switched to Erwin, Wasey, Ruthrauff & Ryan.

The campaign to elect Goldwater and vice presidential candidate William E. Miller focused on the threat of "welfarism" and other social problems, suggesting they stemmed from President Johnson's allegedly radical liberalism. In one spot, Goldwater linked domestic violence, pornography, and graft to questionable morals within the Democratic administration. "The national morality by example and by persuasion should begin at the White House and should have good influence to reach out to every corner of the land," Goldwater told viewers. "This is not the case today." The spot concluded with the tagline, "In your heart, you know he's right." In another spot, Goldwater responded directly to critics' charges that he was reactionary and, perhaps, trigger-happy. The candidate was asked, "Mr. Goldwater, what's this about your being called imprudent and impulsive?" Goldwater answered, "It seems to me the really impulsive and imprudent president is the one who is so indecisive that he has no policy at all." Goldwater then contrasted Johnson's foreign policy with that of Eisenhower's, attempting to reinvigorate Cold War paranoia. President Johnson's competitive campaign was far more persuasive and effective, however, contributing to his decisive victory. When it was all over, the Republican Party had not only lost the election but had drained its coffers, having to pay for all of its commercials with cash twenty-four hours in advance of their airing. "As some broadcasters and other creditors have learned," explained *Broadcasting* magazine, "a defeated party's treasurer may be hard to find after an election."[72]

Although national politics deservedly made the headlines, a seminal moment in the history of advertising also took place as 1964 drew to a close. With little fanfare, the popular Burma-Shave road sign advertising campaign came to a close, replaced by more efficient television advertising. Philip Morris, which had acquired the Burma-Shave brand the previous year, quickly recognized that television advertising was necessary to seriously compete against Colgate's Rapid-Shave and Gillette's Foamy in the $100 million shaving cream business. Burma-Shave's roadside campaign, a forty-year tradition, cost about $200,000 a year, an amount which included not only the signs but also payment to farmers for "media space" on their land. Philip Morris planned to spend $1 million in television advertising for Burma-Shave, and was excited about the brand's new siblings, Burma-Bey after-shave lotion and Burma Blockade aerosol deodorant. Introduced in 1926, Burma-Shave was the world's first brand of shaving cream but, by 1964, had become old-fashioned, outdated, and plain tired. The brand's road signs perpetuated these heinous marketing qualities and had become obsolete because, as one

Philip Morris executive explained, "superhighways carry motorists too fast over hill and dale to read the jingles." "Roads are no longer for browsing," added *Sponsor* magazine, "they are for getting places—perhaps even home to watch television." [73]

The burying of one of the most recognizable, if ignored, symbols of American consumer culture of the past was a telling sign of the times as the postwar era drew to a close. The first medium originally dedicated to the principles of commerce had achieved its mission of reviving the American Dream, but a seismic shift was about to rock the nation's cultural landscape. The first generation raised on television and television advertising was poised to reject much of the postwar "psychic air" they had breathed, challenging the fundamental values of their parents. As the baby boom era ended, television advertising too was about to enter a new, less innocent era steeped in the values of the nation's increasingly restless youth, and to help redefine the American Dream once again.

Conclusion

As a defining site of twentieth-century American culture, the first era of television advertising is a vital piece of our history that has been largely neglected. Retracing the steps of postwar television advertising addresses this historical oversight and, in the process, sheds new light on our understanding of our national ethos to consume, both then and now. The American Dream—stalled during the Depression and World War II—blossomed as never before, nourished by the most powerful advertising medium in history. Unlike other media, television was intended to be a medium of advertising from the get-go, specifically designed to grease the wheels of consumerism. Also contrary to print or radio, television advertising carried with it a unique purpose, to raise our national "consumer consciousness" by promoting an ideology grounded in the values of consumption, materialism, and upward mobility. This purpose was achieved beyond anyone's expectations, as television advertising entered the national psyche and became part and parcel of everyday life.

We cannot, then, overestimate the impact television advertising had in shaping our values during this key juncture of American history, values which remain the foundation for who we are as a people. Our social and economic grounding in consumer capitalism, shared by much of the world, is strongly linked to the ideology embedded in commercial television's first two decades. American television and its core ideology of consumption can be seen as Cold War artillery, a form of corporate propaganda that proclaimed the rewards of free enterprise and drew upon nationalistic sentiment. Just as government propaganda instructed Americans to save money during the Depression and told those on the home front to make sacrifices to achieve victory, television advertising in the postwar era linked consuming to the ideological cornerstones of capitalism and democracy. Television advertising thus helped re-establish the American Dream by equating citizenship with consumption, that is, by reinscribing a consumer ethic into the idea of American citizenship. The massest of mass media impelled Americans to spend money, selling the message that doing so was beneficial not only for the individual but also for the nation.

The amazing story of television advertising, however, has been overshadowed by its host medium, television, with the latter credited and blamed for a large share of the cultural dynamics of postwar America. Even after the demise of the single-sponsor system, it was advertisers who brought television to us, using the medium to shape consumer behavior in their favor. The golden age of television was thus in many ways actually the golden age of television advertising, as it was advertisers who brought the shows to viewers. The tremendous impact of television advertising was a function of its being in precisely the right place at precisely the right time, in sync with a number of key social, economic, and demographic trends. Television advertisers' relentless pursuit of a mass audience, homogeneous in nature and middle class in tastes, resonated with the social norms of conformity and consensus. Piped into the landscape of domestic life, television advertising catered to Americans' desire to fill their new homes with symbols of success and happiness. Television advertising not only helped drive the postwar economy, but also shaped and reflected a growing standardization of American culture, beaming the same images and language into homes across the country. By means of its national reach, television advertising was thus instrumental in turning America into a much more homogeneous country. Commercials helped to spread the suburban and, more specifically, the Southern Californian lifestyle across the country, promoting the values of an egalitarian consumer paradise. Cultural standards originating in New York City and Hollywood were disseminated coast-to-coast, impacting local community life. Television advertising was also in synch with the nation's love affair with automobiles and mobility in general, advancing our desire for private transportation and satisfying our perpetual wanderlust.

Although television advertising was designed for a mass audience and delivered on a mass scale, it would be wrong to assume that it was simply a vehicle of consensus or agent of conformity. While it did indeed act on a macro level as a force of homogeneity and standardization, television advertising also functioned on the local level as a force of individualization as consumers constructed their identities through the marketplace. As the loudest voice of capitalism, commercial television thus did indeed exploit the freedom and liberties to be found within consumerism, that each purchase is a form of democracy in action. Rather than being purely a "top-down" form of propaganda, then, television advertising was quite accommodating of diversity, making it clear that each individual was free to choose from the huge array of products and services available in the marketplace. Consumption may have been the common denominator, but how one consumed was up to the individual, deflating the idea that the postwar era, and specifically postwar consumerism, allowed little or no personal expression. When government officials and business leaders promoted (or defended) television advertising as a voice of the American Dream, they cleverly and consistently emphasized the individualistic dimensions of the medium. Without this claim — steeped in the founding principals of the nation — the industry would have likely been subject to even more criticism and regulation.

Outside of its role within the larger culture, commercial television caused a sea change in the history of advertising, leaping beyond print and radio to redefine the terms of the exchange between seller and buyer. With both the risks and rewards of television advertising significantly higher than those of radio, television advertisers exploited the promotional possibilities of a medium created specifically to sell products and services. By integrating commercials into the shows, sponsors also exploited the trust viewers had in stars in the attempt to keep folks from leaving their cushy sofas. Sponsors' initial ability to control program content, a legacy of radio days, represented an exponential leap in the packaging of commerce as entertainment. Television shows were conceived not as entertainment during which to advertise, but rather as advertising vehicles offering entertainment. Driven by this fluid interchange between entertainment and consumerism, postwar America became a place in which it was difficult to say where leisure ended and consumption began. For the first time in the nation's history, perhaps, leisure became articulated as a form of consumerism rather than as what people did when they were not working. Advertising on television was instrumental in forging this new and improved American Dream, serving as the principal voice of a domestic paradigm of pleasure.

One also finds many interesting paradoxes and dichotomies within postwar television advertising, a fair reflection of an era whose complexities have been largely underestimated. Television was initially a medium of the wealthy, with a set considered a luxury item until the early 1950s. This was rather ironic, as television's most vocal critics tended to be the intellectual elite of academics, journalists, and professionals. As the cost of a set dropped, however, television evolved into the massest of mass media, a voice of populist or even "lowest common denominator" thought. The average American owning a television set in the 1950s watched about five hours a day, willing to endure the barrage of commercial messages which were a part of every program. Study after study showed, however, that the man or woman on the street generally held advertisements on television in low regard, believing most to be too long, loud, or irritating. Equally contradictory, most studies also showed that viewers consistently rewarded advertisers by buying their products. Television advertising achieved its objectives despite (or because of) its overly aggressive techniques.

Most symbolic of the aggression of postwar television advertising, however, was the emergence of children as a viable audience and legitimate target market. Television advertising had a symbiotic relationship with the baby boom, as marketers used the medium to turn a generation of children into a generation of consumers. Weaned on television commercials, the products sold by television commercials, and the shows created expressly as advertising vehicles, baby boomers did not become the most consumer-oriented generation in history by chance. The legacy of television advertising during the postwar years lives on not only in the notoriously consumptive habits of forty- and fiftysomethings, but in those of their children, the "echo boom." Today's teenagers (Generation Y) are making their parents look like ascetics, as the former benefit from a booming economy and eagerly embrace the symbolic trappings of the good life. This ripple effect of postwar television advertising will have implications well into the twenty-first century.

The long-term effects of postwar television advertising can be traced directly back to the tremendous power held by those in the industry. Postwar advertising culture almost immediately achieved iconic status, driven in large part by the new, exciting medium of television. There were plenty of men in advertising before 1946, after all, but no men in gray flannel suits. Never before did, and perhaps never again will, the universe of advertising attract so much attention, both positive and negative. Advertising people became seen as heroes or villains, depending on your view, labeled as either leaders of a noble democratic cause or hucksters and hidden persuaders. Stealing and giving back to other artistic forms, television advertising emerged as a new, legitimate avenue of creative expression. The big money to be had in television commercials swayed creative talent from other fields to apply their trade in the art of persuasion, while entertainers' role as brand spokespeople expanded dramatically, redefining the very nature of what it meant to be a star. With a televisual testimonial or plug, entertainers' fame and ubiquity grew in scope and speed as never before, but at the expense of a certain mystique or sense of glamour. The celebrity of today is viewed more than ever as a spokesperson for a cluster of brands (think Michael Jordan), a status set in motion by postwar television advertising. The tentacles of television advertising reached into a plethora of institutions in postwar America, as related fields adapted to the demands of the new medium. Leading social scientists worked their research magic into new theories and techniques devoted to the psychology of the marketplace. The new research blood injected into the business arena gave Corporate America a different set of tools to work with, tools required to satisfy increasingly savvy consumers. Today's "professional" consumer can be traced back to some of the consumerism survival skills developed by Americans during the postwar years, when television advertising emerged as the atomic bomb of marketing weapons.

As the back end of the marketing process, the retail arena too reacted to what was going on in the front end. Television advertising's ability to "presell" consumers shifted the responsibilities of the retailer away from direct selling toward inventory management, with market coverage of commercials dictating what goods the retailer should carry. Professional and collegiate sports also adapted, with game clocks reset to suit the temporal constraints of television advertising where time literally meant money. Perhaps even more important was the effect television advertising—an agent of the private sector—had on public life. The unique vocabulary of television advertising, expressed through sight and sound, became an alternative form of public discourse, a cultural Esperanto equipping Americans with a new language of consumerism. Events previously considered within the civic arena—from the Rose Bowl to space launches—became literally commercialized, brought to us by private corporations. Public affairs were eagerly co-opted by television advertising, no longer just news but opportunities for companies to shape public opinion, gain consumer goodwill, or lobby for a particular cause. Public service announcements were at the crossroads of the private and public sectors, television advertising's rather modest effort to fulfill the medium's mission to serve the greater community. Although not a particularly powerful force in the postwar years, PSAs would make a major mark on the television landscape of the much more socially aware counterculture that lay ahead.

Television advertising's intersection with politics too blurred the lines between the private and public interests, as election committees looked to Madison Avenue to sell their candidates to Americans. The parallel universe of election campaigns used the familiar model of commercial television, creating a democracy of the political marketplace where consumers expressed their choice not with dollars but with votes. It's almost unthinkable today that even a local congressperson or state representative could get elected without the help of television advertising. The clearest exchange between private and public sectors within television advertising, however, was the intervention by various governmental arms when it became readily apparent that sponsors, agencies, and broadcasters could not regulate themselves. The quiz show scandals were almost inevitable, as the pressures and profit motive of commercial television pushed advertisers to bend the rules until they broke. Trained in the art of presenting a version of reality that was "more real than reality," advertisers created a fictionalized account of what was supposed to or believed to be truth. To sponsors, quiz shows and program content in general were not just entertainment but also advertisement, and thus a plastic art that could be manipulated for advantage. This gap between sponsors' and the government's vision was too wide, causing the system to crash and leading to the development of a new, more balanced paradigm of commercial television.

The quiz show scandals were just the most sensational of the abuses or crimes committed by commercial television in the postwar years. Brash, abrasive, and loud, many commercials were derived from the George Washington Hill school of advertising, in which getting noticed took precedence over everything else. To many viewers abroad, American-style advertising was the Ugly American, kin to the overweight tourist in Bermuda shorts and a Hawaiian shirt or worse, an imperialistic invader with hegemonic intent. In reality, postwar television advertising was not much worse than prewar advertising; because of its amazing reach, however, and because it was delivered directly into viewers' homes, it was nearly impossible to ignore the frequently offensive nature of television advertising. Carnival barkers had hawked medicine tonic a half-century before the first commercial ever aired (also drawing the wrath of government officials), but such salespeople did not have the ability to pitch their product to 25 million people at once sitting in their living rooms or at their kitchen tables.

Concentration of power is a dangerous thing, history has shown over and over, a tenet which proved to be true in the case of postwar commercial television. At both an industry level and as a media vehicle, the power of television advertising during its first era was highly concentrated, accounting for some of its various sins and the negative social consequences it caused.

Critics of free market capitalism would look to television advertising not as a mostly democratic institution capable of empowering consumers through the freedom of the marketplace but rather as a force that furthered economic inequalities and promoted a shallow interpretation of status. Critics of consumer culture would argue that television advertising helped create our disposable society, where replacing things that are still perfectly functional has become the norm. One cannot argue that television advertising spread the harmful effects of the automobile (more Americans died in car accidents during the 1950s than during World War II) and smoking, each a major component of the advertising business and everyday life in postwar and contemporary America. Television advertising can thus be held partly responsible for damaging the health and well-being of both individuals and the environment, a fact only recently reflected by legal action today. Puffery to enhance the attributes of a product is one thing, but outright deception, lying, and covering up of research to promote the sale of harmful products is unforgivable.

Also unforgivable is television advertising's tacit endorsement of racism. Like most institutions of postwar America, television advertising did not live up to its guiding principles of democracy, freedom, and equality. Television advertising became less racist only when blacks demanded their right to be a part of it. Television, in fact, has yet to fully live up to America's pluralistic mission, with African Americans and other minorities often pushed to the margins of commercial television. Although inexcusable, it should not be surprising that television advertising reflected and helped spread social norms regarding race in the postwar era. Commercial television's aim for the direct center of the national bull's-eye was an overt attempt to attract as large an audience as possible. As its chief method of measurement and pricing—cost per thousand—implied, television advertising was a pure instrument of mass culture, designed to appeal first and foremost to white, middle class viewers.

As a product of consensus ideology, television advertising reflected many other central themes of postwar America. Narrow gender roles and contained sexual mores were embedded in television advertising narratives, reinforcing the male-as-breadwinner and female-as-housewife cultural stereotypes. Leveraging Americans' trust in experts, advertisers often used demonstration techniques or quoted statistics, which served as scientific, quantifiable "proof" that their claims of efficacy or competitive superiority were true. Many advertisers also positioned their products around the theme of progress, capitalizing on our vision of America as a place of perpetual social and economic improvement. New models of cars were always better than last year's models, and breakthrough medical technologies seemed to occur with unusual frequency. Underlying this theme was a belief that endless prosperity and unlimited abundance lay just around the corner, the postwar expression of America's eternal optimism. Although these were certainly important themes, it was, of course, Americans' penchant to consume that advertisers tapped into most clearly and compellingly. With the American Dream grounded in a patriotic form of consumerism, television advertising shamelessly promoted an endless cycle of consumption and leisure. Between its beginnings as a precocious prodigy and its emergence as some of the psychic air we breathed, television advertising became an integral piece of the American experience. Although long gone from the airwaves, the television advertising of postwar America lives on, a powerful and enduring part of our individual and national identities.

Notes

Abbreviations

MTR = The Museum of Television and Radio, New York City and Beverly Hills
HHC = Hal Humphrey Collection, University of Southern California Cinema-
Television Library, Los Angeles
UCLA = University of California, Los Angeles Film and Television Archive

Introduction

1. Michael Kammen, *American Culture American Tastes: Social Change and the Twentieth Century* (New York: Knopf, 1999), 19.

2. Robert J. Samuelson, *The Good Life and Its Discontents: The American Dream in the Age of Entitlement* (New York: Vintage, 1997), 19–21, 33.

3. Lawrence R. Samuel, *Pledging Allegiance: American Identity and the Bond Drive of World War II* (Washington, D.C.: Smithsonian Institution Press, 1997), 50; David Halberstam, *The Fifties* (New York: Villard, 1993), 506; Karal Ann Marling, *As Seen on TV: The Visual Culture of Everyday Life in the 1950s* (Cambridge, Mass.: Harvard University Press, 1994), 134.

4. Marling 134; Kammen 58; Halberstam 506, 496.

5. George Lipsitz, *Time Passages: Collective Memory and American Popular Culture* (Minneapolis: University of Minnesota Press, 1990), 42–44.

6. Lipsitz 46.

7. Lipsitz 43–45.

8. Lipsitz 45–46.

9. William Boddy, *Fifties Television: The Industry and Its Critics* (Urbana: University of Illinois Press, 1990), 155. Boddy notes that television advertising overtook that of radio in 1952 and print in 1955; Kammen 174.

10. Douglas T. Miller and Marion Nowak, *The Fifties: The Way We Really Were* (Garden City, N.Y.: Doubleday, 1977), 346–352; Ien Ang, *Living Room Wars: Rethinking Media Audiences for a Postmodern World* (London: Routledge, 1996), 56.

11. Kammen 166.

12. Kammen 59.

13. Michele Hilmes, *Hollywood and Broadcasting: From Radio to Cable* (Urbana: University of Illinois Press, 1990), 140; Michele Hilmes, *Radio Voices: American Broadcasting, 1922–1952* (Minneapolis: University of Minnesota Press, 1997), 273; Boddy 94–5, 168; Susan Smulyan, *Selling Radio: The Commercialization of American Broadcasting, 1920–1934* (Washington, D.C.: Smithsonian Institution Press, 1994), 90; Erik Barnouw, *The Sponsor: Notes on a Modern Potentate* (New York: Oxford University Press, 1978). In *Radio Voices*, Hilmes discusses in depth broadcasting's first incarnation of the "magazine concept," specifically Mary Margaret McBride's radio show of the 1930s and 1940s, while Smulyan credits cooking expert Ida Bailey Allen with what appeared to be the first magazine style radio format. For more on sponsorship in radio, see Barnouw's *The Golden Web: A History of Broadcasting in the United States, 1933–1953* (New York: Oxford University Press, 1968) and *A Tower in Babel: A History of Broadcasting in the United States to 1933* (New York: Oxford University Press, 1966).

14. Boddy 160; Christopher Anderson, *Hollywood TV: The Studio System in the Fifties* (Austin: University of Texas Press, 1994), 87; Michael Curtin, *Redeeming the Wasteland: Television Documentary and Cold War Politics* (New Brunswick, N.J.: Rutgers University Press, 1995), 21.

15. Halberstam 501. Good sources on the general history of advertising include the following: Harry Wayne McMahon, *The Television Commercial* (New York: Hastings House, 1957); Stuart Ewen, *Captains of Consciousness: Advertising and the Social Roots of Consumer Culture* (New York: McGraw-Hill, 1976); Daniel Pope, *The Making of Modern Advertising* (New York: Basic Books, 1983); Michael Schudson, *Advertising, The Uneasy Profession: Its Dubious Impact on American Society* (New York: Basic Books, 1984); Stephen Fox, *The Mirror Makers: A History of American Advertising and Its Creators* (New York: William Morrow, 1984); Roland Marchand, *Advertising the American Dream: Making Way for Modernity, 1920–1940* (Berkeley: University of California Press, 1985); T. J. Jackson Lears, *Fables of Abundance: A Cultural History of Advertising in America* (New York: Basic Books, 1994); and James B. Twitchell, *Adcult USA: The Triumph of Advertising in American Culture* (New York: Columbia University Press, 1996).

Chapter 1

1. Erik Barnouw, *Tube of Plenty: The Evolution of American Television* (New York: Oxford University Press, 1990), 83–92. For other general histories of early television, see Jeff Kisseloff, *The Box: An Oral History of Television, 1920–1961* (New York: Penguin, 1995); David E. Fisher and Marshall John Fisher, *Tube: The Invention of Television* (New York: Counterpoint, 1996); Albert Abramson, *The History of Television, 1880–1941* (Jefferson, N.C.: McFarland, 1987); Barnouw, *The Image Empire: A History of Broadcasting in the United States from 1953* (New York: Oxford University Press, 1970); Frank

Sturcken, *Live Television: The Golden Age of 1946–1958 in New York* (Jefferson, N.C.: McFarland, 1990).

2. "The Hot Afternoon When TV Went Commercial," *Sponsor*, July 17, 1961, 34–35, 53. In *The Box*, Lenore Jensen, an early television commercial actress, remembers the Bulova watch commercial as a simple image of a watch with a second sweep hand, with the "Minute Waltz" playing underneath (62).

3. "The 50 Best Commercials," *Entertainment Weekly*, March 28, 1997, 21–39; Patricia Murray, "What a Year of Television Has Taught Lever Brothers about Commercials," *Printer's Ink*, February 9, 1945, 19–21.

4. Karen S. Buzzard, *Electronic Media Ratings: Turning Audiences into Dollars and Sense* (Stoneham, Mass.: Focal Press, 1992), 3; Smulyan 106–107, 118.

5. Marchand 105–107; Buzzard, *Electronic Media Ratings*, 3.

6. Marchand 107; Miller and Nowak 344; "Television Boost," *Business Week*, July 7, 1945, 84–85.

7. "General Foods' Television Committee: What It Is . . . How It Operates," *Sales Management*, May 1, 1947, 65; "Television Boost"; "Boost for Video," *Business Week*, December 8, 1945, 84.

8. "Television Is Ready for the Big Time," *Sales Management*, February 15, 1946, 171–172.

9. "Will Television Commercials Be One-Minute Movie Shorts?" *Sales Management*, April 15, 1946, 84–86.

10. Cdr. E. F. McDonald Jr. and Paul B. Mowrey, "Can Advertising Support Large-Scale Television?" *Printer's Ink*, February 21, 1947, 44–78; Dick Bruner, "Agencies, Sponsors Push Video Activity; 500,000 New Sets to Follow FCC Activity," *Printer's Ink*, March 28, 1947, 84.

11. "General Foods' Television Committee: What It Is . . . How It Operates"; Lipsitz 18.

12. Dr. Donald Horton and Halsey V. Barrett, "Commercials That Click on Television Sports Programs," *Printer's Ink*, October 24, 1947, 46–47.

13. Gilbert Millstein, "TV: High-Frequency Palpitations," *The Nation*, July 26, 1952, 67–69.

14. Thomas Whiteside, "Good (Gulp) to the Last Drop," *Reader's Digest*, November 1947, 114–116; E. P. H. James, "Let's Stop Jumping to Conclusions about Television," *Printer's Ink*, October 15, 1948, 34–60; "New Tool," *Time*, April 19, 1948, 81–82.

15. "Good (Gulp) to the Last Drop."

16. "Sponsors' World," *Time*, August 30, 1948, 53.

17. "Is It Worth It?" *Business Week*, April 16, 1949, 36; "High-Priced Revolution," *Time*, November 29, 1948, 88–90.

18. "Assaying Television," *Newsweek*, January 5, 1948, 56.

19. "Television's Growing Pains," *Business Week*, November 12, 1949, 50–52; "Video

Becomes Big Business; Set Volume to Surpass Radio," *Printer's Ink*, February 18, 1949, 42–45; "Showmanship Is Key to Video Advertising Success," *Printer's Ink*, February 18, 1949, 58–68; "Sales and Service Problems Fade as TV Picks Up Speed," *Printer's Ink*, February 18, 1949, 70–72.

20. "Television's Growing Pains"; Lipsitz 77–96.

21. "TV's Gain Is Radio's Loss," *Business Week*, April 15, 1950, 90.

22. T85:0490, MTR; "TV: High-Frequency Palpitations." For time capsules of postwar advertising culture, see Sloan Wilson's *The Man in the Gray Flannel Suit* (New York: Simon and Schuster, 1955) and Frederic Wakeman's *The Hucksters* (New York: Rinehart, 1946).

23. "Account Switching Worries Agencies," *Business Week*, September 22, 1951, 43–44.

24. Thomas Whiteside, "The Relaxed Sell," *The New Yorker*, June 3, 1950, 70–86.

25. "The Relaxed Sell."

26. "The Relaxed Sell."

27. "A Message from the Sponsor," *Time*, February 16, 1948; Evangeline Davis, "Video, I Love You," *Atlantic*, March 1950, 87; Halberstam 501.

28. Gilbert Seldes, "Three—Count 'Em—Three," *Atlantic*, May 1952, 85–86; "The Relaxed Sell."

29. "The Relaxed Sell." Creative license was also used for in the development of "original" music for television. In writing the theme song for *Texaco Star Theater* in 1948, Buddy Arnold claims in *The Box*, he lifted Liszt's *Hungarian Rhapsody No. 2* for the song's second section (113–114).

30. "Video, I Love You."

31. Charles W. Morton, "Accent on Living," *Atlantic*, September 1950, 83–84.

32. "Accent on Living."

33. AT:28231.003, MTR; AT:28231.002, MTR.

34. "The Relaxed Sell"; Robert Lewis Shayon, "If It's Art, It's Commercial," *Saturday Review*, November 18, 1950, 34.

35. Hal Humphrey, "Frankenstein Was a Sissy," *The Mirror*, September 5, 1950, 41, File: "Sponsors," HHC; Hal Humphrey, "Ask the Sponsor—He Knows," *The Mirror*, June 12, 1951, 41, File: "Sponsors," HHC.

36. "The TV Pitchmen," *Time*, June 18, 1951, 55–56; see Steven Watts, *The Magic Kingdom: Walt Disney and the American Way of Life* (New York: Houghton Mifflin, 1998), for more on Disney culture.

37. AT:23625.003, MTR; Hal Humphrey, "There's Gold in Those Plugs," *The Mirror*, April 7, 1952, 45, File: "Commercials," HHC.

38. AT:28299.017, MTR; AT:28231.020, MTR; AT:28231.004, MTR.

39. "If It's Art, It's Commercial"; AT:23625.001, MTR; Lipsitz 90; T80:0055, MTR; Marchand 109. Cast members of *Mama*, sponsored by Chase and Sanborn Coffee, also sipped coffee at the end of their show, notes Kisseloff in *The Box* (302).

40. Clark Agnew, "Too Many TV Commercials Are Just Radio with Pictures Added," *Printer's Ink,* April 15, 1949, 32–34; Terry Armstrong, "Seven Ways Television Commercials Are Asking Folks to Buy," *Sales Management,* September 15, 1949, 105–111.

41. Hal Humphrey, "Give It to Us Straight," *The Mirror,* September 18, 1952, 57, File: "Commercials," HHC.

42. Hal Humphrey, "Better Mousetraps Wanted," *The Mirror,* January 31, 1951, 19, File: "Commercials," HHC; Hal Humphrey, "Actors Make Lousy Pitchmen," *The Mirror,* May 16, 1951, 41, File: "Commercials," HHC; for more on Benny, see Jack and Joan Benny's *Sunday Nights at Seven: The Jack Benny Story* (New York: Warner Books, 1990) and Irving A. Fein, *Jack Benny: An Intimate Biography* (New York: G. P. Putnam's Sons, 1976); Marchand 109.

43. UCLA.

44. AT:23625.002, MTR.

45. T86:1316, MTR; T91:0053, MTR; T87:0403, MTR.

46. "The Open Hands," *Time,* December 22, 1952, 49.

47. T88:0030, MTR; T87:0402, MTR; "Better Mousetraps Wanted"; "Actors Make Lousy Pitchmen"; "Give It to Us Straight."

48. Hal Humphrey, "Plugs, Plugs, and More Plugs," *The Mirror,* June 27, 1951, 24, File: "Commercials," HHC; T:25331, MTR.

49. Ellen Seiter, *Sold Separately: Children and Parents in Consumer Culture* (New Brunswick, N.J.: Rutgers University Press, 1993) 104; T85:0316, MTR; David Buckingham, *Children Talking Television: The Making of Television Literacy* (London: Falmer, 1993) and Buckingham, *Moving Images: Understanding Children's Emotional Responses to Television* (Manchester, U.K.: Manchester University Press, 1996); T:34388, MTR; T:34389, MTR; T:17792, MTR. "We were hucksters. You might say we were real whores," conceded Buffalo Bob Smith in Gary H. Grossman's *Saturday Morning TV* (New York: Dell, 1981). For more on *Howdy Doody,* see Stephen Davis's *Say, Kids! What Time Is It? Notes from the Peanut Gallery* (Boston: Little, Brown, 1987) and Buffalo Bob Smith's and Donna McCrohan's *Howdy and Me: Buffalo Bob's Own Story* (New York: Plume, 1990).

50. Lynn Spigel, *Make Room for TV: Television and the Family Ideal in Postwar America* (Chicago: University of Chicago Press, 1992), 50–60. Although television deprivation for children was a concern, experts were also worried about the ill effects of television overexposure, Spigel notes. Hal Humphrey, *The Mirror,* November 17, 1950, 45, File: "Untitled," Hal HHC; *KTTV Television News Letter,* January 1952, File: "Sponsors" HHC.

51. "Beer in Salt Lake City," *Newsweek,* November 12, 1951, 105.

52. Goodman Ace, "People Who Live in Paper Houses," *Saturday Review,* February 9, 1952, 26.

53. AT84:0012.001, MTR.

54. AT:21960.003, MTR; Halberstam 224.

55. "Westinghouse Girl," *Time,* August 4, 1952, 46-47; "The Big Pitch," *Newsweek,* June 16, 1952, 96-98. For a complete study of presidential campaign advertising, see Kathleen Hall Jamieson's *Packaging the Presidency: A History and Criticism of Presidential Campaign Advertising* (New York: Oxford University Press, 1992). See also Edwin Diamond's *The Spot: The Rise of Political Advertising on Television* (Cambridge, Mass.: MIT Press, 1992) and Philip Gold's *Advertising, Politics, and American Culture* (New York: Paragon House, 1987).

56. Hal Humphrey, "What Won't They Sell Next?" *The Mirror,* October 31, 1952, 47, File: "Commercials," HHC; "The Big Pitch"; T84:0147, MTR.

57. Goodman Ace, "Going, Going, Gone," *Saturday Review,* March 22, 1952, 31-32; Wayne Oliver, AP press release, March 26, 1952, File: "Sponsors," HHC.

58. Milton R. Moskowitz, "Radio in Eclipse," *The Nation,* December 20, 1952, 581; Spigel 75-78.

59. "Going, Going, Gone"; Wayne Oliver, AP press release, March 26, 1952, File: "Sponsors," HHC.

60. "The Big Pitch."

61. "Radio in Eclipse"; "The Big Pitch"; "You're Being Sold — But You Don't Know It," *Business Week,* October 27, 1951, 148-149.

62. AT:23625.005, MTR.

63. "Trade Winds," *Saturday Review,* February 2, 1952, 4; Hal Humphrey, "Doctors Sore at TV Quacks," *The Mirror,* July 16, 1952, 45, File: "Commercials," HHC.

64. "Advice to Advertisers," *Time,* May 28, 1951, 63-64.

65. "The Big Pitch"; Gilbert Seldes, "The Commercial as a Work of Art," *Saturday Review,* September 20, 1952, 35-36. See Seldes's *The Great Audience* (New York: Viking, 1950) and *The Public Arts* (New York: Simon and Schuster, 1956).

66. "Seven Ways Television Folks Are Asking Folks to Buy"; AT:39038.018, MTR; AT39038.019, MTR; AT39038.017, MTR.

67. AT:21960.002, MTR.

68. "The Commercial as a Work of Art"; see Michael Kammen's *The Lively Arts: Gilbert Seldes and the Transformation of Cultural Criticism in the United States* (New York, 1996) for more on Seldes and his earlier work.

69. "The Big Pitch."

Chapter 2

1. "Speaking of Pictures," *Life,* April 27, 1953, 18-19.

2. "5 Years of TV — A Study of Sight, Sound, Motion," *Printer's Ink,* January 29, 1954, 58-64; Lipsitz 73.

3. Karen S. Buzzard, *Chains of Gold: Marketing the Ratings and Rating the Markets* (Metuchen, N.J.: Scarecrow, 1990) 32-33; Kammen 50; "Who's Going to Foot the Bill?" *Business Week,* May 23, 1953, 43-44.

4. "Who's Going to Foot the Bill?" For more on the networks and their personalities, see Stuart Lewis Long, *The Development of the Television Network Oligopoly* (New York: Arno, 1979).

5. The ratio of live to film broadcasts in 1953 was 78:22, according to Hilmes in *Hollywood and Broadcasting* (151); "5 Years of TV"; "The TV Switch," *Newsweek,* July 27, 1953, 71.

6. "Nets Scramble for More," *Business Week,* September 12, 1953, 29–30.

7. "Satisfied Customers," *Time,* September 28, 1953, 69. In *The Box,* Al Durante, a J. Walter Thompson executive, states that the legendary *Kraft Television Theatre* was created as a way for the company to introduce its new product, Cheez Whiz; "Nets Scramble for More"; Louis F. Thomann, "Old Commercials Were Good, but TV Advertiser Changes," *Printer's Ink,* February 25, 1955, 31.

8. Philip Hamburger, "Television is a Puzzlement," *The New Yorker,* April 10, 1954, 111–113; Anderson 87.

9. "Television is a Puzzlement"; Anderson 87.

10. "U.S. Steel's House Stars on TV Show," *Business Week,* May 8, 1954, 50; Hal Humphrey, "Anniversaries and Girdles," *The Mirror* April 29, 1954, File: "Commercials," HHC.

11. "The Cruel Camera," *Newsweek,* February 28, 1955, 59; "Why TV Sponsors Sputter," *TV Guide,* October 30, 1953, 20–21.

12. "The Cruel Camera."

13. "The Cruel Camera"; Hal Humphrey, "Oh, the Compatible Air!" *The Mirror,* November 6, 1953, 29, File: "Commercials," HHC.

14. "The Cruel Camera."

15. *New Republic,* June 14, 1954. Billy Gray, Bud on *Father Knows Best,* explains in *The Box* that despite Scott Paper's sponsorship of the show, toilet paper could never be shown. "That would suggest that people had assholes [and] if they did, [the show's producers] would have to admit that people take shits" (345).

16. "Why TV Sponsors Sputter," *The Nation,* December 20, 1952.

17. *New Republic,* June 14, 1954; Lipsitz 71.

18. Frank Orme, "TV Commercials," *The Nation,* April 4, 1953, 289.

19. "TV Commercials."

20. "TV Commercials," T:27688, MTR. See Michael D. Murray and Donald G. Godfrey, eds., *Television in America: Local Station History from across the Nation* (Ames: Iowa State University Press, 1997) for more on the fascinating story of KTLA; "TV Time Salesmen at KABC-TV, Channel 7, Hollywood, Carry New Portable TV Sets for Selling Television Shows," Channel 7 (KABC-TV, Los Angeles) News press release, October 21, 1955, File: "Sponsors," HHC.

21. Marya Mannes, "Channels: Those D—n Commercials," *The Reporter,* March 2, 1954, 40–42.

22. "Channels: Those D—n Commercials"; Marchand 100.

23. C. Lester Walker, "How to Stop Objectionable TV Commercials," *Reader's Digest*, November 1953, 71–72; "Insufferable," *Newsweek*, February 1, 1954, 75.

24. Kammen 111; Gilbert Seldes, "Heckling the Hucksters," *Saturday Review*, January 30, 1954, 28; "Insufferable"; "Ought to Be a Law," *Newsweek*, April 12, 1954,

25. "Insufferable"; "Ought to Be a Law." For more on Bernays's (a nephew of Sigmund Freud) ideas, see his "The Theory and Practice of Public Relations: A Resume," in *The Engineering of Consent*, edited by Bernays (Norman: University of Oklahoma Press, 1955) and his *Biography of an Idea: Memoirs of Public Relations Counsel* (New York: Simon and Schuster, 1965).

26. "Who Sees What?" *Newsweek*, November 16, 1953, 75; Ang 56–57.

27. "$100 Million down the Drain," *Time*, October 11, 1954, 103.

28. Hal Humphrey, *The Mirror*, February 16, 1955, File: "Untitled," HHC. See Marchand's *Advertising the American Dream* for an extensive discussion on the cultural gap between advertising men and the public during the 1920s and 1930s.

29. *Business Week*, May 28, 1955, 146.

30. "Channels: Those D—n Commercials"; AT84:0012.002, MTR; AT21968.005, MTR.

31. AT:23625.016, MTR; AT:38536.005, MTR; AT:28231.018, MTR.

32. "The Commercial Touch," *Commonweal*, June 19, 1953, 265; *The New Republic*, June 14, 1954.

33. "Jingles for Britain," *Newsweek*, September 26, 1955, 106. See R. W. Burns, *British Television: The Formative Years* (London: Peregrins, 1986) and H. H. Wilson, *Pressure Group: The Campaign for Commercial Television in England* (New Brunswick, N.J.: Rutgers University Press, 1961) for more on the rise of television in the United Kingdom; Charles W. Morton, "Accent on Living," *Atlantic*, May 1955, 86–87; Robert Wernick, "Jingles for Britain," *Life*, October 3, 1955, 135–145; "Plugs for Plugs," *Newsweek*, July 12, 1954, 52.

34. "Jingles for Britain" (*Newsweek*); "The Other Knob," *Fortune*, September 1955, 71–72; "British TV," *Business Week*, September 17, 1955, 88–96; Blake Ehrich, "British TV: How Decorous Can Ads Get?" *The Reporter*, January 19, 1954, 29–33.

35. *New Republic*, June 14, 1954.

36. Milton Moskowitz, "Alas, Poor England! Commercials are Coming . . .", *The Nation*, November 21, 1953, 425–426; "British TV" (*Business Week*).

37. *The New Republic*, June 14, 1954; "Jingles for Britain" (*Life*); "The Alternative," *Time*, August 16, 1954, 65–66.

38. "Plugs for Plugs"; "The Alternative."

39. Goodman Ace, "There Will Always Be a Sponsor," *Saturday Review*, April 16, 1955.

40. "The Invasion," *Time*, August 29, 1955, 37; "A Thick Skin?" *Newsweek*, October 3, 1955, 59.

41. "C-Day," *Time,* October 3, 1955, 57; "British TV" (*Business Week);* "A Thick Skin?"

42. "British TV" (*Business Week*).

43. Joseph J. Seldin, "Selling the Kiddies: TV Admen's Master Stroke," *The Nation,* October 8, 1955, 305; Buckingham, *Children Talking Television.*

44. "Selling the Kiddies"; Kammen 166.

45. Goodman Ace, "Smoke Gets in Your Ears," *Saturday Review,* February 28, 1953, 41. Ace was the head writer of *The Buick-Berle* show in the mid-1950s. For more Acisms, track down his *The Book of Little Knowledge: More Than You Want to Know about Television* (New York: Simon and Schuster, 1955).

46. "Ban Liquor Drinking on Michigan TV?" *The Christian Century,* March 24, 1954; Goodman Ace, "Play Beer!!!" *Saturday Review,* April 3, 1954, 42.

47. Wally Fingal, "NARTB Report Impresses Politicos," *Printer's Ink,* May 6, 1955, 64.

48. "Does 'Beer Belong' to Radio-TV, or Radio-TV Belong to Beer?" *The Christian Century,* May 25, 1955.

49. AT:38536.006, MTR.

50. "5 Years of TV"; "Television's Gain Is Other Media's Loss," *Business Week,* April 9, 1955, 62–68; "Admen Rejigger Budgets as TV Grabs Ball," *Business Week,* October 16, 1954, 146–148.

51. "Television's Gain Is Other Media's Loss."

52. "Television's Gain Is Other Media's Loss."

53. Anderson 85; T81.0112, MTR; "Admen Rejigger Budgets as TV Grabs Ball."

54. Goodman Ace, "No Parking!" *Saturday Review,* December 11, 1954, 28; Marling 136.

55. AT:28299.012, MTR; AT28231.013, MTR.

56. AT27859.003, MTR; AT:28231.005, MTR; AT27859.005, MTR. For more on postwar car culture, see *Cruiseomatic: Automobile Advertising of the 1950s,* compiled by Yasutoshi Ikuta (San Francisco: Chronicle Books, 1988); Halberstam 475.

57. "No Parking!"

58. AT:21811.025, MTR.

59. UCLA.

60. "Death of the Salesman?" *Time,* January 31, 1955, 52; AT88:1214, MTR; T:19738, MTR; T88:0031, MTR; T91:0247, MTR.

61. T:33389, MTR; Hal Humphrey, "Mr. Fonda Turns Pitchman," *The Mirror,* June 21, 1954, part 2, 3, File: "Commercials," HHC.

62. "5 Years of TV"; Hal Humphrey, *The Mirror,* December 3, 1954, part 2, 10, File: "Actors as Pitchmen," HHC.

63. "Actors as Pitchmen."

64. "Death of the Salesman?"

65. "The Fat Silhouette," *Time,* December 26, 1955, 46.

Chapter 3

1. "The New Cyclops," *Business Week,* March 10, 1956, 91–94; for a full discussion of the government's attempt to "sell the future while the present was out of stock," see *Pledging Allegiance;* "Television's Gain Is Other Media's Loss."

2. "The New Cyclops"; "Television's Gain Is Other Media's Loss."

3. "The New Cyclops"; Lawrence M. Hughes, "Free Choice or Free TV?" *Saturday Review,* February 22, 1958, 39–66.

4. Halberstam 506.

5. Hal Humphrey, "Orange Juice Drowns Roses," *Mirror-News,* January 6, 1956, File: "Commercials," HHC.

6. Alfred Bester, "So Good It's Almost Mediocre," *Holiday,* March 1956, 76–82.

7. T78:0307, MTR; T83:0354, MTR.

8. Richard F. Dempewolff, "Backstage Wizardry of the TV Commercials," *Popular Mechanics,* February 1957, 121–316; "So Good It's Almost Mediocre."

9. "Backstage Wizardry; "So Good It's Almost Mediocre."

10. "So Good It's Almost Mediocre." The seminal work on postwar Southern California culture is Kenneth T. Jackson's *Crabgrass Frontier: The Suburbanization of the United States* (New York: Oxford University Press, 1985).

11. "Hucksters in Britain," *Time,* February 20, 1956, 56–58; "British TV with an American Lilt," *Business Week,* October 20, 1956, 112–123.

12. "British TV with an American Lilt"; "Advertisers Race to Book Time as Britain Succumbs to Commercial TV," *Business Week,* July 20, 1957, 55; "Spots before Their Eyes," *Time,* July 28, 1958, 45.

13. "The New Cyclops"; Halberstam 629.

14. "The New Cyclops"; Daniel Seligman, "Revlon's Jackpot," *Fortune,* April 1956, 136–244.

15. "Revlon's Jackpot"; Halberstam 629.

16. "Revlon's Jackpot."

17. "Necessarily Boring," *Newsweek,* March 4, 1957,

18. "Queen of Commercials," *Newsweek,* January 21, 1957, 90. June Graham, another leading commercial actress of the 1950s, claims that seven women (herself, Meade, Joyce Gordon, Vivian Ferrar, Betsy Parker, and Kathi Norris "did 90 percent of all the commercials" (*The Box,* 537); "The Unobtrusive Beauties," *Time,* June 11, 1956, 47–48.

19. Hal Humphrey, "Sexy Girls Can't Sell Soap," *Mirror-News,* August 9, 1957, File: "Commercials," HHC.

20. Walter Goodman, "Social Science on Madison Avenue," *Commentary,* April 1957, 374–378.

21. "Social Science on Madison Avenue."

22. "Social Science on Madison Avenue." For more on Dichter and his theories of motivation, see his *The Strategy of Desire* (Garden City, N.Y.: Doubleday, 1960), *Handbook of*

Consumer Motivations: The Psychology of the World of Objects (New York: McGraw-Hill, 1964), and *Motivating Human Behavior* (New York: McGraw-Hill, 1971).

23. Halberstam 506–507.

24. Buzzard, *Electronic Media Ratings,* 2; "Pay-TV Seen as Relief for Advertisers," *Editor & Publisher,* September 7, 1957, 26; Hal Humphrey, "Webb's 'Ark' Is Listing," *Mirror-News,* December 14, 1956, part 2, 3, File: "Commercials," HHC; Hal Humphrey, "Viewers' Thirst Gives Sponsors Nightmares," *Mirror-News,* November 7, 1956, part 2, 3, File: "Commercials," HHC; Hal Humphrey, "That Old Liver Bile Just Keeps Rollin' Along," *Mirror-News,* December 3, 1958, File: "Commercials," HHC.

25. "Sexy Girls Can't Sell Soap"; Marling 9–49.

26. Marchand 96–97; "Star Performers Will Do More Selling on TV No Matter What the Critics Say," *Printer's Ink,* December 20, 1957, 34–39.

27. "Star Performers Will Do More Selling on TV No Matter What the Critics Say."

28. Arthur Bellaire, Norman King, and Rollo Hunter, "What Are the Prime Considerations in Using a Star?" *Sponsor,* November 29, 1958, 56–76; "Star Performers Will Do More Selling on TV No Matter What the Critics Say"; AT:23817.004, MTR.

29. A. L. Hollender, "How Valuable Is a Star's Name in a TV Commercial?" *Sponsor,* April 19, 1958, 46–48; "What Are the Prime Considerations in Using a Star?"; Marling 84.

30. "What Are the Prime Considerations in Using a Star?" "Star Performers Will Do More Selling on TV No Matter What the Critics Say."

31. Joe Csida, "Know Thy Star," *Sponsor,* July 12, 1958, 16–19.

32. "Know Thy Star."

33. UCLA.

34. UCLA.

35. "Viewers' Thirst Gives Sponsors Nightmares."

36. AT:21968.003, MTR; AT:21969.002, MTR.

37. AT:21960.007, MTR; "The Television Commercial, a Status Report," *Television Magazine,* July 1959, 43–83; "Maypo's TV Spots Open Up New Markets," *Printer's Ink,* May 29, 1959, 48–49.

38. "TV Commercial Built on Sand," *Business Week,* April 20, 1957, 73–81.

39. "TV Commercial Built on Sand"; AT:38536.009, MTR; Halberstam 226.

40. "TV's 64-Million-Dollar Question," *U.S. News & World Report,* August 9, 1957, 55–57; *Business Week,* October 16, 1954; "TV Programmers Play It Safe," *Business Week,* June 29, 1957, 108–114; Miller and Nowak 344.

41. Boddy 157; "The $10 Million Show," *Newsweek,* July 1, 1957, 46; "TV Programmers Play It Safe."

42. T85:0672, MTR; T85:0673, MTR; T77:0463, MTR; T79:0095, MTR.

43. Cynthia Lowry, "You'll Wonder Where the Sponsor Went," AP Newsfeature, July 23, 1958, File: "Sponsors," HHC; "TV's 64-Million-Dollar Question."

44. "TV Programmers Play It Safe." For the full Du Mont story, see Gary Newton Hess, *An Historical Study of the Du Mont Television Network* (New York: Arno, 1979; "TV's 64-Million-Dollar Question"; *Sponsor,* November 27, 1957.

45. Hal Humphrey, "It's the Viewer Who Pays Anyway," *Mirror News,* February 12, 1958, part 2, 4, File: "Sponsors," HHC.

46. Ray Conners, "Plymouth Salesmen Attend Unique Meeting," press release, January 24, 1958, File: "Sponsors," HHC.

47. Hal Humphrey, "The Sponsor Isn't TV's Real Villain," *Mirror News,* March 29, 1958, File: "Sponsors," HHC.

48. "Taboos, Sponsors Stifle Good TV; Divorce of Ads from Play Needed, Script Writer Says," *Advertising Age,* March 31, 1958. Serling fans should investigate Joel Engel's *Rod Serling: The Dreams and Nightmares of Life in "The Twilight Zone"* (Chicago: Contemporary Books, 1989) and Serling's own *Patterns* (New York: Simon and Schuster, 1957).

49. "From Radio/TV Jingle to Popular Song," *Sponsor,* June 14, 1958, 39; "Commercials First," *Sponsor,* February 8, 1958, 27–50.

50. "Commercials First."

51. Steuart Henderson Britt, "Subliminal Advertising — Fact or Fantasy," *Advertising Age,* November 18, 1957, 103–106, File: "Commercials — Old Stuff," HHC; NARTB press release, November 13, 1957, File: "Commercials — Old Stuff," HHC. Seminal sources on subliminal advertising include Vance Packard's *The Hidden Persuaders* (New York: D. K. McKay, 1957) and Wilson Brian Key's *Subliminal Seduction* (New York: New American Library, 1973).

52. "The Lovable Hucksters," *Newsweek,* December 29, 1958, 60; "Commercials First"; "The Jingle Jangle," *Time,* May 6, 1957, 50–53.

53. T:43483, MTR; Miller and Nowak 362; "McGuires Join Sales Ranks in Deal with Coke," *Advertising Age,* January 12, 1959; "The Jingle Jangle."

54. "The Jingle Jangle"; Halberstam 502.

55. "From Radio/TV Jingle to Popular Song"; "Use as Ad Jingle 'Cheapens' Tune, Judge Decides," *Advertising Age,* August 18, 1958.

56. "Can TV Come of Age?"

57. "Land of the Rising Plug," *Time,* July 28, 1958, 45.

58. "The Secret Commercial," *Time,* July 1, 1957, 65; "The Mammoth Mirror," *Time,* October 12, 1962, 87.

59. "It Was a Rough Year"; AT:28231.007, MTR; AT:24831.017, MTR.

60. Colin Campbell, "Should the Star Give the Commercial?" *Broadcasting,* June 9, 1958, 113; AT:28299.007, MTR; AT21921.012, MTR; Halberstam 505.

61. "TV Programmers Play It Safe"; "Bad Timing," *Time,* August 12, 1957, 40.

62. "Buick Sought Real M.D.s for TV, but Now Won't Use 'Em," *Advertising Age,* November 24, 1958, 1–87.

63. "Free Choice or Free TV?"; "Now Sponsors Call the Tune," *Business Week,* April

19, 1958, 53–58; "Time on Their Hands," *Time,* July 28, 1958, 45; "TV Nets Scramble for Fall Sponsors," *Business Week,* August 9, 1958, 47–50.

64. Boddy 158; Smulyan 90; Anderson 86; Hilmes, *Hollywood and Broadcasting,* 140; Hilmes, *Radio Voices,* 285. Thomas Whiteside discusses Weaver and the birth of the magazine concept in "The Communicator II: What about the Gratitude Factor?" *The New Yorker,* October 23, 1954, 43–44. Also see Vance Kepley Jr., "The Weaver Years at NBC," *Wide Angle,* April 1990, 46–63, and Weaver's own (with Thomas M. Coffey) *The Best Seat in the House* (New York: Knopf, 1994).

65. "TV Nets Scramble for Fall Sponsors." For more on the history of ABC, see Sterling Quinlan's *Inside ABC: American Broadcasting Company's Rise to Power* (New York: Hastings House, 1979) and Leonard Goldenson's and Marvin J. Wolf's *Beating the Odds: The Untold Story Behind the Rise of ABC: The Stars, Struggles, and Egos That Transformed Network Television* (New York: Scribner's, 1991).

66. "Now Sponsors Call the Tune."

Chapter 4

1. "It Was a Rough Year"; "That Old Liver Bile Just Keeps Rollin' Along."

2. "We Must Respect, Use, and Even Cherish TV," *Sponsor,* May 30, 1959, 37–39.

3. "We Must Respect, Use, and Even Cherish TV."

4. "Deception on TV," *The New Republic,* October 19, 1959, 3–4. Note that using a different method of computation, the *Historical Statistics of the United States* reports that television advertising expenditures multiplied about five times (from about $330 million to $1.6 billion) between 1951 and 1960; "Ad Men React: Many Words, No Words," *Business Week,* October 10, 1959, 56–60; "The Television Commercial, a Status Report"; Halberstam 500, 503; Miller and Nowak 345.

5. AT:21888.017, MTR; AT:21964.031, MTR; AT:21888.003, MTR; "Magic Minutes," *Newsweek,* April 22, 1963, 92.

6. "Poll of Ad Men Pulls Blasts at TV for Light Programs and Heavy Commercialism"; Anderson 87; T88:0045, MTR; T82:0389, MTR; T78:0293, MTR; T85:0954, MTR; T84:0330, MTR; T:07720, MTR; T80:0232, MTR.

7. "TV Is Cure for Decline in Art of Selling: Barrett," *Advertising Age,* October 5, 1959; "The Television Commercial, a Status Report."

8. "The Television Commercial, a Status Report."

9. "Will They or Won't They?" *Newsweek,* April 4, 1960, 71–72; "Trying Ads Out on the Road," *Business Week,* May 7, 1960, 123–127.

10. Robert Horton, "The Economic Squeeze on Mass TV," *The Reporter,* April 28, 1960, 14–20; Buzzard, *Chains of Gold* 75; Ang 57.

11. "The Television Commercial, a Status Report"; "The Blurb at Any Cost," *Newsweek,* August 24, 1959, 52; "The Television Commercial, a Status Report"; Bernard Asbell, "The Sixty-Second Sell," *The Reporter,* September 17, 1959, 56–58.

12. "Deception on TV"; "Quiz Probe May Change TV," *Business Week,* November 7,

1959, 32. For an overview of the quiz show scandal, see Kent Anderson, *Television Fraud: The History and Implication of the Quiz Show Scandals* (Westport, Conn.: Greenwood, 1978).

13. "Cosmetics: TV's $126 Million Sweetheart," *Sponsor,* June 27, 1959, 33–74; "The Economic Squeeze on Mass TV." For an insider account of the quiz show scandal, see Joseph Stone's and Tim Yohn's *Prime Time and Misdemeanors: Investigating the 1950s T.V. Quiz Scandal—A D.A.'s Account* (New Brunswick, N.J.: Rutgers University Press, 1992).

14. Philip Cortney, "Responsibility of Television to the People," *Vital Speeches of the Day,* February 1, 1960, 252–254.

15. "Quiz Probe May Change TV."

16. Dael Wolfle, "Science Proves . . .", *Science,* November 18, 1960, 1457; *The New Yorker,* December 3, 1960; John Crosby, "What You Can Do to Make Poor TV Better," *Ladies Home Journal,* November 1960, 136. For a full treatise by Crosby, see his *Out of the Blue: A Book about Radio and Television* (New York: Simon & Schuster, 1952). He looks back on these early days in "It Was New and We Were Very Innocent," *TV Guide,* September 22, 1973, 5–8.

17. "Trick or Treat," *The New Republic,* November 9, 1959, 6–7; "Turning the Wrong Knob," *Commonweal,* November 20, 1959, 229–230; "The Economic Squeeze on Mass TV"; Curtin 70.

18. "Admen Face the TV Issue," *Business Week,* November 21, 1959, 116–120.

19. "The Sixty-Second Sell"; Hal Humphrey, "TV Film Ad Tricks Told," *Mirror News,* November 16, 1959, part 1, 9, File: "Commercials—Old Stuff," HHC.

20. "What You Can Do to Make Poor TV Better." An in-depth study of the FCC during the latter postwar years is James L. Baughman's *Television Guardians: The FCC and the Politics of Programming, 1958–1967* (Knoxville: University of Tennessee Press, 1985); "Diet for Commercials"; Hal Humphrey, "Garry Moore Allergic to the 'Hard Sell,'" *Mirror-News,* March 25, 1959, part 1, 16, File: "Commercials," HHC.

21. "Diet for Commercials."

22. "Notes and Comment," *The New Yorker,* November 19, 1960, 41; "You Pay to See Plugs," *Newsweek,* December 12, 1960, 88.

23. "The TV Scene," *The Catholic World,* August 1957, 386.

24. *The New Yorker,* December 3, 1960.

25. *The New Yorker,* December 3, 1960.

26. "Quiz Probe May Change TV."

27. Robert Lewis Shayon, "John's Other Advertiser," *Saturday Review,* July 16, 1960, 33.

28. "Ad Men React: Many Words, No Words." For divergent views on how to best skin the postwar advertising cat, see Rosser Reeve's *Reality in Advertising* (New York: Knopf, 1961) and Bob Levenson's *Bill Bernbach's Book* (New York: Villard, 1987).

29. "The Economic Squeeze on Mass TV." Other examples of auto-paranoia included

Chevrolet's refusal to allow a pioneer to "ford" a river and Chrysler's objection to the mentioning of Abraham Lincoln's name on one of its shows, Kisseloff notes (501).

30. "Madison Ave.'s Program Taboos," *Variety,* October 26, 1960, 28, File: "Advertising," HHC.

31. "Madison Ave.'s Program Taboos."

32. "Madison Ave.'s Program Taboos." In *The Box,* Pat Buttram, Gene Autrey's sidekick (and later Mr. Haney on *Green Acres*), remembers that Autrey always chewed gum on his show because Wrigley was the sponsor. "Of course, the bad guys never chewed gum," Buttram added (276).

33. "Madison Ave.'s Program Taboos."

34. T89:0159, MTR; UCLA; "'Stop Smoking, Start Bathing' is Benny Show Motif," *Advertising Age,* October 12, 1959, 71; Halberstam 503–504.

35. UCLA; T89:0141, MTR; T89:0145, MTR.

36. "Garry Moore Allergic to the 'Hard Sell'"; Maurine Christopher, "Mrs. FDR Only Newest 'Anti-Tuneout' Ad Star," *Advertising Age,* February 23, 1959, 1B.

37. "Viewer Sees 30 Ads in Night; Handle TV Copy with Care, Bellaire Book Says," *Advertising Age,* July 20, 1959, 8.

38. "TV Hosts Send Polaroid Sales Soaring," *Printer's Ink,* November 6, 1959, 50–54. Dave Garroway integrated other sponsors' products into *The Today Show.* Joe Culligan of the NBC sales department once persuaded Garroway to place a piece of Saran Wrap over the camera lens to show viewers how clear the product was (*The Box,* 371).

39. Hal Humphrey, "Commercials Play Like Uncle Tom's Cabin," *Mirror-News,* April 4, 1960, File: "Commercials," HHC.

40. Hal Humphrey, "Hints for Sponsors Looking for Images," *Times-Mirror* Syndicate press release, June 27, 1960, File: "Sponsors," HHC.

41. AT:23625.011, MTR.

42. "Mrs. FDR Only Newest 'Anti-Tuneout' Ad Star"; Thomas L. Stix, "Mrs. Roosevelt Does a Commercial," *Harper's Magazine,* November 1963, 104–106.

43. "TV Is Cure for Decline in Art of Selling: Barrett"; "Sales Chart Says Bert & Harry TV Ads Sell: Graham," *Advertising Age,* February 1, 1960.

44. "How TV Rejiggers Market Areas," *Business Week,* February 20, 1960, 87–90.

45. *Business Week,* January 17, 1959, 72–78.

46. AT:28231.006, MTR.

47. AT:28231.011, MTR; AT:28231.010, MTR; AT:28231.008, MTR.

48. AT:21921.006, MTR; AT:21921.009, MTR; "Fox Exit Leaves No Surviving Members of First Edsel Team," *Advertising Age,* July 20, 1959, 8.

49. AT:21888.011, MTR; AT:21888.010, MTR. For more on Volkswagen's breakthrough ads, see Frank Ransome, *Think Small: The Story of Those Volkswagen Ads* (Brattleboro, Vt.: S. Greene Press, 1970) and Robert Glatzer, *The New Advertising: The Great Campaigns from Avis to Volkswagen* (New York: Citadel Press, 1970). Excellent studies of 1960s "countercultural" advertising are Larry Dobrow's *When Advertising*

Tried Harder. The Sixties: The Golden Age of American Advertising (New York: Friendly Press, 1984) and Thomas Frank's *The Conquest of Cool: Business Culture, Counterculture, and the Rise of Hip Consumerism* (Chicago: University of Chicago Press, 1997).

50. AT84:0012.008, MTR; AT84.0012.007, MTR.

51. AT84.0012.005, MTR; AT84.0012.003, MTR; AT84.0012.004, MTR.

Chapter 5

1. "Pepsi-Cola Plans Big Radio-TV Splash," *Broadcasting*, February 13, 1961, 32-33.

2. "Pepsi-Cola Plans Big Radio-TV Splash." For more on Pepsi and the "cola wars," see J. C. Louis and Harvey Z. Yazijan, *The Cola Wars* (New York: Everest House, 1980), Roger Enrico and Jesse Kornbluth, *The Other Guy Blinked: How Pepsi Won the Cola Wars* (New York: Bantam Books, 1986), and "Cola Wars" in Richard Tedlow's *New and Improved: The Story of Mass Marketing in America* (Basic Books, 1990).

3. "How Much Do You Know about the $75 Million TV Commercials Industry?" *Sponsor*, July 16, 1962, 25-48; "Network TV Clients: 376," *Broadcasting*, April 17, 1961, 37; Curtin 216; "The Mammoth Mirror," 85-90.

4. "Truth and TV." For Newton Minow's views on the failure of commercial television, see his *Equal Time: The Private Broadcaster and the Public Interest* (New York: Atheneum, 1964).

5. "Taste, Sponsorwise," *Time*, October 6, 1961, 61.

6. Thomas M. Garrett, "TV: Who's to Blame?" *America*, January 27, 1962, 556-557.

7. "Taste, Sponsorwise." *Camel News Caravan* also had tight restrictions regarding the depiction of smoking. In *The Box*, Reuven Frank, a writer for the NBC show, recalls such broadcasting taboos as "No Smoking" signs and cigar smokers (save for Winston Churchill). Arthur Holch, the senior editor of the show, adds that people never died of cancer, but "of a long illness" (366).

8. "Taste, Sponsorwise"; "TV Sponsors Tell Their Story to the FCC."

9. "Lip Movers and Others," *Newsweek*, October 23, 1961; "Time Buying and TV," *The New Republic*, October 30, 1961, 8. For more Conisms, see his *With All His Faults: A Candid Account of Forty Years in Advertising* (Boston: Little, Brown, 1969) and *Fairfax Cone's Blue Streaks: Some Observations, Mostly about Advertising* (Chicago: Crain Communications, 1973).

10. Robert W. Sarnoff, "Creativity in Television," *Vital Speeches of the Day*, April 1, 1960, 382-384; "Lip Movers and Others"; "Time Buying and TV"; John Bartlow Martin, "The Master Planners," *Saturday Evening Post*, November 4, 1961; Hal Humphrey, "More Commercials on TV May Be Just What We All Needed," *Los Angeles Mirror*, April 20, 1961, part 3, 6, File: "Commercials," HHC.

11. "TV and Public Service: A Proposal for Action."

12. "TV: Who's to Blame?"

13. Hal Humphrey, "Minow Hits Blurbs but Who's Excited?" *Los Angeles Times*, Au-

gust 1, 1962, File: "Commercials," HHC; "Toning Down Yule Toy Ads," *Business Week,* October 13, 1962; "Christmas Commercials for Children," *Consumer Reports,* November 1961, 638–640.

14. "TV Commercials: Wonderful World of Make-Believe"; "Christmas Commercials for Children."

15. "Maxwell House Helps Push Toy Coffee Serving Set," *Broadcasting,* April 10, 1961, 42; Seiter 103.

16. Fred Danzig, "Television in Review," UPI, October 31, 1961, File: "Commercials — Old Stuff," HHC; "Still More TV for Toys?" *Broadcasting,* June 25, 1962, 46.

17. "Panel Hits TV for Toys; Sees Improvement," *Advertising Age,* June 25, 1962. See Bob Hodge's and David Tripp's *Children and Television: A Semiotic Approach* (Stanford, Calif.: Stanford University Press, 1986) for more on the effects of televisual "indoctrination" of children.

18. "Christmas Commercials for Children."

19. *Time,* December 9, 1961; "Bearding Commuters," *Newsweek,* May 21, 1962; "The Mammoth Mirror."

20. "Commercialsville," *The New Yorker,* May 13, 1961, 32–33; "Bless the Commercials," *Time,* May 12, 1961, 44–45A; AT:21888.015, MTR.

21. AT:38536.012, MTR; "Magic Minutes."

22. AT:21960.013, MTR; AT:33680.005, MTR; "The Serious Business of Being Funny," *Television Magazine,* February 1961, 42. Ogilvy's approach to advertising is well documented in his *Confessions of an Advertising Man* (New York: Atheneum, 1963) and *On Advertising* (New York: Vintage, 1985).

23. "The Serious Business of Being Funny"; "Ad Men React: Many Words, No Words."

24. "Chun King's Humor Pays Off," *Broadcasting,* February 27, 1961, 30–31; "'Negative' Sell: It Can Produce," *Printer's Ink,* May 12, 1961, 40–42.

25. "'An Hour of Freberg Is That Much Better Than 20 Seconds,'" *Broadcasting,* January 15, 1962, 34; "Saul Bass, Leading Set and Industrial Designer, to Design Production for Stan Freberg's Chun King Special," ABC News press release, November 8, 1961, File: "Commercials — Old Stuff," HHC; *Newsweek,* May 2, 1962; "The Mammoth Mirror."

26. 107 "B.B.B. & H.," *Time,* September 28, 1962, 96; "Brotherly Love," *Newsweek,* November 5, 1962, 85. For some great Bob and Ray humor, see Bob Elliott's *From Approximately Coast to Coast . . . It's the Bob and Ray Show* (New York: Atheneum, 1983).

27. "How Much Do You Know about the $75 Million TV Commercials Industry?"; William O'Hallaren, "Spot Announcement," *Atlantic,* August 1961, 88–89; "The Master Planners."

28. "Music to Sell by Hits $18-Million Note," *Business Week,* September 8, 1962, 68–70.

29. "Commercialsville"; "Lyres for Hire," *Time,* April 21, 1961, 69.

30. "Tip Top Jingle Money Makers," *Sponsor*, April 30, 1962, 32-50; "Everybody's Singing Along with Mitch," *Broadcasting*, April 10, 1961, 40-41.

31. "Lyres for Hire."

32. "Say It with Music," *Broadcasting*, February 13, 1961, 34.

33. "How to Be Rich through a Pencil," *Time*, August 31, 1962, 48.

34. "Whose Voice?" *Newsweek*, June 11, 1962, 88.

35. Peter Bart, "Too Much Too Often," *Saturday Review*, August 11, 1962, 35.

36. "Too Much Too Often"; Letter from W. H. Tankersley, CBS director of program practices, to Hal Humphrey, July 25, 1962, File: "Commercials—Old Stuff," HHC.

37. "Too Much Too Often"; "Product Protection Peace Pact," *Broadcasting*, July 2, 1962, 23.

38. "The Yap Gap," *Time*, April 28, 1961, 74; "Too Much Too Often"; "And Now, a WORD . . . ," *Newsweek*, October 29, 1962, 82.

39. "TV's Vital 20 Seconds," *Dun's Review and Modern Industry*, February 1962, 65-72.

40. "The Death of a (TV) Salesman?" *Broadcasting*, February 13, 1961, 27-28; Hal Humphrey, "Serling: Cheers to Beers to Jeers," *Los Angeles Times*, May 30, 1962, File: "Commercials," HHC.

41. "Kovacs: He Made TV Selling Fun," *Printer's Ink*, April 13, 1962, 58-60. Kovacs fans might hunt down Diana Rico's *Kovacsland: A Biography of Ernie Kovacs* (New York: Harcourt Brace, 1991) and David G. Walley's *The Ernie Kovacs Phile* (New York: Bolder, 1975).

42. "Kovacs: He Made TV Selling Fun."

43. "Kovacs: He Made TV Selling Fun."

44. AT:231.009, MTR; "The Serious Business of Being Funny."

45. T81:0129, MTR; T82:0338, MTR.

46. Peter Bart, "The Hidden Sell," *Saturday Review*, July 14, 1962, 50-51.

47. "The Hidden Sell."

48. *Saturday Review*, August 11, 1962; AT:21888.009, MTR.

49. "Bearding Commuters"; "Realism," *The New Yorker*, July 28, 1962, 16-18; Hal Humphrey, "'Tobacco Road' Detours to TV," *Los Angeles Times*, November 23, 1962, File: "Commercials," HHC.

50. AT:23831.004, MTR; AT:23831.006, MTR.

51. "TV News Gets into the Money," *Business Week*, June 9, 1962, 50-54; "On TV the 'Lending' is Easy for Xerox Copying Machine," *Broadcasting*, June 18, 1962, 40. For more on the business side of news programs, see Edward Bliss Jr., *Now the News: The Story of Broadcast Journalism* (New York: Columbia University Press, 1991).

52. AT:39038.049, MTR; "TV News Gets into the Money."

53. "TV and Public Service: A Proposal for Action"; "TV News Gets into the Money"; "Can a Sponsor Quit TV?" *Business Week*, November 24, 1962, 29.

54. Donald I. Rogers, "Advertising of 'Enemies,'" *Vital Speeches of the Day,* August 15, 1962, 653–656.

55. "Can a Sponsor Quit TV?"

56. "Can a Sponsor Quit TV?"; "Not Too Much Freedom, However," *The Nation,* December 8, 1962, 386; "Hiss Aftermath: More, Less Sponsor Power," *Printer's Ink,* November 23, 1962, 11–17; "TV Must Fight All Censorship: Minow Has Right to Guard Repute: Frawley," *Advertising Age,* November 26, 1962, 3.

57. Charles W. Morton, "The Worst Commercial," *Atlantic,* May 1962, 104–105; "A Minow is Swimming," *New Republic,* November 6, 1961; Stephen White, "Who Put the Alphabet into the Soup?" *Horizon,* January 1962, 112–113.

Chapter 6

1. "The People Look at Television," *Television Magazine,* March 1963, 47. For the full study, see Gary A. Steiner, *The People Look at Television: A Study of Audience Attitudes* (New York: Alfred A. Knopf, 1963); Norman E. Cash, "Looking at the First 25 Years," *Printer's Ink,* March 20, 1964, 46–50.

2. Neil Hurley, "The TV Commercial: Window on Mass Culture," *America,* January 5, 1963, 13–15.

3. "The TV Commercial: Window on Mass Culture."

4. "The TV Commercial: Window on Mass Culture."

5. "Sure, Advertising is Propaganda — But It's Vital to Freedom, Says Downs," *Sponsor,* August 5, 1963, 46–47.

6. "Looking at the First 25 Years."

7. "Looking at the First 25 Years."

8. John Tebbel, "How Europe Fights Commercial TV," *Saturday Review,* August 10, 1963, 46–47; "The Mammoth Mirror"; "The Master Planners."

9. Miller and Nowak 366; "Black viewers were simply not considered a major or distinctive concern of television broadcasters," claims Michael Curtin in *Redeeming the Wasteland.* "Primary emphasis within the industry was placed instead on attracting a mass audience of white, middle class *consumers*" (Curtin's emphasis; 227).

10. "Yesterday's TV Ad-Viewing Tots Are Now Integration Activists: Hayakawa," *Advertising Age,* August 19, 1963, 1, 75; "Do Advertisers Face a Negro Boycott?" *Printer's Ink,* September 13, 1963, 7–8; "Action-Backed Drive Gets Negroes on TV," *CORELATOR, Congress of Racial Equality,* February 1964, File: "Commercials — Old Stuff," HHC.

11. "Yesterday's TV Ad-Viewing Tots Are Now Integration Activists: Hayakawa."

12. "Do Advertisers Face a Negro Boycott?" General Motors almost pulled out of *Bonanza* when a black character was introduced on the show, Kisseloff observed (503).

13. "Yesterday's TV Ad-Viewing Tots Are Now Integration Activists: Hayakawa."

14. Maurine Christopher, "Integration Drive Gains Momentum in TV Industry," *Ad-*

vertising Age, September 30, 1963, 105; "The Singing Saleswoman," *Ebony,* April 1964, 143–146.

15. "TV: A New Force in Selling to U.S. Negroes," *Sponsor,* August 17, 1964, 44–52; "The Negro Consumer — What Broadcasters Have Learned about Him," *Sponsor,* September 14, 1964, 36–40.

16. "TV: A New Force in Selling to U.S. Negroes."

17. Wallace A. Ross, "What's New in Color Commercials?" *Sponsor,* December 31, 1962, 43–51; "Advertisers Edge into Tint TV as Sets Multiply," *Advertising Age,* January 21, 1963, 3, 54; "Advertisers Report Color Commercials Have Many Fringe Benefits," *Sponsor,* May 13, 1963, 40–41.

18. "What's New in Color Commercials?"; "Advertisers Edge into Tint TV as Sets Multiply"; "Advertisers Report Color Commercials Have Many Fringe Benefits."

19. "What's New in Color Commercials?"; "Advertisers Edge into Tint TV as Sets Multiply"; "Color Commercials: Fidelity Is Hard Work," *Sales Management,* July 5, 1963, 51–65.

20. John T. Murphy, "Color: Bonus for the Commercial," *Printer's Ink,* March 20, 1964, 45–46; AT:28231.016, MTR.

21. AT:25728.006, MTR; "Magic Minutes"; "One-Commercial Bonanza," *America,* October 12, 1963, 406.

22. "New Directions: Travel Turns to TV," *Sponsor,* October 26, 1964, 33–37; Deborah Haber, "The Airlines: In the Air and on It," *Television Magazine,* February 1964, 46–93.

23. "The Airlines: In the Air and on It"; "New Directions: Travel Turns to TV."

24. "The Airlines: In the Air and on It."

25. "Household Products Commercials Feature More 'Realistic' Gals," *Sponsor,* March 18, 1963, 28–45; Lillian Donnelly, "TV Commercials Are Undergoing a Revolutionary Change According to Hollywood's Maxine Anderson," press release, March 2, 1964, File: "Commercials — Old Stuff," HHC.

26. Hal Humphrey, "Housewives Skeptical of TV Counterparts," *Los Angeles Times* Syndicate, release date May 15, 1963, File: "Commercials," HHC.

27. "Housewives Skeptical of TV Counterparts"; "Slice of Life Can Be Dreary or Exciting," *Broadcasting,* April 27, 1964, 41.

28. "Household Products Commercials Feature More 'Realistic' Gals."

29. Bill Davidson, "TV's Prosperous Pitchmen," *Saturday Evening Post,* August 24, 1963, 26–27.

30. "Hollywood Trio Stars in Maxwell House Fall Drive," *Advertising Age,* September 2, 1963, 1; "TV Commercials Are Undergoing a Revolutionary Change According to Hollywood's Maxine Anderson"; Bob Thomas, AP Newsfeature, April 1, 1964, File: "Commercials — Old Stuff," HHC; "Ultra-Identification Not Good, Says Spokesman," *Sponsor,* April 20, 1964, 52–55.

31. Hal Humphrey, "TV Pitchmen to Throw Curves," *Los Angeles Times,* September 3, 1963, part 4, 18, File: "Commercials," HHC.

32. Harry W. McMahan, "Tops of the Year: 1962 Rich in 'Good' TV Ads, but a Beggary for 'Greats,'" *Advertising Age,* January 21, 1963; "What Makes Effective 'Sell,'" *Sponsor,* June 24, 1963, 29-68.

33. Alan Levy, "A 58-Second Film Festival," *The Reporter,* June 20, 1963, 39-42.

34. "Clio, Muse of Huckstery," *Time,* May 31, 1963, 47-48; Robert Lewis Shayon, "Clio's Commercials," *Saturday Review,* June 8, 1963, 52; "A 58-Second Film Festival."

35. Sara Welles, "Sex and the Judges," *Printer's Ink,* May 17, 1963, 50.

36. "Sex and the Judges."

37. "Does It Take Men to Sell Women?" *Printer's Ink,* June 26, 1964, 52; AT:21960.015, MTR. See Spigel's *Make Room for TV* for a full discussion of gender roles and identity within postwar television.

38. "Ads, Not Art," *America,* January 12, 1963, 36; "Clio's Commercials"; Paul Goodman, "Nothing but Ads," *The New Republic,* February 9, 1963, 28-30.

39. "Growing Appreciation of TV's Commercials," *Broadcasting,* June 15, 1964, 58-59; "TV Commercials Can Please, as Well as Sell, Museum of Modern Art Show Proves," *Advertising Age,* April 1, 1963, 100; "TV Getting Too Arty, Warns Mogul," *Sponsor,* March 18, 1963, 50.

40. AT:21888.002, MTR; AT:21960.014, MTR; "Focus on Commercials: How Sublime the Ridiculous," *Television Magazine,* February 1963, 17-20; "Magic Minutes."

41. "Focus on Commercials: How Sublime the Ridiculous"; "Magic Minutes."

42. Letter from Walter Gore to editor, *The New Republic,* May 4, 1963, 37; *SRC Bulletin,* October 1963, vol. 11, no. 9, File: "Commercials — Old Stuff," HHC; "'The Big Difference' in Anacin," *Consumer Reports,* June 1963, 261-262; "'Most Obnoxious TV Spots Contest' Draws Viewers' Nominees," *Advertising Age,* October 14, 1963; Halberstam 225-226.

43. Ralph Tyler, "Television: Modern Medicine Man," *Television Magazine,* November 1964; Charles W. Morton, "The Peanut Butter World," *Atlantic,* April 1963, 129; Jack Kaplan, "A Therapy of Chaos," *Today's Health,* January 1963.

44. "Fewer Commercials," *The New Republic,* April 13, 1963; "22 Straight Commercials," *Newsweek,* April 15, 1963; "Our Timid Watchdog," *Consumer Reports,* March 1964, 110; Richard L. Tobin, "And Now a Word from Our Newscaster," *Saturday Review,* June 8, 1963, 47-48; "22 Straight Commercials"; Goodman Ace, "And Now a Brief Message from . . .", *Saturday Review,* April 25, 1964, 10; Art Buchwald, "Hooray for Commercials!" *Readers' Digest,* May 1964, 27-28.

45. "Toys More Like Toys," *Business Week,* September 28, 1963; "Disparaging Claims and Toys Put under Fire," *NAB Code Authority TV Code News,* January 1964, vol. 3, no. 1, File: "Commercials — Old Stuff," HHC.

46. "Code Authority Approves Revised Toy Guidelines," *NAB Code Authority TV*

Code News, March 1964, vol. 3, no. 3, File: "Commercials — Old Stuff," HHC; A. J. Vogl, "Changing Face of the Children's Market," *Sales Management,* December 18, 1964, 35.

47. Albert R. Kroeger, "Television: Autocrat of the Breakfast Table," *Television Magazine,* November 1963.

48. "Television: Autocrat of the Breakfast Table"; Seiter 103. See also B. M. Young, "New Approaches to Old Problems: The Growth of Advertising Literacy," in *Commercial Television and European Children,* edited by S. Ward, T. Robertson, and R. Brown (Alderhost, U.K.: Gowen, 1986).

49. Arturo F. Gonzalez, "The Moppet Market," *The Reporter,* June 18, 1964, 40–43.

50. "The Moppet Market."

51. Buckingham, *Moving Images* and *Children Talking Television,* 258.

52. "The Moppet Market."

53. Robert Lewis Shayon, "Daniel (Bubblegum) Boone," *Saturday Review,* September 5, 1964, 18; "The Moppet Market"; Buckingham, *Moving Images,* 308; "Daniel (Bubblegum) Boone"; Miller and Nowak 347–348.

54. "Daniel (Bubblegum) Boone."

55. "Can TV Sell for the Movies?" *Sponsor,* July 29, 1963, 35–60.

56. "Can TV Sell for the Movies?"; "The Mary Poppins Bandwagon Rolls," *Sponsor,* December 14, 1964, 27–31.

57. "What Hollywood Doesn't Tell Madison Avenue," *Sponsor,* July 15, 1963, 33–67; "How Admen See Hollywood," *Sponsor,* July 22, 1963, 34–37.

58. "What Hollywood Doesn't Tell Madison Avenue"; "How Admen See Hollywood"; Hal Humphrey, "Sponsor Phobias Now Tranquilized," *Los Angeles Times,* September 6, 1963, File: "Sponsors," HHC; Robert Lewis Shayon, "The Wife Who Wasn't There," *Saturday Review,* October 17, 1964, 27.

59. "Image Builders Go Back to Print," *Business Week,* October 31, 1964, 70. See Curtin's *Redeeming the Wasteland* for a complete discussion of the rise and fall of one of the primary genres of "quality" television, the documentary. Curtin considers documentaries during the postwar years to have been a "Cold War education project" and a "tonic for a nation adrift in aimless consumerism and passive entertainment" (255).

60. Goodman Ace, "That Same Wax of Ball Again . . . ," *Saturday Review,* May 16, 1964, 14.

61. Hal Humphrey, "Sponsorphrenia Rules the Waves," *Los Angeles Times,* July 26, 1963, File: "Sponsors," HHC; "Ultra-Identification Not Good, Says Spokesman."

62. "And Now a Word from Our Newscaster."

63. "And Now a Word from Our Newscaster."

64. "Gulf Oil Co. Is Only Sponsor for Moon-Shot, Vietnam Specials," *Sponsor,* August 10, 1964, 19; George Lazarus, *Chicago Daily News Service,* August 13, 1964, File: "Commercials — Old Stuff," HHC.

65. "Guerilla War on Soap Giants," *Business Week,* August 29, 1964, 50–52.

66. "Guerilla War on Soap Giants"; Lawrence M. Hughes, "How Purex Succeeds against the Giant Soapers," *Sales Management*, January 17, 1964.

67. "What's Good for U.N. Is Good for Xerox," *Business Week*, April 18, 1964, 80–82; "Xerox to Run 90-Minute Shows on TV with One-Sentence Ads," *Printer's Ink*, April 10, 1964, 9. Curtin also has noted Corporate America's interest in bringing television to overseas markets in order to create demand for products made in the States (75).

68. "A 58-Second Film Festival."

69. "Oratorios for Industry," *Time*, July 24, 1964, 42.

70. "Road to the Presidency," *Sponsor*, January 18, 1965, 27–32; "Spotting the Candidates," *Newsweek*, September 21, 1964; AT84:0012.010, MTR; AT84:0012.011, MTR.

71. AT84:0012.009, MTR.

72. "Goldwater Using TV in Primary Campaigns," *Broadcasting*, April 13, 1964, 66; "GOP May Bank Heavily on TV," *Broadcasting*, July 27, 1964, 51; "Spotting the Candidates"; AT84.0012.013, MTR; AT84.0012.012, MTR; "The Most Costly Race in Political History," *Broadcasting*, September 7, 1964, 46–48.

73. "GOP 'Morals' Film Back in Can," *Sponsor*, October 26, 1964, 58–59.

Index

music, 9, 21–22, 24, 40, 43, 50, 72, 80,
    81, 110, 112–114, 153, 166–168, 174, 195,
    198, 200. *See also* jingles
My Friend Irma, 48
My Little Margie, 54
My Sin cologne, 135

NAACP, 186–187
Nabisco, 186, 205
Nash, Ogden, 112
Nash automobiles, 72
National Airlines, 193
National Association of Broadcasters
    (NAB), 154, 158, 159, 203, 204, 213
National Association of Educational
    Broadcasters, 39
National Association of Radio and Tele-
    vision Broadcasters (NARTB), 39, 59,
    77, 79, 111, 133, 134, 203
national identity, xi, xv, 88, 183, 184, 228
National Review, 179
Nationwide Insurance, 178–180
Nat King Cole Show, The, 113
NBC, 3, 17, 27, 30, 32, 33, 34, 35, 37, 38,
    41, 48, 49, 50, 53, 54, 64, 65, 77, 80,
    82, 83, 88, 89, 93, 94, 95, 97, 98, 107–
    108, 117, 118, 119, 120, 134, 159, 173, 177,
    178, 183, 187, 190, 208, 212, 214, 215
Nescafe instant coffee, 80
New Deal, xi, xiii
New Frontier, 153, 181, 184
Newport cigarettes, 166, 168
New Republic, The, 132, 200
newspaper(s), xiv, xviii, 7, 11, 32, 33, 34,
    36, 81, 101, 109, 127, 130, 136, 155, 157,
    192, 193, 202, 209, 210, 213
Newsweek, 43, 161
New Yorker, The, 135, 161
New York Giants, 21, 73
New York Herald Tribune, The, 99, 179
New York Times, The, 17, 99, 144, 198,
    208, 216
New York University, 183, 187
New York Yankees, 73

Nichols, Mike, 143, 162
Nick at Night, xx
Niebuhr, Dr. Reinhold, 62
Nielsen, A. C., 16, 63, 83, 93. *See also*
    Nielsen TV Index
Nielsen TV Index, 127. *See also* Nielsen,
    A. C.
1984, 111
Nippon Electric, 116
Nixon, Richard, 115, 141, 148–149, 179, 183
Norman, Craig & Kummel, 94, 162, 201
Northeast Airlines, 193
Northwest Orient, 193
Nowak, Marion, xv, 8, 123
Nyrun, 94

Ogilvy, David, 162
Organization Man, The, 107
Ogilvy, Benson & Mather, 75, 110, 124,
    144
O'Herlihy, Dan, 174
Old Gold cigarettes, 19, 43, 44
Oldsmobile, 22, 23, 77, 113
online technology, xxi. *See also* Internet
Open End, 206
Oregon Journal, 202
Oreo cookies, 202
Original Amateur Hour, 19
Orwell, George, 111
Ory, Edward "Kid," 114
Oscar awards, 197, 213
Otarion hearing aids, 144

Paar, Jack, xvi, 101–102, 142, 179
Pabst Blue Ribbon Beer, 74
Packard, Vance, xviii, 107, 112
Packard automobiles, 66
Page, Patti, 113
Pajama Game, 166
Pall Mall cigarettes, 19
Pan American World Airways, 193
Papert, Koenig, Lois, 177, 215
Paramount Pictures, 209
Parkay margarine, 107

Parker, Fess, 208
Parker, Frank, 54
Password, 186
Pat Boone Show, The, 146
patriotism, xi, 123, 174, 228
Patterson, Floyd, 118
Peace Corps, 176–177
"Peanuts," 146
Penn, Irving, 153
Pepperidge Farm pastry, 110
Pepsi-Cola, 27, 108, 153, 168
Pepsodent toothpaste, 26, 196
Person to Person, 105, 114, 134
Peter Pan peanut butter, 30
Pet Milk, 32, 54
Pharmaceuticals, Inc., 94–95, 128
Philadelphia cream cheese, 107
Philadelphia Phillies, 4
Philco, 3, 34, 48
Philco Television Playhouse, 32, 48
Philip Morris, 19, 42, 54, 69, 80, 218–219
Piel Brothers (Bert and Harry), xx, 103, 112, 126, 145, 165
Piel's beer, 103, 126, 165, 166, 202
Pillsbury, 30, 53, 82, 216
Playboy magazine, 52
Playhouse 90, 109
Play of the Week, The, 48
plugola, 31–32, 134, 135, 175
plug(s), xvi, 27, 30, 31, 79, 102, 114–115, 133, 134, 135, 175, 225
Plymouth, 96, 109, 117, 125, 147
point-of-sale promotion, 49, 81, 104, 144
Poitier, Sidney, 185
Polaroid cameras, 101, 134, 142
Pond's cold cream, 58
Pontiac, 77
Pontiac Star Parade, 125
Porter, Cole, 113, 166
Portia Faces Life, 52
Post cereals, 51, 205
Postum, 51
Power Elite, The, 107
Prell shampoo, 162

Preminger, Otto, 215
premiums, 72, 205, 209
Presley, Elvis, 97, 125
Previn, Andre, 215
Price, Paul, 59–60
Price Is Right, The, 212
print, xix, 7, 13, 18, 25, 46, 75, 76, 92, 94, 98, 109, 110, 120, 123, 130, 134, 138, 144, 155, 157, 161, 193, 203, 210, 213, 221, 223. *See also* magazines; newspapers
Printer's Ink, xx, 10, 15, 46, 98, 122, 173, 198, 199
Private Eye, 28
Procter & Gamble, 4, 38, 48, 68, 75, 105, 110, 155, 186, 188, 201, 214
Prudential insurance, 155
Psychological Corporation, 126
public relations, 61, 74, 82, 102, 118
public service announcements (PSAs), 100, 176–177, 225
Publisher's Information Bureau (PIB), 75
Puffed Wheat cereal, 211
puffery, xix, 140, 158, 162, 227
Pulse, 126
Purex Corporation, 214–215

Quaker Oats, 72, 205, 211
Quality Drug Stores, 17
Queen Elizabeth, 66
Queen Marie (of Romania), 98

race, xv, 148, 185–189, 227
radio: advertisers, 10, 12, 16, 59, 73; advertising, 13, 22, 25, 27, 33, 76, 112, 144, 221; advertising billings, 38; advertising by Northwest Orient, 193; advertising to African Americans, 187; advertising to children, xv, xvi, 32, 71–72, 205, 206; announcers, 90, 196; and Arthur Godfrey, 30; audience and listenership, 15, 16; and "Aunt Jenny," 99; British, 67, 71; commercialization of, xix, 3, 92; copywriters, 20; costs, 9, 13–14, 16; cross-marketing, 160; departments, 8;

disk jockeys, 134, 167; effectiveness, 12; expenditures, 74, 75, 76; household penetration of, 122; impact on advertising business, 17–18; integrated advertising, 28–29; intrusiveness, 138; media selling, 60; and media "spill," 91; as medium, 223; networks, xiv, xvii, 39, 75; and plugola, 31; popularity of, xvi; premiums, 72, 205; revenue, 48; and sponsor system, xiii, 223; stations, 11, 39, 168; structure of, 5–7, 18, 48, 120; and testimonial advertising, 98; time, 75; as uni-dimensional medium, 25, 192; voice-over talent, 168

Radio and Television Executives Society, 62

Raleigh cigarettes, 155

Ralston Purina, 145, 205

Randall, Tony, xviii

Rapid-Shave shaving cream, 218

Rathbone, Basil, 99

rating(s), xvii, 19, 49, 63, 82, 83, 94, 97, 102, 109, 110, 120, 121, 122, 127, 128, 129, 133, 149, 156, 173, 177, 178, 212

Raymond, Gene, 78, 101

RCA, 3–4, 35, 113, 189, 190

RDX, 94

reach, 16–17, 49, 110, 127

Reader's Digest, 141

Reagan, Ronald, 82, 100, 136

recall, 11, 63, 72, 105, 166, 197

Red Buttons Show, The, 47, 52, 77

Red Scare, 75. *See also* Cold War

Reed, Donna, 143

Reeves, Rosser, 36, 202

Reiner, Carl, 89

Remco Toy Company, 159

Remington electric shaver, 65

Reporter, The, 60, 133, 198

retail(ers), 15, 76, 93, 105, 144–145, 160, 164, 197, 225

Revlon, 93, 128–129, 132, 155

Revson, Charles, 129

Revson, Martin, 129

Rheingold beer, 13, 80, 112–113

Riesman, David, 107

Rinso detergent, 4, 6

Robinson, Edward G., 196

Robinson, Jackie, 185

Rodgers, Richard, 50, 215

Rogers, Donald I., 179

Rome, Harold, 112, 166, 167

Romney, George, 174

Ronson lighters, 13

Roosevelt, Eleanor, 144

Royal Drene Shampoo, 110

Royal pudding, 72

Ruby, Jack, 214

Ruthrauff & Ryan, 4, 8. *See also* Erwin, Wasey, Ruthrauff & Ryan

Sahl, Mort, 162

Sales Management, 9, 42, 191

Salvo detergent, 201, 202

Samuelson, Robert J., x

Sandburg, Carl, 136

San Francisco College, 187

Sanka coffee, 27, 51, 167

Saran Wrap, 93, 203

Sarnoff, Robert W., 108

Sarong Girdle, 51, 198

Satina, 51

Saturday Evening Post, 217

Saturday Review, xx, 73, 211, 213

Schaefer's Beer, 73, 80

Schick Safety Razor, 180

Schlesinger, Arthur, 154

Schlitz beer, 42, 168, 172, 186, 202

Schlitz Playhouse of Stars, 48

Schweppes tonic water, 75

Schwerin, Horace (Schwerin Research Corporation), 41, 63–64, 95, 126, 172, 190, 194, 197, 202

Schwinn bicycles, 135

S. C. Johnson & Company, 122, 156

Scotkins paper napkins, 56

Scott, Raymond, 112

Screen Actors Guild (SAG), 165, 195